OUT of CONTEXT

DANIEL BALDERSTON

OUT of CONTEXT

Historical Reference and the Representation

of Reality in Borges

Duke University Press   *Durham and London 1993*

© 1993 Duke University Press

All rights reserved

Printed in the United States of America on acid-free paper ∞

Typeset in Galliard by Keystone Typesetting, Inc.

Library of Congress Cataloging-in-Publication Data

appear on the last printed page of this book.

For José Bianco

and Enrique Pezzoni

in memoriam

Contents

Acknowledgments

This book has developed slowly, and a great number of people have made suggestions along the way. Special thanks to Sylvia Molloy, Gerald Martin, Evelyn Fishburn, Eduardo Paz Leston, Andrés Avellaneda and Noé Jitrik for their challenges to get things right and to three good friends who generously read multiple versions of this work: Gwen Kirkpatrick, Marina Kaplan, and Francine Masiello. To John Rouse, for help with translations from the German. To my parents, for allowing me to use their ranch house near Loyalton, California, during the fall of 1990, where, far from the "mundanal ruido," I was able to write most of the book, and to Tulane University for support during that sabbatical semester. To the librarians (especially Judy Sokol and Jane Dixon of the interlibrary loan staff) at the University of Nevada-Reno for their good humor and helpfulness. To Eduardo Santa Cruz for help with the preparation of the index. And to Reynolds Smith of Duke University Press for seeing this through.

Earlier versions of some portions of the book have appeared in the following journals: bits of chapters 1, 2, 3 and 9 as "Historical Situations in Borges" in *MLN* (1990), reprinted by permission of Johns Hopkins University Press; part of chapter 3 in a Spanish version by Eduardo Paz Leston and Ana María Torres as "Los senderos de lo histórico: Una nueva lectura de Borges" in *Primer Plano,* the literary supplement of *Página 12* (18 August 1991), with commentaries by Ricardo Piglia and Nicolás Rosa, reprinted by permission of Tomás Eloy Martínez and the publishers of *Página 12*; a Spanish version of chapter 5 as "Cuento (corto) y cuentas (largas) en 'La escritura del dios'" in a special journal issue of *Cuadernos Hispanoamericanos* (1992), reprinted by permission of the Instituto de Cooperación Iberoamericana.

The map of India appears thanks to the generosity of Professor Josef Opatrný, director of Latin American Studies at the Charles University in Prague. It is taken from Johannes Blaeu, *Novus Atlas* (Amsterdam, 1647), and is reproduced by permission of the Clementinum Library.

Nur dann zeig' ich, dass ich einen Schriftsteller verstanden habe, wenn ich in seinem Geiste handeln kann; wenn ich ihn, ohne seine Individualität zu schmälern, übersetzen und mannigfach verändern kann.

—Novalis, fragment 2005

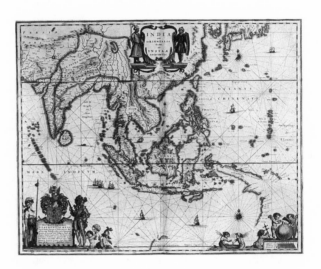

He saw a map of India as in a daze. Suddenly sure of himself, he touched one of the tiniest letters. A ubiquitous voice said to him: "The time of your labor has been granted."—Borges, "The Secret Miracle"

1

Introduction: History, Politics, and Literature

in Borges

¿Y el muerto, el increíble?
Su realidad está bajo las flores diferentes de él
y su mortal hospitalidad nos dará
un recuerdo más para el tiempo
y sentenciosas calles del Sur para merecerlas despacio
y brisa oscura sobre la frente que vuelve
y la noche que de la mayor congoja nos libra:
la prolijidad de lo real. (29)[1]

And the dead man, the incredible one? His reality lay beneath flowers different from himself and his mortal hospitality will give us one more memory for time and sententious streets in the South to be savored slowly and a dark gust on the forehead that looks back and night that frees us from the greatest anguish: the prolixity of the real.

The hallmark of Borges criticism is provided by the title of Ana María Barrenechea's important 1957 book, *La expresión de la irrealidad en la obra de Jorge Luis Borges* [The Expression of Irreality in the Work of Jorge Luis Borges]. "Borges," for many readers and critics, means "irrealidad," and the adjectives that have been created from the surname seem to refer to the unreal, the fictive, even the fictive to the second or third degree. Since Borges positions himself in the essays in *Discusión* [Discussion] and *Otras inquisiciones* [Other Inquisitions] in opposition to the social realist mode of narrative fiction that was dominant in Latin America[2] at the time of the

composition of *Ficciones* [Ficciones] and *El Aleph* [The Aleph], it is perhaps
not surprising that readers and critics, eager to have it one way or the other,
have embraced his "fantastic literature" or denounced him as escapist,[3] both
reactions which assume that the stories have nothing significant to say
about reality, history, or politics. To be sure, Sylvia Molloy's notion of a
vaivén [movement back and forth] in Borges (here, between reality and
fantasy) (*Letras* 194)[4] and Marina Kaplan and Davi Arrigucci's attention to
the grounding of "Tlön, Uqbar, Orbis Tertius" and "Biografía de Tadeo
Isidoro Cruz" [Biography of Tadeo Isidoro Cruz] in historical and cultural
realities[5] are signs that it should now be possible to reconsider the question
of the relation of Borges's fictions to realities beyond the text.[6] Similarly,
my Borges index (*The Literary Universe of Jorge Luis Borges*) and Evelyn
Fishburn and Psiche Hughes's recent Borges dictionary should quiet those
who have been assuming—wrongly—that all of those bookish references
in Borges's stories and essays are pure invention.[7]

Perhaps it would be useful to quote a few critics:

> In Borges, once the external world has vanished and with it, in conse-
> quence, *our reality,* the only secure possible mooring besides the self,
> the only term of the relation that is left, is irreality, which, by a simple
> change of sign, becomes in turn the only Borgesian reality. Thus, then,
> for Borges—and here we are threatened by paradox—the only reality
> is irreality. (Ferrer 59, emphasis in original)

> Borges takes away the "real" weight of history, situating it in a mythic
> horizon, negating it. When he places the whole episode (and, we
> might say, the whole period) in a place outside of the concrete and the
> factic, outside of the historical, he deprives it of all concrete impor-
> tance, of every possibility of influencing reality, of forming part of the
> historical process. . . . Once again, Borges negates reality. (Borello,
> *Peronismo* 180)

> Borges has assembled philosophical and literary schools, theologians
> and poets, murderers and saints, and has endowed them with literary
> equality. Historical and non-historical events and personalities have
> shed their traditional myths and taken on new mythical raiment.
> Borges' allegiance is not to historical truths. The primary purpose of
> all his motifs is to provide joy for the "fiction maker" and the selected
> group of seers who will recognize a fictitious web in the no less
> fictitious history recorded by man. (Sosnowski, "God's Script" 381)

The Borges fiction is . . . a context-free paradigm which can be re-activated through reading at any time and under any circumstances. (Franco 62)

Borges trivializes historical study, and this devaluation then becomes a necessary step in the freeing of the fictions from all external determinations. (Franco 69)

We have watched an admirable writer at work at the task of destroying reality and turning us into shadows. We have analyzed the process of dissolution of the concepts on which human beings found belief in their concrete being: the cosmos, personality and time. We have seen besides the horrifying presence of the infinite and the disintegration of substance into reflections and dreams. (Barrenechea, *Expresión de la irrealidad* 202)

In the stories of Borges . . . reality is seen "sub specie aeternitatis," that is to say, not the singular but the general, not individual beings but archetypes. Such a vision of reality must perforce be organized in a system; Borges uses systems already established by philosophy and theology. (Alazraki, *Prosa narrativa* 89)

Fiction [for Borges] is abstract and artificial rather than representational or mimetic. (Balderston, *El precursor velado* 176)

This catalog could be continued more or less indefinitely, yet it is—to borrow the title of the final book on Bolívar of the Venezuelan historian Vicente Lecuna (discussed in chapter 8)—a "catalog of mistakes and slanders." To refute Berkeley, Dr. Johnson kicked a stone (Boswell 1: 315); to refute the "irrealists," I will need a whole book,[8] but for starters I shall quote the end of Borges's essay "Nueva refutación del tiempo" [New Refutation of Time]:

Negar la sucesión temporal, negar el yo, negar el universo astronómico, son desesperaciones aparentes y consuelos secretos. Nuestro destino (a diferencia del infierno de Swedenborg y del infierno de la mitología tibetana) no es espantoso por irreal; es espantoso porque es irreversible y de hierro. El tiempo es la sustancia de que estoy hecho. El tiempo es un río que me arrebata, pero yo soy el río; es un tigre que me destroza, pero yo soy el tigre; es un fuego que me consume, pero yo soy el fuego. El mundo, desgraciadamente, es real; yo, desgraciadamente, soy Borges. (771)

> To deny temporal succession, to deny the self, to deny the astronomi-
> cal universe, are apparent acts of desperations and secret consolations.
> Our destiny (unlike the hell of Swedenborg or the hell of Tibetan
> mythology) is not frightening because it is unreal: it is frightening
> because it is irreversible and ironclad. Time is the substance of which I
> am made. Time is a river that sweeps me away, but I am the river; it is a
> tiger that tears me apart, but I am the tiger; it is a fire that consumes
> me, but I am the fire. The world, unfortunately, is real; I, unfortu-
> nately, am Borges.

To refute the "irrealist" position more fully it will be necessary to examine some of the stories in considerable depth;[9] taking at face value assertions from *Otras inquisiciones* like the one just quoted has led too often to the creation of an aesthetic "system" (of the kind mentioned—and practiced—by Alazraki) that is then imposed on the stories.

In this book I will study seven stories: three from *Ficciones* ("Pierre Menard, autor del Quijote," 1939 [Pierre Menard, Author of *Don Quixote*], "El jardín de senderos que se bifurcan," 1941 [The Garden of Forking Paths], and "El milagro secreto," 1943 [The Secret Miracle]), three from *El Aleph* ("La escritura del dios," 1949 [The God's Script], "Historia del guerrero y de la cautiva," 1949 [Story of the Warrior and the Captive], and "El hombre en el umbral," 1952 [The Man in the Threshold]), and one from *El informe de Brodie* ("Guayaquil," 1970).[10] My readings of these stories will involve the reconstruction of lost or hidden contexts through attention to historical references and "circumstantial details," but first I would like to reexamine the notions on representation and history in a series of key Borges texts and then provide a brief survey of some of the ideas on historical knowledge that seem most important to Borges and to my readings of his stories.

In an essay that is widely considered Borges's most important (albeit extremely dense and arbitrary) statement on narrative theory, "La postula-ción de la realidad" (1931) [The Postulation of Reality], he argues that one of the methods of creating verisimilitude in narrative "consiste en imaginar una realidad más compleja que la declarada al lector y referir sus deriva-ciones y efectos" (219) [consists in imagining a reality more complex than the one made explicit to the reader and then to tell of its consequences and effects], and that another involves the use of "pormenores lacónicos de larga proyección" (221) [laconic details that cast long shadows]. Both of these methods involve transgressing what formalist critics of whatever variety would consider the limits of the text and asking the reader to consider its silences and unrealized implications.[11] This is in fact what Borges and his friend and longtime collaborator, Adolfo Bioy Casares, themselves propose in the reported conversation at the beginning of "Tlön, Uqbar, Orbis Tertius":

> Bioy Casares había cenado conmigo esa noche y nos demoró una vasta polémica sobre la ejecución de una novela en primera persona, cuyo narrador omitiera o desfigurara los hechos e incurriera en diversas contradicciones, que permitieran a unos pocos lectores—a muy pocos lectores—la adivinación de una realidad atroz o banal. (431)

> Bioy Casares had had dinner with me that night and we were engaged in a vast argument about how to accomplish a novel in the first person, the narrator of which would omit or disfigure the facts and enter into various contradictions, which would permit some readers—very few readers—to guess at an atrocious or banal reality.

Indeed, in "Tlön" itself such a horrible or banal reality can be glimpsed at the end of the story, when the narrator proposes to dedicate his days to an improbable Quevedian translation of *Urne Buriall* instead of attending to a world dominated by fascism, dialectical materialism, and that new faith, Tlönism (443).[12]

What I propose to do here is to show how an imaginative reading of Borges's texts that is attentive to historical and political context can discover implications in those texts that considerably complicate the picture we have had up to now of the "postulation of reality" in Borges.[13] The texts I have chosen have often been used in discussions of the fantastic or of self-conscious textuality. While I do not deny these elements of Borges's fiction, I would argue that the interest of the stories is considerably heightened by attention to the historical and political elements, elements that can then be put in counterpoint to the others.

For example, Borges's complex discussions of time have been reduced in much of the criticism to notions of circularity, though his major writings on the subject (including "Historia de la eternidad" [History of Eternity], "Nueva refutación del tiempo," "El jardín de senderos que se bifurcan," and "El milagro secreto") assert that ideas of circular and nonlinear time are pleasant metaphysical diversions but that those who interest themselves in these notions are themselves mortal. For instance, it is more interesting to say, as Sosnowski does, that Hladík's "*Vindication of Eternity* must have been demonstrated to him on 29 March 1939" (*Borges y la cábala* 83), holding the notions of temporality and eternity in tension, than to have it one way or the other, as in Alazraki ("In 'The Secret Miracle' Hladík's destiny reaches its culmination, but not within human time, but instead in God's time" [*Prosa narrativa* 17]). In the case of "El jardín de senderos que se bifurcan," it is surprising how often Stephen Albert's theory of parallel universes has been taken as an explanation of the text, a detective story that begins with the news of the death of a German spy and ends with the murder of Stephen Albert a few hours later, and the whole of which is (or at least pretends to be) a gloss on a reference to a history of the Great War; if all things were equal, as Albert would have it, the narrative tension and suspense of the story would vanish.[14]

The phrase from "La postulación de la realidad" that speaks of "a more complex reality" fits a contextual reading of the kind I undertake here in an interesting sense: to get a sense of that greater complexity it is necessary not only to find the "source" of the intertextual reference (the passage in Liddell Hart's *History of the World War, 1914–1918* referring to torrential rains in the Ancre region, for instance) but also to open up the reference, to reconstruct it more fully than the older "source study" would find necessary. Any of the chapters of this book will serve as a demonstration of this idea, but perhaps the richest (and most perverse) is chapter 2, the reading of "Pierre Menard." Though the first step in a reading of this kind is to discover the specific sources (William James on "history, the mother of truth," Julien Benda on militarism, and so forth), the real beginning occurs when these referents are woven together into webs or constellations. In this way, a new text (a parallel fiction, perhaps) is proposed, one in which the implicit referents are made explicit. Connections with history and politics are reestablished; the "dialogues of the dead" are heard again.

Of course this is not so different from how the writing of history has been described. When Paul Valéry says that the past and the future are the greatest of human inventions (*History* 96–97, 122), when Michel de Certeau describes the "historiographical operation" as a writing that "places a population of the dead on stage" (99), what is at work is the interplay between mute and inert "facts" and the human imagination that creates stories or pictures.[15] The difference between this book and a work of historiography is that I—like the writer I am studying—take pleasure in mixing references to "reality" and to "fiction." In his essay on Hawthorne, Borges writes: "A Hawthorne le gustaban esos contactos de lo imaginario y lo real" (674) [Hawthorne liked such contacts between the imaginary and the real]. Fictions out of history, history composed of fiction—a principle of confusion seemingly reigns. What I will show in this book is the extent to which a more precise sense of how this cosmic confusion works will deepen our understanding of the stories, particularly those in *Ficciones* and *El Aleph*.

In a discussion of the function of reference in metafiction, Linda Hutcheon writes:

> It is the metafiction reader's perception of these superimposed levels of reference that directs him/her into, through, and *out of* the text, the text as language. In other words, in metafiction, the only way to make any mimetic connection to *real* referents, as I have defined them here, would be on the level of *process,* that is, of the act of reading as an act of ordering and creating. The encoding within the text itself of the decoder and his/her role acts as a set of instructions to the *reader who exists in the real world* and who, though implicated directly by the existence of this narratee or surrogate addressee *within* the text, is actually an existing being, an interpreting, deciphering being, outside the work of art. . . . If we insist on wanting to speak of fiction's real referents, which by Frege's definition must exist in the real world, metafiction teaches us that it is going to have to be on another level: the *process* may indeed turn out to be "referential" in this sense, and in a way that the *products* can not be. (10–11, emphasis in original)

Similarly, de Certeau, in his discussion of the challenges to narrative history within historiography, writes: "If therefore the story of 'what happened' disappears from scientific history (in order, in contrast, to appear in popular history), or if the narrative of facts takes on the allure of a 'fiction' belonging to a given type of discourse, we cannot conclude that the reference to the real is obliterated. This reference has instead been somewhat displaced" (43).

The referential "process" that Hutcheon speaks of, which operates through a "reader who exists in the real world" (whatever one's friends or colleagues may think!), is the one studied by Borges in "La postulación de la realidad," above all in the discussion of the techniques that force the reader to posit absent causes or absent effects not mentioned in the text. Similarly, the "displacement" of reference in the historiographical examples studied by de Certeau suggests that historiography cannot escape the positing of a "lost whole," which is a necessary fiction (and is necessarily a fiction). Suzanne Gearhart writes: "The relationship between fiction and history articulated here is one in which neither term can be reduced to the other because each is part of the process by which the other is constituted" (27). The reading of Borges's fiction articulated here grows out of this sense of mutual implication.

In "El pudor de la historia" [The Modesty of History] Borges—rather bemusedly—tells of Goethe's assertion on 20 September 1792, when he saw the Prussian army defeated by the French, that a new epoch in the history of the world had begun and that he and his friends had been witnesses to its birth. Borges comments:

> Desde aquel día han abundado las jornadas históricas y una de las tareas de los gobiernos (singularmente en Italia, Alemania y Rusia) ha sido fabricarlas o simularlas, con acopio de previa propaganda y de persistente publicidad. Tales jornadas, en las que se advierte el influjo de Cecil B. de Mille, tienen menos relación con la historia que con el periodismo: yo he sospechado que la historia, la verdadera historia, es más pudorosa y que sus fechas esenciales pueden ser, asimismo, durante largo tiempo, secretas. (754)

> Since that day there has been an abundance of historic occasions and one of the tasks of governments (particularly those of Italy, Germany, and Russia) has been to fabricate them or simulate them, with lots of prior propaganda and persistent publicity. Such occasions, in which the influence of Cecil B. de Mille can be noted, have less to do with history than with journalism: I have suspected that history, real history, is more modest and that its essential dates can therefore remain secret for a long time.

The events that he mentions in the essay, seemingly minor or secret but having important consequences, include Aeschylus's introduction of a second actor into the Greek drama (that is, the introduction of dialogue) and a dialogue (recorded by Snorri Sturluson in the *Heimskringla*) between two brothers fighting on opposite sides in a battle near York. On the latter episode, Borges comments that its importance is due not to the heroism of the actors but to the fact that it was written down by Snorri Sturluson, a descendant of the losing side of the battle:

> No el día en que el sajón dijo sus palabras, sino aquel en que un enemigo las perpetuó marca una fecha histórica. Una fecha profética de algo que aún está en el futuro: el olvido de sangres y de naciones, la solidaridad del género humano (756)

Not the day that the Saxon spoke those words, but the one when an enemy of his recorded them, marks a historical date. A date prophetic of something that is still in the future: the forgetting of blood and of nations, the solidarity of the human race.

Similarly, Borges's approach to the historical events in relation to which he sets the action of his stories is often oblique. Thus, he writes a story not about the meeting between San Martín and Bolívar in Guayaquil in 1822 but about the struggle between two historians for access to a crucial document; in "El jardín de senderos que se bifurcan," he does not write directly about the battle of the Somme but tangentially—and suggestively—in the margins of a major account of that battle; in "Tlön, Uqbar, Orbis Tertius," he writes not about the ideologies of totalitarianism but about a world unthinkable in any other terms. His approach is not unlike de Certeau's observations on the newer kinds of history writing:

> The historian is no longer a person who shapes an empire. He or she no longer envisages the paradise of a global history. The historian comes to circulate *around* acquired rationalizations. He or she works in the margins. In this respect the historian becomes a prowler. In a society gifted at generalization, endowed with powerful centralizing strategies, the historian moves in the direction of the frontiers of great regions already exploited. He or she "deviates" by going back to sorcery, madness, festival, popular literature, the forgotten world of the peasant, Occitania, etc., all these zones of silence. (79, emphasis in original)

Although Borges's first book of narrative fiction, *Historia universal de la infamia* (1935) [Universal History of Infamy], plays in its title with the Hegelian (and Kantian) notion of "universal history," the stories of the Tichborne Claimant, Billy the Kid, the widow Ching, and others parodically deflate the claims of Hegelian approaches to grand designs or universal patterns in world history.[16] In fact, Borges never tires of acknowledging his debt to Schopenhauer, whose pages blasting "Hegelian pseudophilosophy" and its "attempt . . . to comprehend the history of the world as a planned whole" (*World* 2: 443) as the work of "fools . . . shallow fellows and Philistines incarnate" (2: 444–45) could hardly be more vitriolic. For Schopenhauer, the historical event is "absolutely particular" (2: 440) and as such is irreducible to a "philosophy of history": "in so far as history always has for its object only the particular, the individual fact, and regards this as the exclusively real, it is the direct opposite and counterpart of philosophy, which considers things from the most universal point of view, and has the universal as its express object" (2: 441). Also, for Schopenhauer history approaches fiction: "History is therefore the more interesting the more special it is, but also the less trustworthy; and thus it approximates in all respects to a work of fiction" (2: 441).[17]

A number of the other thinkers whose writings on history Borges cites—Russell, William James, Valéry—also express distrust of the "grand design" of Hegelian universal history and insist on the notion that any design found in history is a mental construct. Russell, for instance, writes: "For all facts are equally true; and selection among them is only possible by means of some other criterion than their truth" (*Basic Writings* 522); later in the same 1904 essay "On History" he adds: "The past alone is truly real: the present is but a painful, struggling birth into the immutable being of what is no longer. Only the dead exist fully" (527). He argues that the study of history is useful in helping us "to view the present as already past" (525) but cautions the reader of historical narrative that "a history written after the event can hardly make us realize that the actors were ignorant of the future; it is difficult to believe that the late Romans did not know their empire was about to fall, or that Charles I was unaware of so notorious a fact as his own execution" (522).

James, in the essay that is the source of Menard's pragmatic formulation of the phrase "la historia, madre de la verdad" [history, the mother of truth],[18] argues that "the stream of time can be remounted only verbally" (*Essays in Pragmatism* 167) and that the historian does not write "facts" but *makes* truth out of facts: "The 'facts' themselves meanwhile are not *true*. They simply *are*" (171). Valéry similarly speaks of the insignificance of historical "facts" but argues (in terms very similar to Russell's) that the study of history helps us to view ourselves historically (*History* 124–25).[19] In the logbook of Monsieur Teste, he writes: "History is food for vulgar, credulous minds, in which imagination simply unfolds. Events annoy me, bore me, whether they are public or private. The 'greater' they are, the more stupid" (*Monsieur Teste* 128). Though Borges does not call "great" world historical events stupid in "El pudor de la historia," there is a degree of similarity to Monsieur Teste's position.[20]

Borges, reader of Schopenhauer, James, Valéry, and Russell, is clearly in sympathy with these rather skeptical approaches to matters of historical fact and (like them) values history for its pragmatic worth. Historical situations are useful to him in a special sense, though: they are linked to prior and subsequent situations, and notions of historical causality (however dubious in philosophical terms) imply narrative plots. If Borges writes (in "El arte narrativo y la magia" [Narrative Art and Magic]) that "el problema central de la novelística es la causalidad" (230) [the central problem of novel writing is causality], or shows (in "La postulación de la realidad") the means by which a narrative can be constructed in relation to absent causes or effects, then historical situations, whose seemingly ironclad nature does not withstand scrutiny, offer fascinating possibilities for narrative fiction. Thus, in "El Zahir" [The Zahir], "no hay hecho, por humilde que sea, que no implique la historia universal y su infinita concatenación de efectos y causas" (594) [there is no event, no matter how simple, that does not imply all of universal history and its infinite concatenation of effects and causes]; thus, in "La esfera de Pascal" [Pascal's Sphere], "quizá la historia universal es la historia de la diversa entonación de algunas metáforas" (638) [perhaps universal history is the history of the varying intonation of certain metaphors].[21]

The essay on Pascal, like so many others in *Otras inquisiciones,* is a reflection on the textual nature of the universe; however playful the reference to Hegelian "universal history" here, the tracing of the changing "intonation" of the metaphor of the universe as an infinite sphere is presented as a sort of history of *mentalités.* Over and over again, the essays in *Otras inquisiciones* are intimately concerned with history, however construed.[22] Thus, the essay on Quevedo opens with a reflection on the parallels between history and literature: "Como la otra, la historia de la literatura abunda en enigmas" (660) [Like the other kind of history, the history of literature abounds in enigmas]. "Magias parciales del Quijote" [Partial Magic of *Don Quixote*] ends: "En 1833, Carlyle observó que la historia universal es un infinito libro sagrado que todos los hombres escriben y leen y tratan de entender, y en el que también los escriben" (669) [In 1833, Carlyle observed that universal history is an infinite sacred book in which all human beings write and read and try to understand, and in which they are also written].[23] In "El espejo de los enigmas" [The Mirror of Enigmas], another tracing of the "diversa entonación" of a metaphor, Borges writes: "De ahí a pensar que la historia del universo—y en ella nuestras vidas y el más tenue detalle de nuestras vidas—tiene un valor inconjeturable, simbólico, no hay un trecho infinito" (720) [It is not a big step from this one to think that the history of the universe—and within it our lives and the smallest detail of our lives—has an inestimable symbolic value], while the second sentence of the essay on Beckford's *Vathek* opens with the phrase, "Tan compleja es la realidad, tan fragmentaria y tan simplificada la historia" (729) [So complex is reality, so fragmentary and simplified is history]. Similarly, in "De alguien a nadie" [From Someone to Nobody], Borges recalls the same chapter of *The World As Will and Representation* as discussed above: "Schopenhauer ha escrito que la historia es un interminable y perplejo sueño de las generaciones humanas; en el sueño hay formas que se repiten, quizá no hay otra cosa que formas" (739) [Schopenhauer has written that history is the interminable and uneasy dream of the generations of human beings; in sleep there are forms that are repeated, perhaps there are nothing but forms],[24] while the "Nueva refutación del tiempo," which ends with the admission that we experience time as "irreversible and ironclad" (771), earlier seeks to "refute" time through the discovery of a moment out of sequence: "¿No basta *un sólo término repetido* para desbaratar y confundir la historia del mundo, para denunciar que no hay tal historia?" (769, emphasis in original) [Isn't *a single repeated term* sufficient to disperse and confuse the history of the world, to reveal that there is no such history?].[25]

In *The Political Unconscious,* Jameson writes: "History is *not* a text, not a narrative, but . . . as an absent cause, it is inaccessible to us except in textual form, and . . . our approach to it and to the Real itself necessarily passes through its prior textualization, its narrativization in the political unconscious" (35). This formulation—which follows Lacan in supposing a gap between the realms of the Imaginary and the Symbolic, on the one hand, and the Real, on the other, a gap that cannot be closed by means of language and representation[26]—is surprisingly close to Borges's position in the important poem "El otro tigre" [The Other Tiger] from *El hacedor* (1960) [Dreamtigers]. The speaker in the poem stalks a tiger, first in the Library (in texts)—but that tiger consists of "símbolos y sombras, / Una serie de tropos literarios / Y de memorias de la enciclopedia" (824) [symbols and shadows, a series of literary tropes and of memories of the encyclopedia], and is thus not the "tigre fatal" of his search. Next, the speaker refers to a "real" tiger in Sumatra or Bengal, "pero ya el hecho de nombrarlo / Y de conjeturar su circunstancia / Lo hace ficción del arte y no criatura / Viviente de las que andan por la tierra" (825) [but already the fact of naming it and of conjuring up its circumstance turns it into a fiction of art and not a living creature like those that stalk the earth]. The final stanza reads:

> Un tercer tigre buscaremos. Este
> Será como los otros una forma
> De mi sueño, un sistema de palabras
> Humanas y no el tigre vertebrado

Que, más allá de las mitologías,
Pisa la tierra. Bien lo sé, pero algo
Me impone esta aventura indefinida,
Insensata y antigua, y persevero
En buscar por el tiempo de la tarde
El otro tigre, el que no está en el verso. (825)

We shall search for a third tiger. This one will be like the others a form of my dream, a system of human words and not the vertebrate tiger that, beyond all mythologies, stalks the earth. I know it well, but something obliges me to set out on this indefinite, senseless, and ancient adventure, and I persevere in searching afternoon after afternoon for the other tiger, the one that is not in the verse.

Referential language and narrative cannot "reach" that tiger, and (as with the intermediary stages that are interposed in the versions of Zeno's paradox reviewed in "La perpetua carrera de Aquiles y la tortuga" [The Perpetual Race of Achilles and the Tortoise] and "Avatares de la tortuga" [Avatars of the Tortoise]) each attempt to name or represent it results in the interpolation of yet another "interpretant," to use Charles Sanders Peirce's term. Yet, this recognition of the inadequacy of language to refer to objects need not imply (as it seems to for most of the critics of Borges) that the objects do not exist.[27] In "El otro tigre" Borges suggests that the writer's attempt to refer to something is an endless, and constantly frustrated, process.

Paul Fussell observes of a detail in "El Aleph" that Borges "gets it profoundly right as usual" (183), and the precision of the references to the most varied events of the past in the stories is astounding. Yet it is not the precision of Funes, who says: "Mi memoria, señor, es como vaciadero de basuras" (488) [My memory, sir, is like a garbage heap]. The details have been chosen or invented for what they connote, for the circumstances or contexts they suggest.[28] In one of his essays on Dante, Borges writes: "La precisión que acabo de indicar no es un artificio retorico; es afirmación de la probidad, de la plenitud, con que cada incidente del poema ha sido imaginado" (*Nueve ensayos dantescos* 88) [The precision I have just mentioned is not a rhetorical artifice; it is a proof of the integrity, of the plenitude, with which each incident of the poem has been imagined]. And this precision, this attention to context, shows up the error of those critics who looked for certain constant themes in Borges's work (for example, Alazraki). Compare the following:

En el suelo, apoyado en el mostrador, se acurrucaba, inmóvil como una cosa, un hombre muy viejo. Los muchos años lo habían reducido y pulido como las aguas a una piedra o las generaciones de los hombres a una sentencia. ("El Sur" 528)

On the floor, leaning against the counter, a very old man, motionless as an object, was curled up. The many years had reduced and polished him like water a stone or the human generations a saying. [The South]

A mis pies, inmóvil como una cosa, se acurrucaba en el umbral un hombre muy viejo. Los muchos años lo habían reducido y pulido como las aguas a una piedra o las generaciones de los hombres a una sentencia. ("El hombre en el umbral" 613)

At my feet, motionless as an object, a very old man was curled up in the threshold. The many years had reduced and polished him like water a stone or the human generations a saying. [The Man in the Threshold]

This "coincidence" has been read as evidence of Borges's conviction that time is circular, that one person is all humanity, that the individual does not exist, and so forth. But to do so is not to attend to the texts in which the sentences appear. In the one, the "ageless" man in the threshold in India turns out to control the narrative, and the British soldier who sees him in terms of a stereotyped "agelessness" is fooling himself. In the other, the old gaucho is one of the "adjectives or attributes" (to use a phrase that describes the things that surround—and define—Azevedo Bandeira in "El muerto" [548] [The Dead Man]) that will allow Dahlmann to discover his Argentine destiny. The differences between India and Argentina are highlighted by the repetition of the same sentence;[29] if we learn nothing else from Pierre Menard's *Quixote,* it should be obvious that the same words need not signify the same thing.[30]

The research and writing of this book have followed two contrary directions, both of which are discussed in "Pierre Menard, autor del Quijote": the desire to recover the fullness of Borges's knowledge of his historical subjects at the time of the composition of the stories discussed here and the recognition that historical knowledge of those subjects has advanced in the last few decades and that I am situated in my own time, not in Borges's. Thus, in writing about "La escritura del dios," I have labored to discover what Borges—in 1949—could have read about Maya culture and the Spanish conquest of Guatemala at the same time that I have been acutely aware that Maya studies have been revolutionized in the years since, and my notes often register these gaps; a similar double positioning is present in the other chapters.

Issues that have mattered to my generation—decolonization, the Vietnam War, the Central American conflicts, the splintering of the socialist bloc, the unraveling of populist projects in Latin America, the radical questioning of the imperial designs of the United States, the war in the Persian Gulf—will find more than an echo in my discussions of stories from *Ficciones* and *El Aleph,* written between 1939 and 1952, which deal with such distant events as the Indian Mutiny of 1857, the Spanish invasion of Guatemala, and the Boxer Rebellion in China. By inclination and training I feel the attraction of an ideal of "pure scholarship," of annihilation of the self before the matter being studied, yet this book is also an act of undermining ivory towers, using the Menardian techniques of deliberate anachronism and equivocal attribution. In chapter 7 on "El hombre en el umbral" I have not shied away from the current theoretical discussions of Orientalism and postcolonial discourse, and similar echoes will be heard throughout. Though I have made nothing up (not even the book by Pierre Menard on the psychoanalysis of handwriting), I have enjoyed playing with the permutations and combinations of the texts I have read, and now I know much better what fun Borges had at the time of writing.

Why have I devoted fifteen years to the study of Borges (and three books), when the critical consensus has been that he is an "escapist" writer? Partly, of course, because I am convinced that the consensus is profoundly mistaken, and that Borges, even Borges, cannot but write out of context. (I am turning that phrase inside out here, deliberately.) His writing is intimately marked by the experience of twentieth-century Argentine history and politics, by life in Europe during World War I and just after, by association with figures as passionate (and as radically different from one another) in ideological stance as were Leopoldo Lugones, Macedonio Fernández, Victoria Ocampo, María Rosa Oliver, and José Bianco.

I have been slow in becoming certain about the nature of this project. My first work on Borges was done in the era of what we might call "high structuralism," as it existed in universities in the United States, and emphasized self-referentiality, the fantastic, the web of intertextual (but always literary) reference. Yet even in my dissertation on Borges and Stevenson, *El precursor velado,* written more than ten years ago, I was beginning to break out of that mold: in my chapter on the representation of the Tichborne Claimant in *Historia universal de la infamia* I was compelled by curiosity and responsibility to look far beyond the encyclopedia article that was the explicit source of the Borges story, though I did not make the sort of use of what I found that I would make now. Similarly, the preparation of an index to references in Borges, *The Literary Universe of Jorge Luis Borges,* published in 1986, made me ponder the nature of reference to "reality" in this writing, though I was still comfortable with describing the writing as a game with texts. The turning point came about the same time, in "The Mark of the Knife," when I worked on the motif of the scar in "La forma de la espada" [The Shape of the Sword], an essay not included here but already pointing in the direction of my current work: the scar in the story is a textual mark, to be sure, but an irreducible mark referring beyond narrative (and narrativity) to the experience of personal and political violence. Similarly, when I wrote in "Dichos y hechos" on Borges's relation to the "penny dreadfuls" of Eduardo Gutiérrez I was beginning to consider the debate enacted in his writing between the professions of arms and letters.

I am not the only one who has thought long and hard about a contextualized reading of Borges; Davi Arrigucci and Marina Kaplan have written admirable essays on "Biografía de Tadeo Isidoro Cruz" and "Tlön, Uqbar, Orbis Tertius," respectively, that are parallel to my project here, and Evelyn Fishburn and Psiche Hughes, in their wonderful Borges dictionary, explore the question of referentiality in the stories in a way I find helpful and persuasive. Scholars whose work has most deeply influenced mine are L. A. Murillo, James Irby, Sylvia Molloy, and Noé Jitrik. I doubt that any of these people would fully endorse the project articulated here, but I hope the creative misreading I have made of their work will be taken as a sign of how much I value it.

My title acknowledges the charge made when I have presented parts of this project at a variety of campuses and conferences—that I am taking things out of context. Indeed. The quotation from Kafka's diary entry for Christmas Day, 1911 ("Since people lack a sense of context, their literary activities are out of context too" [qtd. in Mark Anderson 261]) could be restated: "Since critics lack a sense of context, their literary activities are out of context too." But perhaps we can follow Bloom's hints on misreading and gloss Kafka to be saying (like his contemporary, the Jewish doctor in Vienna) that critics and writers always write out of (that is, from) their own context, from their immediate circumstances, even if every attempt is made to blur or erase that context. Kafka, Beckett, Eliot, Robbe-Grillet, Borges: we are only beginning to be able to read what is under erasure.[31] The recovery of the "context" in, surrounding, and outside a text, then, is a necessary stage in the interpretation of the text, yet speaking of it is necessarily transgressive, a "return of the repressed."

My attempts to historicize Borges's works may have a certain polemical force because history still constitutes a scandal for literary theory: something irreducibly beyond the text, although (as Jameson says) it may be accessible to us only through texts. The scandal that history constitutes for literature (or that narrative fiction—and theory—constitute for history, as in the work of Hayden White) is rather like the scandal that the notion of material reality causes the philosophers of Tlön.[32] And here is what happens when the boundary between the two is opened:

> El contacto y el hábito de Tlön han desintegrado este mundo. Encantada por su rigor, la humanidad olvida y torna a olvidar que es un rigor de ajedrecistas, no de ángeles. Ya ha penetrado en las escuelas el (conjetural) "idioma primitivo" de Tlön, ya la enseñanza de su historia armoniosa (y llena de episodios conmovedores)[33] ha obliterado a la que presidió mi niñez; ya en las memorias un pasado ficticio ocupa el sitio de otro, del que nada sabemos con certidumbre—ni siquiera que es falso. (443)

> The routine contact with Tlön has made the world disintegrate. Enchanted by its rigor, humanity forgets once and again that it is the rigor of chess players, not of angels. Already the (hypothetical) "primitive tongue" of Tlön has made its way into the schools, already the teaching of its harmonious history (full of moving episodes) has obliterated the history that presided over my childhood; already in memory a fictitious past occupies the place of the other past, of which we know nothing with certainty, not even that it is false.

The narrator of the story pretends to know better, to be able to distinguish a true History from these new historical fictions. The authorial irony, however, is borne out by the fact that the description of this "fictitious past" perfectly accords with the skeptical approaches to historical truth discussed earlier. For Pierre Menard, for instance, "La verdad histórica . . . no es lo que sucedió; es lo que juzgamos que sucedió" (449) [Historical truth . . . is not what happened; it is what we judge to have happened]. The world is "disintegrated" by this approach, yet the fragments can be made to cohere in a design that may not exist outside the mind; so, even the world itself may be judged to be the mind's will and representation. This "disintegration" is for Borges as characteristic of the writing of fiction as it is of the writing of history.

2

Menard and His Contemporaries: The Arms

and Letters Debate

A society rises from brutality to order. As barbarism is the era of *fact,* so the era of order must necessarily be the reign of *fiction*—for there is no power capable of founding order on the mere coercion of bodies by bodies. Fictional powers are needed for that.—Paul Valéry, *History* 215

John Frow has written: "Borges's 'Pierre Menard, Author of *Don Quixote*' is a perfectly serious joke that we are still learning how to take seriously" (170).[1] In that spirit, then, here is the story of how a French symbolist from Nîmes came to rewrite several fragments of *Don Quixote,* and some new hypotheses on the significance of that project.

First, to sketch out Menard's generation.[2] Since his first publications date from the late 1890s and he gravitated in symbolist circles, it is not unreasonable to imagine him born in the 1860s or 1870s. His contemporaries thus include Maurice Barrès (1862–1923), Romain Rolland (1866–1944), Julien Benda (1867–1956), Marcel Schwob (1867–1905), Paul Claudel (1868–1955), André Gide (1869–1951), Paul Valéry (1871–1945), Marcel Proust (1871–1922), Léon Blum (1872–1950), Charles Péguy (1873–1914), Colette (1873–1954), and Henri Barbusse (1874–1935). Of these, Menard seems to have been in contact only with Valéry, whose origins in Sète and Montpellier perhaps linked him to the symbolist of Nîmes. Valéry was close to a number of the others, and his intercession perhaps saved Menard from provincial isolation. Though Menard published the two versions of his symbolist sonnet in *La Conque* in 1899, seven years after that magazine had ceased publication, he was linked through that shell of a review with Valéry, Gide, and Blum, all of whom had been important there, and of course with the journal's editor, Pierre Louÿs (Valéry, *Oeuvres* 1: 1532–34; Lacouture 8). His later publications in the *Nouvelle Revue Française* date from the period when the journal was led first by André Gide and then by Jean Paulhan and Julien Benda;[3] Menard's later polemic with Benda about "arms and letters" confirms that they had some contact (presumably through the *Nouvelle Revue*) during the 1920s.

The paper trail left by the rest of Menard's "visible work" shows the extent to which he was involved in the intellectual milieu of his place and time. For instance, it is not hard to discover a series of links between his works and those of his friend from Montpellier. Menard's initial publications in *La Conque*—two different versions of the same sonnet—obey Valéry's dictum in the 1927 preface to his *Album de vers anciens:* "It is known that the author is no enemy of a system of successive and unending transformations of a work, and that he considers a poem to be an inexhaustible inward object prone to infinite rewritings and changes of mind" (*Oeuvres* 1: 1533). The poem Menard perversely chose to rewrite in alexandrines, "Le Cimetière marin" [The Marine Cemetery], which Valéry had of course written intentionally in an unusual metric form with ten syllables, as he explains in a later essay (1: 1503),[4] contains a stirring stanza on the cruelty of Zeno for having condemned Achilles to immobility (1:151). Zeno's paradox so interested Menard that in 1917 he published *Les problèmes d'un problème* [The Problems of a Problem]. The narrator of the story does not give the date of the second edition of this work, in which Menard "renueva los capítulos dedicados a Russell y a Descartes" [445] [revises the chapters dedicated to Russell and to Descartes], but the revision probably occurred after the 1920 publication of the Valéry poem.[5] The article Menard wrote on possible changes in the game of chess, which he proposes, recommends, discusses, and then rejects (445), parallels Valéry's discussion of a card game: "Instead of playing a straightforward card game with destiny, as we used to do, knowing the rules, knowing the number of cards and face cards, we are now in the position of a player who discovers with amazement that his partner's hand contains face cards he has never seen before, and that the rules of the game change with every deal" (*History* 175–76). And even his handwritten list of verses whose power depends on punctuation echoes Valéry's recollection of Stendhal making fun "of certain learned men he had met: despotism had driven them to take refuge in discussing the commas in a text of Ovid" (*History* 210).

Menard's apparent dilettantism—his writings on mathematics, metrics, chess, art, fashionable society, symbolic logic, philosophy, linguistics—was not unusual in the period before the Great War. Léon Blum, for instance, during the time between his work as a lawyer in the defense of Émile Zola for his part in the Dreyfus affair (1898) and the discovery of his vocation as a socialist leader (1914), wrote several volumes of literary criticism and theater reviews, a study of Stendhal (1914), and *Nouvelles Conversations de Goethe avec Eckermann* (1901) [New Conversations of Goethe and Eckermann], a work in which Goethe discusses contemporary politics and all sorts of other things. Julien Benda, who is mentioned in the text as the author of *La Trahison des clercs* (1927) [The Betrayal of the Intellectuals], in the years before the war published philosophical reflections on the Dreyfus affair (*Dialogues à Byzance,* 1900 [Dialogues in Byzantium]) and an attack on Bergson's intuitive philosophy (*Bergson ou une philosophie de la mobilité,* 1912 [Bergson or a Philosophy of Mobility]). Georges Sorel (1847–1922),[6] the syndicalist thinker who was one of Benda's main targets in *La Trahison des clercs,* wrote on the death of Socrates, pragmatism, the Bible, the decline of the Roman Empire, Vico, mathematics, a medieval bridge near Perpignan, and metaphysics as well as on violence, Marxism, the Dreyfus case, and syndicalist theory. But the most protean figure of all was Menard's friend Valéry, who wrote on politics, art, music, history, philosophy, military troop training, political economy, and, of course, literature.

Menard's *curriculum vitae* for the period from 1899 to 1914 is not all that different from those of his generational cohorts.[7] What does set Menard apart from the others—at least until we reach the discussion of his version of chapter 38 of the first part of *Don Quixote*—is the fact that Menard was able to stay, to use Romain Rolland's unhappy phrase, "au-dessus de la mêlée": none of the items in the bibliography of his "visible work" concerns history or politics. He wrote nothing about the Dreyfus affair, the Crusades, French nationalism, socialism, the French Revolution, or the Great War (unless one considers his 1917 book on Achilles and the tortoise to be an oblique discussion of the battle of Verdun), and this silence sets him apart from all of the contemporaries listed above. Menard was, however, only biding his time, as we shall see.

The great swerve in Menard's career from "visible" to "invisible" works begins after the Armistice. When Menard first contemplates rewriting *Don Quixote,* his first impulse is "conocer bien el español, recuperar la fe católica, guerrear contra los moros o contra el turco, olvidar la historia de Europa entre los años de 1602 y de 1918, *ser* Miguel de Cervantes" (447) [to know Spanish well, to recover the Catholic faith, to battle with the Moors or the

Turks, to forget the history of Europe between the years of 1602 and 1918, to *be* Miguel de Cervantes]. The conception of the project, then, can reasonably be dated as taking place in late 1918 or in 1919. However, the narrator gives two bits of information that suggest that the project came into sharper focus a few years later:

> Dos textos de valor desigual inspiraron la empresa. Uno es aquel fragmento filológico de Novalis—el que lleva el número 2005 en la edición de Dresden—que esboza el tema de la *total identificación* con un autor determinado. Otro es uno de esos libros parasitarios que sitúan a Cristo en un bulevar, a Hamlet en la Cannebière o a don Quijote en Wall Street. Como todo hombre de buen gusto, Menard abominaba de esos carnavales inútiles. (446, emphasis in original)

> Two texts of unequal value inspired his enterprise. One is that philological fragment of Novalis—the one numbered 2005 in the Dresden edition—which sketches out the theme of *total identification* with a given author. The other is one of those parasitic books that situate Christ on a boulevard, Hamlet on the Cannebière, or Don Quixote on Wall Street. Like every man of good taste, Menard hated such frivolous carnivals.

The Dresden edition of Novalis's *Fragmente* was not published until 1929, but the text does not say that Menard consulted that particular edition; the fragment in question, "Pflichtenlehre des Lesers" [The Ethics of Reading], declares: "I only show that I have understood an author when I can act in his spirit; when, without diminishing his individuality, I can translate him and transform him in many ways" (644).[8] The second of the foundational texts has been taken by Emilio Carilla (*Jorge Luis Borges* 37n) to be Enrique Méndez Calzada's *Jesús en Buenos Aires* (1922). I would hope instead that the reference is to a "libro parasitario" that would have been more likely to come to Menard's attention because of its publication to great scandal and acclaim in Paris in that same year, 1922—Joyce's *Ulysses*.[9] In either case, let us assume that Menard undertook the composition of *Don Quixote* in a serious way in 1922, but that most of the extant fragments date not from the first years of apprenticeship in the great work but from the years immediately preceding Menard's death. The narrator[10] ends the obituary with a note on the date and place of its composition: "Nîmes, 1939."[11] Since there is also reference in the text to a letter from Menard to the narrator dated 30 September 1934, it would appear that Menard undertook the writing of chapters 9, 22, and 38 in the mid- to late 1930s: during the civil war in neighboring Spain (the subject, of course, of his novel) and the period of European rearmament before World War II.

Chapter 9 of Menard's *Quixote* includes the famous sentence on "la verdad, madre de la historia" that Menard rewrote under the tutelage of William James.[12] It also contains an anxious reflection on literary modernity—Don Quixote's library included modern books so perforce "su historia debía de ser moderna" (92) [his history should be modern]—and a passing reference to Freud and other "sabios . . . que no solamente escribían sus hechos, sino que pintaban sus más mínimos pensamientos y niñerías, por más escondidas que fuesen" (92) [wise men . . . who not only write the facts, but also paint their slightest thoughts and childish fancies, no matter how concealed they may be].[13] Menard makes a telling remark on his own useless labor, that of rewriting an already existent book, when he says that "aun a mí no se me deben negar [respetos], por el trabajo y diligencia que puse en buscar el fin desta agradable historia" (93) [even I cannot be denied respect for the labor and diligence I have invested in searching for an ending for this pleasant history]. It is also in this chapter that Menard mentions the manuscript of Cide Hamete Benengeli: "Otras algunas menudencias había que advertir, pero todas son de poca importancia y que no hacen al caso a la verdadera relación de la historia, que ninguna es mala como sea verdadera" (95) [Some other trifles should be mentioned, but they are all of little importance and do not bear on the true account of the story, for no story is bad as long as it is true]. Here, he expresses the same skeptical approach to historical truth as that summarized by the narrator of the obituary in the words: "La verdad histórica, para él, no es lo que sucedió, es lo que juzgamos que sucedió" (449) [Historical truth, for him, is not what happened, it is what we judge to have happened]. The reference to the "verdadera relación de la historia" prepares the reader for the urgent and immediate pertinence of chapter 38.

Chapter 22, the adventure of the galley slaves, was written by Menard only in part. It is easy to guess which part it is, though, given Menard's anxiety of influence. It is in this chapter that Don Quixote meets up for the first time with Ginés de Pasamonte, who informs him that he has written his own life's story "por estos pulgares" (208) [with these thumbs, that is, by himself] and compares his version with that of other examples of the picaresque genre. When Don Quixote asks whether the book is finished, Ginés answers: "¿Cómo puede estar acabado . . . si aún no está acabada mi vida? Lo que está escrito es desde mi nacimiento hasta el punto que esta última vez me han echado en galeras" (209) [How can it be finished . . . if my life is not yet finished? What is written goes from my birth until the last time I was thrown in the galleys]. We recognize Menard's self-reflexive irony here, as well as his sense of the fragmentation that literature and time suffer in the modern world. Also, the pun on "galeras" (the prison galley ships but also galley proofs) hints at Menard's sense that publication is an act of violence, a public rape of the author: hence his decision not to publish his masterpiece, *Don Quixote*.

The most important of the three chapters, however, is chapter 38, the discourse on arms and letters. The narrator of the obituary comments that the decision in favor of arms is justifiable in Cervantes (or in Quevedo) but more difficult to understand in Menard: "¡Pero que el don Quijote de Pierre Menard—hombre contemporáneo de *La trahison des clercs* y de Bertrand Russell—reincida en esas nebulosas sofisterías!" (449) [But that the Don Quixote of Pierre Menard—a contemporary of *The Betrayal of the Intellectuals* and of Bertrand Russell—should slide back into those murky sophistries!]. In what follows I will try to situate Menard's contribution to the debate on pacifism and militarism, a debate carried on with great vigor in the period from 1914 to 1939 by Rolland, Barbusse, Benda, Sorel, and a variety of others in France, as well as by Russell and Woolf in England, Gandhi in India, Hašek in Czechoslovakia, and Liebknecht, Luxemburg, and Remarque in Germany.[14] To limit the scope of the discussion, I will concentrate on the French debates on the issues of war and peace (or "arms and letters," as Menard prefers to put it), though I will bring in Bertrand Russell since he is explicitly mentioned in the text.

Modern pacifism[15] came into being as we know it around the time of World War I, first in the writings of Tolstoy, William James ("The Moral Equivalent of War," 1912), and Gandhi, then notably in the writings of Romain Rolland, particularly *Au-dessus de la mêlée* (the English version of which appeared as *Above the Battle* in 1916),[16] and of Bertrand Russell, who spent some time in prison in Britain because of his opposition to militarism and who wrote a volume against war during this period (*Why Men Fight*, 1917). The period after the war was marked by the notable pacifist writings of Erich Maria Remarque (*Im Westem nichts Neues*, 1929)[17] and of Aldous Huxley (*Ends and Means*, 1932) and by the pacifist resolution of the Students' Union at Oxford in 1933. It is interesting to note that pacifist discourse evolved from a high-toned humanitarian appeal to civilized values in Rolland and the James essay (echoed by Russell's *Why Men Fight*)[18] to the ever more pragmatic discussions of the relation between opposition to war and the desire for change in civil society (in Woolf's *Three Guineas*, Gandhi's numerous writings on the theme, Huxley, and A. J. Muste); the essay by James is ironically the least pragmatic of the series, except perhaps for his suggestion (later institutionalized as the "alternative service" performed by conscientious objectors) that human impulses to aggression should be recognized and organized toward socially beneficial ends.

In the years that concern us here, there were important debates within the French Socialist party between pacifist and militarist factions; tragically, the most eloquent of the French pacifist Socialists, Jean Jaurès, was assassinated in 1914, and the surviving leaders of the party were to wrestle over the issue of pacifism, particularly during the Great War and in the painful period of the civil war in Spain when Léon Blum was prime minister in France of a Popular Front government (Lacouture 107–11, 215–20, 305–58). The Communist party, though based on a theory of revolutionary violence, was obedient to the dictates from Moscow that postponed the moment of insurrection and asserted that the party was the party of peace. (This was to change to some extent at the time of Stalin's decision to authorize the formation of the international brigades to aid the Republican government in Spain, and Communist militants were active in the resistance to Vichy and the Nazi army of occupation.) The only groups that actively supported an aesthetics and politics of force were the nationalist groups on the right such as the Action française, the sympathizers with Italian and German fascism, and that peculiar ideological hybrid who was Georges Sorel, author of a 1908 book, *Reflections on Violence,* that is one of Benda's main targets in *La Trahison des clercs* (and later, at the end of his life, an admirer—and mentor—of both Mussolini and Lenin [Roth 141–211]). Thus, in the writings of Maurras, Barrès,[19] Céline, and Brasillach one finds celebrations of force not radically unlike those of Marinetti in Italy, the Freikorps writers in Germany,[20] or Wyndham Lewis in England.[21] Valéry's position will be taken up a bit later.

Julien Benda's book *La Trahison des clercs,* published in 1927, became something of a cause célèbre at the time (though not to the same extent as Rolland's essays published during the war). In the book Benda argues that the intellectual (the "clerc" of his title) must strive for a voice that is free of nationalism and xenophobia, even at the risk of conflict with society. If the intellectual leaves the ivory tower of pure speculation and meditation, it should only be in order to take stands on matters of pure moral principle, such as the cause of Truth in the Dreyfus affair; there should never be the taint of mundane "politics" or self-interest. Benda's argument is rather convoluted in what he attacks Barrès and Sorel for what he judges to be their sordid prostitution of the intellect in the service of political interest but does not rule out all political involvement. In fact, in the years after the publication of *Trahison*, Benda often complained that he had been misread, and he was outspoken in his defense of the Spanish Republic and active in a variety of left-wing efforts in the years after World War II (Schalk 39–46; Sarlo 135; Aznar Soler and Schneider 16–19, 237–39).[22] Benda reserves some of his harshest words for Romain Rolland, whose "mystical pacifism" he deplores in terms as strong as those he uses to attack the militarist intellectuals like Barrès and Sorel. His own position is a pacifist one, but he would divorce pacifism from appeals to sentiment and instead make it part of a return to the abstract morality of liberalism as he construes it.

Against Barrès and company, Benda writes: "It is certainly something new to see men of thought preaching the abasement of the toga before the sword, especially in the country of Montesquieu and Renan" (*Betrayal* 82). A bit later, he attacks militarism for assuming a pragmatic guise:

> This exhortation to concrete advantages and to that form of soul which procures them, is expressed by the modern "clerk" in another very remarkable teaching: By praise of the military life and the feelings which go with it, and by contempt for civil life and the morality it implies. We know the doctrine preached in Europe during the past fifty years by its most esteemed moralists, their apology for war "which purifies," their veneration for the man of arms "the archtype [*sic*] of moral beauty," their proclamation of the supreme morality of "violence" or of those who settle their differences by duels and not before a jury, while they declare that respect for contracts is the "weapon of the weak," the need for justice the "characteristic of slaves." (101–2)[23]

But he is not hopeful that war will be eliminated. In fact, the militarization of Europe during World War I seems to him a prologue of things to come: "Men will not revise their values for wars which only last fifty months and only kill a couple of million men in each nation. One may even doubt whether war will ever become so terrible as to discourage those who love it, the more so since they are not always the men who have to fight" (155–56). Note that he poses the choice not between the "profession of arms" and the "profession of letters" (or "the toga" and "the sword") but between those intellectuals who support war and political conflict and those who choose to rise above such things; the soldiers themselves, as he notes with savage irony, are not parties to this debate.

Russell's initial writings on militarism are explicitly indebted to William James's "Moral Equivalent of War," as when he writes: "Blind impulse is the source of war, but it is also the source of science, and art, and love. It is not the weakening of impulse that is to be desired, but the direction of

impulse towards life and growth rather than towards death and decay"
(*Why Men Fight* 12–13). He moves beyond James, though, when he bases
his discussions on the experiences of "active pacifists," of conscientious
objectors and noncooperators, during the war (17), as well as on the
experiences of those who sought to participate willingly in the conflict
(49n), and he is quite concrete about the links between militarization and
state power (and elsewhere in the book considers the links between capital-
ism and militarism): "The excessive power of the State, partly through
internal oppression, but principally through war and the fear of war, is one
of the chief causes of misery in the modern world, and one of the main
reasons for the discouragement which prevents men [*sic*] from growing to
their full mental stature" (65–66). Unlike Benda, though, he thinks that
intellectuals are more prone to feelings of nationalism and militarism than
others because they are more aware of what is happening beyond the
frontiers of the nation: "Only educated men [*sic*] are likely to be warlike at
ordinary times, since they alone are vividly aware of other countries or of
the part which their own nation might play in the affairs of the world. But it
is only their knowledge, not their nature, that distinguishes them from their
more ignorant compatriots" (82).

Here Russell turns upside down the idea of the moral superiority of the
intellectual that we saw in Benda. Indeed, he takes a pessimistic view of
human nature (though, like James, he thought it possible to organize
human aggression toward positive ends): "The ultimate fact from which
war results is the fact that a large proportion of mankind have an impulse to
conflict rather than harmony, and can only be brought to cooperate with
others in resisting or attacking a common enemy" (113).[24] In the final essay
in the book, "What We Can Do," Russell writes: "War, at its outset,
integrates the life of a nation, but it disintegrates the life of the world, and
in the long run the life of a nation too, when it is as severe as the present
war" (255). He argues that the pacifist cannot be required to come up with a
specific program in the midst of a world war (though his program evidently
mixes individual moral decision with a restructuring of the world economy,
the educational system, marriage, and institutionalized religion): "Until
the war is ended there is little use in detail, since we do not know what kind
of world the war will leave" (266). Years later, in his *History of Western
Philosophy*, Russell would quote with approval these famous words by Karl
Marx: "The truth, i.e., the reality and power, of thought must be demonstrated in practice. The contest as to the reality or non-reality of a thought
which is isolated from practice, is a purely scholastic question. . . . Philoso-

phers have only *interpreted* the world in various ways, but the real task is to *alter* it" (784, emphasis in original).

Similarly, in *Why Men Fight,* Russell insists on an active concept of truth, that intellectuals must use their talents to change the world: "It is necessary to create a new hope, to build up by our thought a better world than the one which is hurling itself into ruin. Because the times are bad, more is required of us than would be required in normal times. Only a supreme fire of thought and spirit can save future generations from the death that has befallen the generation which we knew and loved" (270–71). The pacifist philosopher, then, is not "au-dessus de la mêlée" but is involved in a work of social transformation that seeks to be the "moral equivalent of war."[25]

Georges Sorel, whose *Réflexions sur la violence* (1908) so outraged Julien Benda, asserted that the violence of the oppressed was a revolutionary act, though Russell bemusedly notes in his history of philosophy that Sorel "used Bergsonian irrationalism to justify a revolutionary labour movement having no definite goal"[26] and asserts that Sorel himself was so lacking in direction that he went from revolutionary syndicalism to monarchism (791).[27] Sorel was particularly impatient with parliamentary Socialists, who seemed to him "a group of intellectuals, who through the utilisation for their own ends of both the state and the proletariat, had established a position of power for themselves" (Jennings 131).[28] Sorel wrote: "Everything may be saved, if the proletariat, by their use of violence, manage to re-establish the division into classes, and so restore to the middle class something of its former energy" (98). Sorel argues, then, not for violence by the intellectual but for violence by the proletariat against the class to which the intellectual belongs. It is dizzying to rethink *Don Quixote* from this perspective, since neither the use of violence by the knight-errant nor the repressive force of the state is justified, but the many acts of popular *ressentiment* (usually against the knight, such as the various incidents involving the *pícaro* Ginés de Pasamonte) are celebrated as expressions of positive energy. In fact, Sorel's contribution to the arms and letters debate turns out to be rather more complicated than expected; he was in favor of class violence but opposed to war because "international conflicts . . . generally result in a compromise, a negation of the ends of violence" (Horowitz 124). Thus, though Sorel may seem the most prominent spokesman for the point of view expressed by Menard's Don Quixote in the arms and letters debate, he argues not for the "profession of arms" against the "profession of letters" but against both professions.

Valéry's meditations on the world after the Great War were centered on the theme of order and chaos, as exemplified by the epigraph that opens this chapter, taken from his preface to Montesquieu's *Lettres persanes*. In "The Crisis of the Mind" (1919), Valéry writes these somber words:

> Standing, now, on an immense sort of terrace of Elsinore that stretches from Basel to Cologne, bordered by the sands of Nieuport, the marshes of the Somme, the limestone of Champagne, the granites of Alsace . . . our Hamlet of Europe is watching millions of ghosts.
>
> But he is an intellectual Hamlet, meditating on the life and death of truths; for ghosts, he has all the subjects of our controversies; for remorse, all the titles of our fame. He is bowed under the weight of all the discoveries and varieties of knowledge, incapable of resuming this endless activity; he broods on the tedium of rehearsing the past and the folly of always trying to innovate. He staggers between two abysses— for two dangers never cease threatening the world: order and disorder. (*History* 28–29)

Unsurprisingly, Valéry's writings during the period between the world wars speak for the party of order: often for the League of Nations on an international scale, on occasion for dictatorship at the national level. Though he is careful in his writings in favor of the idea of dictatorship to say that he speaks in the abstract, not in the concrete (as in his preface to a book on the Portuguese dictator Salazar [*History* 233–40]), and though his friend Salvador de Madariaga tries to paint him as an internationalist and a liberal (*History* xxi–xxxvi), he shares with Fernando Pessoa, Wyndham Lewis, Marinetti, and others a basic sympathy for the corporativist ideal. His son François is at pains to explain his friendship with Marshal Pétain: "Having by chance been designated in 1931 to receive Marshal Pétain into the French Academy with the traditional eulogy,[29] Valéry became his friend and, by forcing his pen perhaps, made of the Marshal the prototype of the warrior as a man of intellect" (*History* xiv).[30] His friendship with Pétain seems to have remained intact under the Vichy government.[31] He himself had written on troop training in the last years of the nineteenth century; Pétain must have seemed larger than life for him, a heroic example of a soldier-intellectual.

For Russell and Benda (but not for Sorel) the debate is not between the soldier and the writer but between the militarist intellectual and the pacifist intellectual. One of the striking features of Menard's text is the ways in which the new "class" (or "social category," as Régis Debray would prefer [21]) of the intelligentsia is inscribed in the "arms and letters" debate in chapter 38 of *Don Quixote*. For Cervantes—as for Camões and Garcilaso before him and Quevedo after—the categories of "soldier" and "poet" were not mutually exclusive, but for the men of Menard's generation the two professions were clearly delineated, so that when Péguy died in the battle of the Marne in 1914, it was after he had made a choice against literature (as would also be true in 1940 in the case of Sartre's friend Paul Nizan [Schalk 71–73]). One reason for the vehemence of Benda's book and the reactions to it was the new self-consciousness of the intellectuals as a group—a group to which one could be faithful, a group one could betray.

Now, what does Menard have to say about the role of the intellectual in a conflict-ridden world? One curious aspect of the discourse he composes for Don Quixote is that he almost ignores the claims of the pacifist intellectual. He recognizes as a "laberinto de muy dificultosa salida" (1: 392) [labyrinth very difficult to escape from] the fact that soldiers are more expensive to keep than intellectuals because the latter can be rewarded with jobs while the former "no se pueden premiar sino con la mesma hacienda del señor a quien sirven" (1: 392) [cannot be rewarded except with the very estate of the leader they serve].[32] The debate between arms and letters turns on which is more important to the modern state:

> Dicen las letras que sin ellas no se podrían sustentar las armas, porque la guerra también tiene sus leyes y está sujeta a ellas, y que las leyes caen debajo de lo que son letras y letrados. A esto responden las armas que las leyes no se podrán sustentar sin ellas. (1: 392)

> Letters say that without them arms cannot be sustained, because war also has its laws and is subject to them, and laws fall within the province of letters and intellectuals. To this, arms answers that laws cannot be sustained without them.

In words that must have been written in the difficult decade of the 1930s rather than in the more optimistic 1920s, Menard adds:

> Con las armas se defienden las repúblicas, se conservan los reinos, se guardan las ciudades, se aseguran los caminos, se despejan los mares de cosarios [sic], y finalmente, si por ellas no fuese, las repúblicas, los reinos, las monarquías, las ciudades, los caminos de mar y tierra estarían sujetos al rigor y a la confusión que trae consigo la guerra el tiempo que dura y tiene licencia de usar de sus previlegios [sic] y de sus fuerzas. (1: 392)

> Arms are used to defend republics, to preserve realms, to guard cities, to secure roads, to clear the seas of pirates, and finally, if it were not for

them, republics, realms, monarchies, cities, the roads of sea and land
would be subject to the harshness and confusion that war brings for
the time it lasts and has license to make use of its privileges and of its
forces.

Most of the rest of the discourse has to do with the danger faced by the
soldier, a danger the intellectual supposedly does not face (though Menard
could not have been thinking here of Lorca, Freud, Benjamin, or Babel).
He laments that warfare itself has changed in modern times, particularly
with the development of artillery, which he calls a "diabólica invención" (1:
393) [devilish invention],[33] though he neglects to mention such other
diabolic inventions as the machine gun or mustard gas, which surely contributed as much to taking away the ancient nobility of the profession of
war.[34] Menard's Don Quixote, then, expresses a naive love of warfare for its
own sake, an attitude quite out of tune with the intellectual currents of the
day, except—and the qualification gives one pause—for the nationalist
intellectuals in the Fascist countries of the 1930s. It is perhaps Menard's
ultimate irony, dying as he does on the eve of World War II, that his knight-
errant should be enthusiastic about modern war much in the fashion of
Marinetti or Wyndham Lewis. One presumes that in the lost latter half of
his novel he shows the "Knight of the Sad Countenance" disabused of these
warlike enthusiasms.

An important issue sidestepped by Menard in his *Quixote* is the debate
about nationalism, one of the central terms of intellectual debate in the
period between the Dreyfus affair and World War II and an issue often
intertwined with the debate on pacifism and militarism. To be sure, choosing to write about Spain instead of France frees him of the explicit need to
take sides in that debate, though for both the nationalist novelist Maurice
Barrès (in his travel book on Spain, Italy, and Scandinavia, *Du sang, de la
volupté et de la mort,* 1894 [Of Blood, Sensual Pleasure, and Death])[35] and
the internationalist André Malraux (in his novel of the Spanish civil war,
L'Espoir, 1937 [Hope]) writing about Spain proved to be a convenient way
of writing about France.[36] The narrator writes:

> El fragmentario Quijote de Menard es más sutil que el de Cervantes.
> Este, de un modo burdo, opone a las ficciones caballerescas la pobre
> realidad provinciana de su país; Menard elige como "realidad" la tierra
> de Carmen durante el siglo de Lepanto y de Lope. ¡Qué españoladas
> no habría aconsejado esa elección a Maurice Barrès o al doctor Rodrí-
> guez Larreta! Menard, con toda naturalidad, las elude. En su obra no

hay gitanerías ni conquistadores ni místicos ni Felipe Segundo ni autos de fe. Desatiende o proscribe el color local. Ese desdén indica un sentido nuevo de la novela histórica. Ese desdén condena a *Salammbô,* inapelablemente. (448)

The fragmentary *Quixote* of Menard is more subtle than that of Cervantes. The latter, in a clumsy way, opposes fictions of knights-errant to the poor reality of his country; Menard has chosen as "reality" the land of Carmen during the century of Lepanto and of Lope. What Spanish caprichos would not have come to the pen of Maurice Barrès or Dr. Rodríguez Larreta as a consequence of this choice! Menard, with all naturalness, avoids them. In his work there are no gypsy scenes or conquistadors or mystics or Philip the Second or autos-da-fé. He is indifferent to local color or forbids it altogether. Such scorn condemns *Salammbô* without recourse.

This passage makes clear the extent to which discourse about Spain was part of French Orientalism,[37] though this is a theme not studied by Edward Said in his important book on the subject. Spain for Mérimée and Barrès was an exotic Other, and, because of its proximity to France, Spain was an Other that guaranteed French claims to be the true heirs to Roman ideals of clarity, order, and civilization (hence its importance to nationalists like Barrès).[38] This exotic Spain was emphatically not the one described by Malraux and Menard, though it would be rash to assimilate Menard's novel to the literature of the international brigades.[39]

Valéry writes: "In the public press the news is of such diversity, incoherence, and intensity" (*History* 203). This observation is confirmed by a look at the newspapers for the week of Pierre Menard's letter to the narrator in which he asserts: "Mi propósito es meramente asombroso" (447) [My proposal is merely astonishing]. That letter is dated 30 September 1934; had Pierre Menard looked at the newspaper that day he would have found news from Moscow of the celebrations of the seventieth anniversary of the First International, while the newspaper of the previous day would have told of war games observed in the mountains of León by the president of Spain (ominously, and prophetically, the games were fought by a "Red, or defending, army" and a "blue, or invading, army" [*New York Times* 29 September 1934]) and of the retirement of Miguel de Unamuno from his university professorship. The next day's paper reported a Eucharistic Congress in Buenos Aires, at which three thousand pilgrims prayed for the end of the Chaco War, Hitler's pledge to continue German rearmament despite economic difficulties, defiant moves by the Generalitat in Barcelona against the Madrid government, that "penitent" kulaks were to be allowed by Stalin to recover their civil rights, and that a friendly conversation had taken place in Sofia between the kings of Yugoslavia and Bulgaria (*New York Times* 1 October 1934). Nothing in the news of those several days would suggest that a week later the spotlight of world attention would be directed to Pierre Menard's neighborhood, for it was at Marseilles, on La Cannebière (a boulevard mentioned in the story [446]), on 9 October 1934, that King Alexander of Yugoslavia and the French foreign minister, Louis Barthou, were assassinated by a Croatian terrorist reputedly in the pay of Mussolini. The assassination of the Yugoslav king did not have the immediate grave consequences of a similar assassination in Sarajevo in 1914, but the death of the French foreign minister led to the appointment of the infamous Pierre Laval as his successor. The stirrings of fascism that were first felt in France in February 1934 on a national level, the promotion of Laval to the post of French foreign minister, and the absorption of Yugoslavia into Fascist Italy's sphere of influence were significant portents of things to come.

For Valéry, however, and apparently also for Menard, historical "facts" of this kind have no significance in themselves. Valéry argues repeatedly against the grounding of history in the study of "facts": "In history, as in everything else, what is positive is ambiguous. What is real lends itself to an infinite number of interpretations" (*History* 124).[40] Both the past and the future are inventions of the human mind (96–97, 122); the study of history is useful because it allows us to look at ourselves historically (124–25). However, the continuity and clarity that Valéry thought formerly sustained the historical imagination have now vanished:

> History as it was formerly conceived was pictured as a group of parallel chronological tables, between which certain transverse accidentals were sometimes marked here and there. A few attempts at synchronization produced no results, apart from a kind of demonstration of their futility. What was happening at Peking in Caesar's time, or on the Zambezi in Napoleon's time, happened on another planet. But *melodic* history is no longer possible. All political themes are now intermingled, and each event as it occurs immediately takes on a number of simultaneous and inseparable meanings. (*History* 115)

The sharp choice offered by Menard's Don Quixote, who asks us to choose the profession of arms or the profession of letters, is hopelessly marked by nostalgia for a former time when such choices could supposedly be made with a sense of moral and intellectual clarity. What is most profoundly quixotic about Menard's hero is his refusal to grapple with the positions actually being taken at the time of writing. There is nostalgia for a time before there were intellectuals,[41] a refusal to entertain the Sorelian distinction between bourgeois (and state) repressive force and proletarian violence, a desire to discuss modern war as if it were still conducted by the rules of dueling. As Menard's Don Quixote himself says: "Y así, considerando esto, estoy por decir que en el alma me pesa de haber tomado este ejercicio de caballero andante en edad tan detestable como es esta en que ahora vivimos" (1: 393–94) [And thus, considering this, I am inclined to say that it weighs on my soul to have chosen this profession of knight-errant in an age as detestable as the one in which we live]. Julien Benda in his more cynical moments might well have agreed with that assessment.

In closing, I would like to discuss two texts that throw an interesting light on Pierre Menard and his *Quixote,* both inexplicably absent from the 1939 obituary. The first is a Borges poem from the 1925 collection *Luna de enfrente* [Moon across the Way]; it was suppressed by the author in later editions of the book and escaped the attention of the author of the obituary (who is not altogether ignorant of Argentine letters, as witnessed by his reference to Larreta's *La gloria de don Ramiro* [The Glory of Don Ramiro])[42] and of later critics. The second is a book by Pierre Menard, published in Paris in 1931; its omission from the bibliography of his "visible" works is very odd indeed.

First, the Borges poem, "Por los viales de Nîmes":

> Como esas calles patrias
> Cuya firmeza en mi recordación es reclamo
> Esta alameda provenzal
> Tiende su fácil rectitud latina
> Por un ancho suburbio
> Donde hay despejo y generosidad de llanura.
> El agua va rezando por una acequia
> El dolor que conviene a su peregrinación insentida
> Y la susurración es ensayo de alma
> Y la noche es benigna como un árbol
> Y la soledad persuade a la andanza.
> Este lugar es semejante a la dicha;
> I yo no soy feliz.
> El cielo está viviendo un plenilunio
> Y un portalejo me declara una música

Que en el amor se muere
Y con alivio dolorido resurje.
Mi oscuridá dificil mortifica la calma.
Tenaces me suscitan
La afrenta de estar triste en la hermosura
Y el deshonor de insatisfecha esperanza.
(*Luna de enfrente* 38)

Like those streets of my country whose solidity in my memory is a call, this row of poplars in Provence extends its easy Latin rectitude across an extensive suburb where there is the assurance and the generosity of the plains. The water flows praying in an irrigation ditch of the sorrow that is appropriate to its unfelt pilgrimage and the murmuring is a rehearsal for the soul and the night is kind like a tree and solitude invites one to go out walking. This place is like happiness; and I am not happy. The sky is living its full moon and from a doorway a tune reaches me, dying in love and with painful relief rising up again. My difficult obscurity mortifies calm. These things continuously cause me the shame of being sad amid beauty and the dishonor of unsatisfied hope.

This poem was apparently written during the Borges family's second European trip (1923–24). Though the biographies are imprecise in their discussions of the itinerary, there were stops in London, Paris, Geneva, Madrid, Andalucía, and Mallorca (Jurado 37; Rodríguez Monegal, *Jorge Luis Borges* 179).[43] At what moment Borges slipped away to see Pierre Menard in Nîmes is not clear, but the poem is unequivocal evidence of the event itself. Perhaps he was after an interview with the author of *Les problèmes d'un problème,* perhaps he had heard rumors of Menard's projected *Quixote.* The language of the poem ("peregrinación," "afrenta," "deshonor") and especially the verse "Y la soledad persuade a la andanza," with its inevitable evocation of knight-errantry, suggest that the shade of Don Quixote presided over the failed encounter and not, say, that of Zeno or Leibniz or John Wilkins. What the poem records with unmistakable force are the misunderstandings that rendered impossible a true "meeting of the minds" between the middle-aged symbolist of Nîmes and the young veteran of the avant-garde and born-again Argentine nationalist.

The description of the landscape around Nîmes describes the young Borges's sense of estrangement from Menard: "su fácil rectitud latina," "su peregrinación insentida." His own sense of difference and remoteness from "Latin clarity" is described as "mi oscuridá difícil," while his sense of disappointment comes through clearly enough in the final verses: "La afrenta de estar triste en la hermosura / Y el deshonor de insatisfecha esperanza." Unlike Rafael Cansinos-Asséns and Macedonio Fernández, Borges's Hispanic mentors in this period, Menard must have seemed aloof and indifferent to his visitor from afar.

That Borges and Menard discussed the latter's projected *Quixote* seems obvious from other signs. In a series of essays published in the 1920s (*El tamaño de mi esperanza* 108–14 [The Extent of My Hope]; *El idioma de los argentinos* 10–13, 139–46 [The Language of the Argentines]), Borges attacks Menard's overly literal view of the text and celebrates Cervantes's "descuidos" (without, of course, mentioning Menard, whose work was still "invisible"). The interview must have taken place early in the development of Menard's project, when the French writer was still intent on turning himself into Cervantes. Menard later came around to Borges's views on Cervantes, as shown by his 1934 letter to the narrator in which he writes: "Mi complaciente precursor no rehusó la colaboración del azar; iba componiendo la obra inmortal un poco *à la diable,* llevado por inercias del lenguaje y de la invención" (448, emphasis in original) [My complacent precursor did not reject the collaboration of chance; he went along composing his immortal work a bit randomly, borne along by the inertia of the language and of invention].

The young Borges, with his conviction that literature had been reinvented by the avant-garde writers of his generation, must have been disconcerted by Menard. Here was a Frenchman who—two decades before the major manifestos of surrealism, Ultraism, creationism, and the other revolutionary movements in modern literature and culture—had written a monograph on images that would not refer to things in the world but instead be "objetos ideales creados por una convención y esencialmente destinados a las necesidades poéticas" (444) [ideal objects created by a convention and essentially destined for poetic needs], yet who entertained himself in the triumphant decade of the avant-garde by rewriting a seventeenth-century Spanish novel. What obstinacy! How out of touch with the spirit of the times!

The *Zeitgeist* did, however, preside over a publication by Menard that the author of the obituary saw fit to pass over in silence, *L'Ecriture et le subconscient: Psychanalyse et graphologie* (1931) [Writing and the Subconscious: Psychoanalysis and Graphology].[44] If earlier we speculated on the presence of Freud in Menard's *Quixote,* this work, suppressed from the bibliography of his published works, establishes beyond a doubt that Menard saw himself as a lesser disciple of the Viennese master.[45] In the opening pages he argues that modern scientific handwriting analysis[46] must come to terms with the teachings of Freudian psychoanalysis, and that when it does, it will in turn be able to make a modest contribution to psychoanalysis itself. On page 110, a sample of Freud's own handwriting is given, previously identified as the original of a letter from Freud to Menard:

> We have been surprised to learn from Freud himself (autograph no. 22, page 110) that psychoanalysts have not yet had recourse to graphology, which would open up so many horizons for them and would permit them to erect their theories on a scientific basis. Graphology, a scientific method of study of the subconscious, permits the resolution of the majority of problems raised by psychoanalysis, especially those regarding the sexual instinct in its normal evolution, in the perversions, inhibitions and sublimations. (86)

On page 111, after the reproduction of part of the letter in question in Freud's crabbed and barely legible script, Menard returns to this point:

> One understands easily enough why Freud has preferred the study of psychoanalysis over that of physiognomy. However, one might be surprised that he had not dreamt of using graphology as a complement to his investigations (Freud. autograph no. 22),[47] graphology being the study of gesture inscribed on paper and thus possessing an objective and consequently scientific basis. (111–12)

Just as the author of Menard's obituary writes, "Me consta que es muy fácil recusar mi pobre autoridad" (444) [It is obvious that it is very easy to deny my meager authority], and thus establishes his own authority through the rhetorical stratagem of protestations of unworthiness, Menard himself is tacitly establishing his own authority as a student of Freudian psychoanalysis, as a writer of the German language (as well as of seventeenth-century Spanish), and as a correspondent of Freud's. The parricidal impulse contained in Menard's references to Freud finds expression in Menard's reproduction of Freud's letter *in Freud's own hand* as well as in French translation and in Menard's paraphrase, for elsewhere in the book Menard provides his reader with the tools for analyzing the analyst (and gives sample analyses of Napoléon, Sade,[48] Santa Teresa of Avila, and a variety of other famous people). A worthy precursor of Derrida (in his analyses of Freud's "magic writing pad" ["Freud and the Scene of Writing"]), Menard provides practical instruction in the analysis of the master's hand.

That the author of the obituary was conscious of this publication of

Menard's but chose to suppress it is evident in his self-conscious reference to Menard's own handwriting. The last of the footnotes to the text reads:

> Recuerdo sus cuadernos cuadriculados, sus negras tachaduras, sus peculiares símbolos tipográficos y su *letra de insecto*. En los atardeceres le gustaba salir a caminar por los arrables de Nîmes; solía llevar consigo un cuaderno y hacer una alegre fogata. (450n, emphasis added)

> I remember his notebooks of graph paper, his black corrections, his strange typographical symbols, and his *insectlike handwriting*. At dusk he liked to go out walking on the outskirts of Nîmes; he used to take with him a notebook and build a merry bonfire.

Perhaps the author of the note was one of the friends or patients of Menard's who were presumably not amused to find samples of their handwriting, together with a discussion of their case histories, made public in *L'Ecriture et le subconscient* (see, for example, the case of the young wives whose sexual satisfaction is reflected in their handwriting [87–94] or the analysis of the handwriting of a young exhibitionist arrested in the Tuileries [114–15]). What motives the author could have had for suppressing reference to two *other* works of Menard's, *Origine thyroïdienne du rhumatisme chronique, progressif et déformant* [The Thyroidal Origin of Chronic, Progressive, and Deforming Rheumatism] and *Conseils pratiques aux jeunes mères* [Practical Advice to Young Mothers], it is beyond the scope of this modest study to surmise.

Menard is insistent on the importance of contingency in the study of personality: an individual does not have a single script, but instead the handwriting will vary to show the impact of circumstance. He says he was able to observe this himself in his study of soldiers in the trenches of the Great War (14) and shows that Napoléon's handwriting bears the marks of his experience: "The simple examination of the signatures and the rubrics of Napoléon (autograph no. 16) in the course of his life permits one to reconstruct the history of the great emperor" (72). He insists on the importance of dress, furniture, and style: "The exterior of an individual is the reflection of his or her interior. One can learn more about customs, tastes and habits of a period by leafing through a photograph album of fashions than by reading a thick book of history" (29). Yet, though the circumstances of one's life may be read in one's script, it is risky to try to extrapolate from the physical evidence: "The graphologist, let us remember, knows nothing whatever of the external conduct of human beings. One should not confuse, as one often does, energy with will. The study of will brings with it a problem of a metaphysical order, that of free will and that of good and evil. The graphologist should not try to find the solution to this problem" (69).

Despite this healthy recognition of the limits of his enterprise, at another point, while analyzing the angle of the script in the last letter written by Marie-Antoinette before she was taken to the guillotine, he happens into an equally thorny problem: "It should be noted that the punctuation is not inserted correctly, something frequently noted in the majority of feminine scripts [*écritures féminines*], which is one of the signs that permits them to be distinguished from masculine scripts [*écritures masculines*]" (105n), and the book ends with a consideration of whether the abstract or the concrete spirit predominates in men or women. Menard, unlike many of his contemporaries, argues that men are more abstract, women more concrete: exactly what a reading of his pages on Don Quixote and Dulcinea would lead one to expect.

Menard's greatest insight is that everything matters in handwriting analysis: "Neither in graphology nor in psychoanalysis are there insignificant signs; all signs acquire importance depending on the manner in which one knows how to examine and interpret them and reconnect them to general causes" (142). He urges his readers to undertake the very exercise to which he devoted himself for so many years—copying: "To fully be cognizant of all of the peculiarities of a script, a good method consists in tracing it and reproducing it with a pen. In this fashion, one sees the differences that exist between the original and the copy or reproduction" (49). As Anthony Grafton has shown in a wonderful recent study, the kinship between criticism and forgery is so close that the best forger is usually the finest textual critic (and vice versa). So it is not particularly surprising that the author of this astute (though at times, perhaps, involuntarily funny) book on the psychoanalytic interpretation of handwriting should be the perpetrator of an identical—but new and improved—version of *Don Quixote*.

As the author of the obituary on Menard was penning his note, Hitler's armies were overrunning Czechoslovakia and then Poland; Franco was driving the last remnants of Republican resistance into prison camps or across the board into southern France (not far from Nîmes); and the factories of Europe, Japan, and the United States were producing those new weapons that Don Quixote so despised. The "arms and letters" debate was never so pertinent, though the winner of the debate—once again, as in 1605—had been determined in advance. Who but Menard would have had the bravura to cast the question in those terms?[49]

3

The "Labyrinth of Trenches without Any Plan" in

"El jardín de senderos que se bifurcan"

Bombardment, barrage, curtain-fire, mines, gas, tanks, machine-guns, hand-grenades—words, words, but they hold the horror of the world.—Remarque 132

All warfare is based on deception.—Sun Tzu 66

An army without secret agents is exactly like a man without eyes or ears.—Chia Lin, qtd. in Sun Tzu 149

In *The Great War and Modern Memory,* Paul Fussell writes:

> Jorge Luis Borges in his short story "The Aleph," that brilliant comic testament to the powers of memory and imagination—and at the same time lament for their limitations—gets it profoundly right as usual. Staring at The Aleph (a thing like and not like a crystal ball), an observer sees all places and events and things simultaneously and from every possible point of view. . . . And Borges, who sometimes gives the impression of knowing everything, singles out an image which brings the essence of the Great War—that is, its multitudinousness—within his vision: in The Aleph, he says, "I saw the survivors of a battle sending out post cards." (183–84)

Fussell goes on to give examples of such battlefield postcards, to explain their precise use, and to explore the peculiar rhetoric of optimism that they embody, a rhetoric based of course on the denial of the realities of trench warfare.[1] Just as the battlefield postcards do not allow the sender to speak of any condition other than being "quite well," so it would seem "El jardín de senderos que se bifurcan" has not left its critics any option except to speak of games with time: to repeat, that is, Stephen Albert's position in the story, deprived of its dialectical punch.[2]

What I propose to do here is radically different—to read the story against the grain,[3] deciphering a series of coded messages having to do with specific events in 1916: the Easter Rising in Dublin, the slaughter of a generation of British, French, and German youths in the "labyrinth of trenches" of the Somme (and of Verdun), the obliteration of a whole string of towns in northern France in a series of ghastly experiments with new technologies of war. I thus propose to restore to the story the rigorous temporality that Yu Tsun speaks of at the beginning:

> Después reflexioné que todas las cosas le suceden a uno precisamente, precisamente ahora. Siglos de siglos y sólo en el presente ocurren los hechos; innumerables hombres en el aire, en la tierra y el mar, y todo lo que realmente pasa me pasa a mí. (472–73)

> Afterward I reflected that all things happen to one now, exactly now. Centuries after centuries and events happen only in the present; innumerable people in the air, on the land, and at sea, and everything that really happens happens to me.

The story begins with a slightly garbled reference to Liddell Hart's *The Real War* (1930), which Borges claimed in October 1940 was one of the works in his library—along with Mauthner's dictionary of philosophy, Lewes's biographical history of philosophy, Boswell's life of Johnson, and Spiller's *The Mind of Man*—that he had reread the most and covered ("abrumado") with marginalia:[4]

> En la página 242 de la *Historia de la Guerra Europea,* de Liddell Hart, se lee que una ofensiva de trece divisiones británicas (apoyadas por mil cuatrocientas piezas de artillería) contra la línea Serre-Montauban había sido planeada para el veinticuatro de julio [*sic*] de 1916 y debió postergarse hasta la mañana del día veintinueve. Las lluvias torrenciales (anota el capitán Liddell Hart) provocaron esa demora—nada significativa, por cierto. La siguiente declaración, dictada, releída y firmada por el doctor Yu Tsun, antiguo catedrático de inglés en la *Hochschule* de Tsingtao, arroja una insospechada luz sobre el caso. (472)

> On page 242 of Liddell Hart's *History of the European War,* it is written that an offensive by thirteen British divisions (backed by 1,400 artillery

pieces) against the Serre-Montauban line had been planned for 24 July [*sic*] 1916, but had to be postponed until the morning of the 29th. The torrential ràins (notes Captain Liddell Hart) caused this delay—an unimportant one, in any case. The following declaration, dictated, reread, and signed by Doctor Yu Tsun, former English professor at the Hochschule of Tsingtao, throws an unexpected light on the case.

Most critics who have written on the story would argue that the most notable error[5] here—ju*l*io for ju*n*io—is itself "nada significativo." Such critics would argue that the incident in Staffordshire—the murder of Stephen Albert by Yu Tsun—did not happen and, even if it had happened, would have had no bearing on the outcome of the battle of the Somme. This begging of the question is curious in light of Borges's declaration in "El arte narrativo y la magia" that "todo episodio, en un cuidadoso relato, es de proyección ulterior" (231) [every episode, in a careful story, is of subsequent importance]. To judge the significance of the error it is first necessary to delve into the "Great Game" of espionage[6] in the midst of a great world conflict.

Though several critics have remarked on the error in the reference to Liddell Hart, only Murillo has attempted an explanation: "I suspect (if the error is not deliberate) that a transcribing or private oversight of sorts is involved" (258). The idea that the error is due to what Stephen Albert (referring to the 602nd Night of the *German* translation of the *Arabian Nights*) calls "una mágica distracción del copista" (477) [a magical moment of absentmindedness by the scribe][7] is less satisfying than Murillo's parenthetical hint, not developed in his book, that the error might be deliberate. I believe that the latter possibility is true, and that the *editor* of the story, who is responsible only for the first paragraph (where the error occurs) and for the footnote on the "hipótesis odiosa y estrafalaria" [odious and outrageous hypothesis] that Runeberg has been murdered by Madden (472n), is being shown up as a careless reader of Liddell Hart. Only a better reader, prepared to go to any lengths to ferret out the truth—only a reader like Stephen Albert or Yu Tsun—is worthy of knowing it.

A possible error in the reference to the page number in Liddell Hart is perhaps a matter of small moment, particularly as Liddell Hart's book was published under two different titles and in numerous editions in Britain and the United States. The confusion of June and July, however, is a different matter, for all the histories of World War I emphasize the extended preparations for the British assault on the German trenches along the Serre-Montauban line,[8] an assault that finally took place at 7:30 A.M. on 1 July

1916.[9] The first day of the battle of the Somme was one of the most costly in world history, and the entire "battle," extending from July to November, resulted in more than a million casualties on the British side alone (Howard Green 11). Thus the editor's mistaking the end of July for the end of June marks him as a very poor reader indeed.

The appalling errors some critics have fallen into precisely out of an unwillingness to read carefully have already been noted.[10] John Sturrock's interesting confession in *Paper Tigers,* on the initial reference to Liddell Hart, reads: "I have not checked this quotation because it does not matter in the least whether it is accurate; Borges needs a datum point and he has provided himself with one" (347). How would the critic know whether the reference mattered without checking it first? The showing up of the editor of Yu Tsun's manuscript as a careless reader is in fact a matter of great importance, but there is much more to the reference. I will first try to reconstruct the circumstances in which the three main characters in the story found themselves in 1916 and then discuss the message Yu Tsun wants to convey to Berlin.

As others have observed, the name of the Chinese spy, Yu Tsun, is that of a character, a student, in Tsao Hsueh-Chin's *Dream of the Red Chamber* or *Hung Lu Meng,* the eighteenth-century novel that Borges discussed in one of his columns in *El Hogar* and that is mentioned here by Yu Tsun himself (475). Ferrer comments on the earlier Yu Tsun (called Chia Yu-Tsun in the Chinese novel): "Later we discover that, despite his seeming extended absence, this Yu Tsun is the one who is behind the whole development and plot of the novel" (181).[11] Chi-Chen Wang reveals in the appendix to his translation of the novel that Chia Yu-Tsun's name "is a homophone for 'fictitious words and uncultivated speech'" (569). No one has remarked, however, on another near homophone (at least to the Western ear) to Yu Tsun's name, that of the author of a work written more than two thousand years ago, *The Art of War* by Sun Tzu. Sun Tzu's work, first translated into French in the eighteenth century, is mentioned in the article on China in the eleventh edition of the *Encyclopaedia Britannica,* with reference to Sun Tzu's chapter on the use of spies (6: 227). Yu Tsun was no doubt educated in Sun Tzu's *Art of War,* that central text of Chinese writing on the subject, and would know Sun Tzu's observations on espionage: "What is called 'foreknowledge' cannot be elicited from spirits, nor from gods, nor by analogy from past events, nor from calculations. It must be obtained from men who know the enemy situation" (145), and, "Secret operations are essential in war; upon them the army relies to make its every move" (149).[12] Griffith, his translator (and a friend of Liddell Hart's), comments:

> Sun Tzu was convinced that careful planning based on sound information of the enemy would contribute to a speedy military decision. . . .
>
> Prior to hostilities, secret agents separated the enemy's allies from him and conducted a variety of clandestine subversive activities. Among their missions were to spread false rumours and misleading information, to corrupt and subvert officials, to create and exacerbate internal discord, and to nurture Fifth Columns. Meanwhile, spies, active at all levels, ascertained the enemy situation. (x–xi)

Interestingly, one of the places that Sun Tzu conquered in his career as a general was Chuan, "now P'o Hsien in modern Shantung" (59n), the very province of origin of Yu Tsun.

The Germans took what was to become Tsingtao (this being the name given the future port city by its Western colonizers)[13] and the surrounding leasehold of Kiaochow in 1897 in retaliation for the killing of two missionaries (*Encyclopaedia Britannica* 6: 202; Schrecker 33–42).[14] In the next few years, they acquired an important sphere of influence in the province of Shantung, though their power outside of the leasehold itself began to disintegrate several years before the outbreak of World War I (Schrecker 140–248). The lavish expenditures by the German navy and by enterprises interested in developing railroads, communications, and ports made Tsingtao "what many considered to be Germany's most successful colony" (Schrecker 249).[15] A large number of schools were founded in the first years of the twentieth century, the most ambitious being the *Gymnasium* and college, the Deutsche-Chinesische Hochschule. The lower school of the Hochschule "provided a five-year course of study with a curriculum consisting of Chinese, German, English, mathematics, history, geography, science, hygiene, technical drawing, physical education, music, and stenography" (Schrecker 244).[16] The German possessions in Tsingtao were seized by the Japanese (who in World War I were allied with the British and French) in early November 1914. Presumably Yu Tsun was willing to be sent on a new assignment—as a spy in England—due to the changed circumstances of his city and the traditional enmity of the northern Chinese for the Japanese and perhaps out of loyalty to the colonial masters who had trained and employed him. That a Chinese former teacher of English would be particularly suited to such an assignment to spy "beyond the trenches" in England is reasonable enough, given that Great Britain at the time had a subject Chinese population of its own. The need others would feel to explain his "difference" from the native population and his presence in the center of the empire would deflect interest from his secret mission.

Yu Tsun makes clear, though, that he is conscious of the complex psycho-dynamics of colonialism. Of his pursuer, Captain Richard Madden, he says:

> Irlandés a las órdenes de Inglaterra, hombre acusado de tibieza y tal vez de traición ¿cómo no iba a abrazar y agradecer este milagroso favor: el descubrimiento, la captura, quizá la muerte, de dos agentes del Imperio Alemán? (472)

> An Irishman in the service of England, a man accused of weakness and perhaps of treason—how could he fail to embrace and be thankful for this miraculous favor: the discovery, the capture, perhaps the death, of two agents of the German Empire?

And of his own colonial situation he writes:

> No lo hice por Alemania, no. Nada me importa un país bárbaro, que me ha obligado a la abyección de ser un espía. Además, yo sé de un hombre de Inglaterra—un hombre modesto—que para mí no es menos que Goethe. Arriba de una hora no hablé con él, pero durante una hora fue Goethe. . . . Lo hice, porque yo sentía que el Jefe tenía en poco a los de mi raza—a los innumerables antepasados que confluyen en mí. Yo quería probarle que un amarillo podía salvar a sus ejércitos. (473)[17]

> I did not do it for Germany, no. That barbarous country, which has forced me into the abject position of being a spy, matters nothing to me. Besides, I know of a man in England—a modest man—who for me is as great as Goethe. I spoke with him no more than an hour, but during that hour he was Goethe. . . . I did it because I felt that the chief looked down on those of my race—on the innumerable ancestors who converge in me. I wanted to prove to him that a yellow man could save his armies.

Yu Tsun's interest in Madden's quandary—the questionable loyalty of the colonized subject whose own country has recently rebelled against the imperial power—no doubt has to do with the interesting parallels between the Boxer Rebellion of 1900 and the Easter Rising in Dublin in April 1916. In any case, Yu Tsun is a very knowledgeable spy, since his statement reveals a surprising familiarity with the case of the leaders of the Easter Rising. Fifteen of the leaders of the Rising, including the poet and political visionary Padraic H. Pearse, had been executed by firing squad in the first days of May, less than two months[18] before the action of the story. One of the charges at the secret court-martial was that the Irish rebels had been part of a "German Conspiracy."[19] Pearse addressed the court-martial as follows:

> As a boy and as a man I have worked for Irish Freedom, first among all earthly things. I have helped to organise, to arm, to train, and to discipline my fellow countrymen to the sole end that, when the time came, they might fight for Irish freedom. The time, as it seemed to me, did come, and we went into the fight. I am glad we did. We seem to have lost. We have not lost. To refuse to fight would have been to lose; to fight is to win. We have kept faith with the past, and handed on a tradition to the future.
>
> I repudiate the assertion of the prosecutor that I sought to aid and abet England's enemy. Germany is no more to me than England is. I asked and accepted German aid in the shape of arms and an expeditionary force. We neither asked for not [sic] accepted Germany [sic] gold nor had any traffic with Germany but what I state. My aim was to win Irish freedom: we struck the first blow ourselves but should have been glad of an ally's aid.
>
> I assume that I am speaking to Englishmen, who value their freedom and who profess to be fighting for the freedom of Belgium and Serbia. Believe that we, too, love freedom and desire it. To us it is more desirable than anything in the world. If you strike us down now, we shall rise again and renew the fight. You cannot conquer Ireland. You cannot extinguish the Irish passion for freedom. If our deed has not been sufficient to win freedom, then our children will win it by a better deed. (O'Buachalla 379–80)[20]

Yu Tsun's stated motives—that he did it not for Germany but to vindicate his Chinese ancestors—echo Pearse's repudiation of Germany ("Germany is no more to me than England is") and his celebration of his own national tradition. The celebration of ancestors is connected for both men with the vindication of a debased and colonized national identity and with the founding or discovery of a tradition that will carry on into the future (or, as Yu Tsun would say after his conversation with Albert, into the innumerable futures).

Yu Tsun's intellectual curiosity, then, is wide-ranging, since he is well informed not only about the British artillery park on the Ancre but also about Chinese and Western theories of war, German and Chinese literature, and the still-secret details of the court-martial of Padraic Pearse and the other Irish patriots. And his astuteness is unbounded, since not only is he capable of killing a man named Albert to indicate the site of the artillery park in France, but also he skillfully weaves words and ideas from Pearse's statement in the court-martial in Dublin into his own statement. In so doing he shows his superiority not only to his chief in Berlin but to his pursuer, Captain Richard Madden.

Madden's case is less interesting, at least on the surface. His problem was exactly what Yu Tsun has perceived: to prove his own loyalty to a discredited colonial master. The Easter Rising had been put down quickly and ruthlessly and the fuller struggle for independence was still several years away, but the fact that a rebellion had burst out at all in the oldest colony of the great world empire was itself a watershed in history. William Butler Yeats was to write a few months later, in the famous poem "Easter, 1916," that:

> MacDonagh and MacBride
> And Connolly and Pearse
> Now and in time to be,
> Wherever green is worn,
> Are changed, changed utterly:
> A terrible beauty is born. (182)

And in a less familiar poem, "Sixteen Dead Men," Yeats addresses the very "German question" that Pearse spoke to in the court-martial:

> You say that we should still the land
> Till Germany's overcome;
> But who is there to argue that
> Now Pearse is deaf and dumb? (182)

Even an English observer could not help but notice the mood of crisis. Charles Carrington writes in *Subaltern's War,* "May and June 1916 mark to the historian a crisis in the war. The Irish Rebellion, the Battle of Jutland, the death of Kitchener in quick succession filled the English newspapers with vague alarms" (27). No wonder Madden should feel threatened, as Yu Tsun says: "Irlandés a las órdenes de Inglaterra, hombre acusado de tibieza y tal vez de traición" (472).

Madden's problem is thrown into sharper relief by his presumed ancestry.[21] His namesake, Richard Robert Madden, was a British official who strongly identified himself with Irish culture and with the abolitionist movement. One of his many works was a two-volume *History of Irish*

Periodical Literature. In the preface to that work, Captain Madden's name-sake writes:

> For my part I do not think there is any country in Europe in which it is more desirable to foster and encourage, to patronize and protect, literary tastes and intellectual recreations than Ireland, unhappily circumstanced as that country is, the great bulk of the food and the property of the land being transmitted to another—the former consumed, and the latter spent in a foreign land; without a resident nobility and gentry, the natural patrons in every independent country of literature, art, and science. (1: 7)

Madden adds that the "'English Pale' Government, planted in Ireland, differed not materially from the colonial English rule of the planters in the West Indies" (1: 13), an observation that doubtless serves to connect his writings on Ireland with his writings on Caribbean slavery. There is a delicate echo of Swift's "Modest Proposal" in this preface, in the way the vocabulary of eating is linked to the enterprise of British colonialism in Ireland and elsewhere. Madden closes his preface with the observation that, though the work is "purely and simply literary" in design (1: 81) and for that reason he had endeavored "to abstain from the introduction into it of politics and polemics" (1: 82), he was unable to do so: "The progress of literature is so mixed up with that of civilization, and the interests of the latter are so interwoven with those of liberty—civil and religious—that the writer who deals with one subject, must of necessity take the other into consideration" (1: 82).[22]

This Richard Madden is most important to Latin American letters because of his mission to the Caribbean. Edward Mullen writes that Madden was "an Irish physician who was employed by the British Colonial office from 1833 to 1839 in Jamaica and Cuba" (5). During his period in Cuba, when he was charged with trying to end Spanish and North American involvement in the slave trade, Madden became closely linked to the group of Cuban abolitionist writers that met in the home of Domingo del Monte, a group that included Cirilo Villaverde and Anselmo Suárez y Romero. It was there that Madden made the acquaintance of the black poet Juan Francisco Manzano, who was soon persuaded by the abolitionist group to write an autobiography.[23] Madden's translation of Manzano's autobiography, *Life of the Negro Poet, Written by Himself. And Translated from the Spanish by R. R. M.,* was published in English in 1840; the original Spanish remained unpublished until 1937, though Manzano's life was to serve as inspiration for Suárez y Romero's sentimental novel *Francisco* in 1839 and of course more recently for the Cuban film *El otro Francisco* (1975) [The Other Francisco], a film in which Madden appears as a character in the abolitionist *tertulia*.[24]

If Captain Richard Madden were related to this namesake, then, his English superiors would have reason to suspect his loyalty to the Crown, particularly in the volatile period just after the Easter Rising, since the earlier Madden had been unequivocally pro-Irish and firmly opposed to colonialism and slavery.[25] It seems almost uncanny that the critique of the theory of superior and inferior races central to Madden's writings on slavery[26] should reappear in a cryptic form in the Borges story, in which both Yu Tsun and Madden are serving despised colonial masters, at once seeking to prove the abilities of their races while at the same time reinforcing by their actions the position of the colonial masters.

Stephen Albert's case is also complicated by his contradictory feelings about his nationality and calling.[27] Having gone to China as a Christian missionary, he is now a missionary of Chinese culture in the West, even preserving several odd volumes of the "Enciclopedia Perdida que dirigió el Tercer Emperador de la Dinastía Luminosa y que no se dio nunca a la imprenta" (476) [Lost Encyclopedia that the Third Emperor of the Luminous Dynasty had directed and which was never printed]. Giles's article on Chinese literature in the *Encyclopaedia Britannica* tells of the destruction of the two Nanking copies of this enormous work, the *Yung Lo Ta Tien,* when the Ming dynasty collapsed during the Manchu invasions in 1644; it adds laconically that "a similar fate overtook the Peking copy, with the exception of a few odd volumes, at the siege of the legations in 1900" (6: 230).[28] Since the date in question is that of the Boxer Rebellion, it is obvious that Stephen Albert ("Algo de sacerdote había en él y también de marino" [476] [There was something of the priest in him and something of the seaman]) was up to something more than preaching the gospel in China; he too had played his part in the "Great Game" of espionage.[29]

Besides the obvious association of Stephen Albert with the town in northern France, the name Albert is linked to the historical period because it was the name of the Belgian king from 1909 to 1934, the only European monarch who actually served in World War I at the head of an army. Since Belgium was one of the first victims of the war, unhappily caught on the way from Germany to France, it is fitting that the name of the Belgian king be remembered in that of the hapless Sinologist, whose only fault was his surname.[30]

The town of Albert was situated, as John Masefield says in *The Old Front Line,* at "a central point in the reckoning of distances" and was "by much the most important town within an easy march of the battlefield" (78). He adds: "It is not now (after three years of war and many bombardments) an attractive town; probably it never was" (78). Its best known landmark was a golden statue of Virgin and Child on the tower of the cathedral. Early in the war a German shell hit the tower, weakening the pedestal on which the Virgin stood; the Virgin lurched forward, hanging at a right angle to the tower for the duration of the war. Thus, Howard Green writes of the Golden Virgin that "more than any other single place or monument, this is the symbol of the Somme" (67). Masefield adds, "Perhaps few of our soldiers will remember Albert for anything except this diving Virgin" (79). H. G. Wells, in turn, writes in a 1917 book:

> It betrays no military secret to say that commonly the rare tourist to the British offensive passes through Albert, Albert which is at last out of range of the German guns after nearly two years of tribulation, with its great modern red cathedral smashed to bits and the great gilt Madonna and Child that once surmounted the tower now, as every one knows, hanging out horizontally over the road in an attitude that irresistibly suggests an imminent dive upon the passing traveler. (116)

The reason why the Golden Virgin was a landmark was that bombardment and trench warfare left few others on the landscape; the "woods" that appear on Liddell Hart's maps rapidly ceased to be anything but collections of mud, splinters, and grisly stumps. For example, Carrington's *Subaltern's War* contains a pair of striking photographs of the village of Passchendaele in Belgium, the center of the "third battle of Ypres" in 1917. The aerial photograph before the battle shows a town, roads, orchards, fields; the photograph taken after the battle shows nothing but a splotchy blur (213). Similarly, Henri Barbusse writes in *Under Fire,* "The trenches that run in this valley have a look of earthquake crevasses, and as if whole tombs of uncouth things had been emptied on the ruins of the earth's convulsion. And there, where no dead are, the very earth is cadaverous" (278), and H. G. Wells writes, "The villages of this wide battle region are not ruined; they are obliterated" (77). As Tim Travers says in a recent study of the battle of the Somme, "Time and again the same story was told in late September and October [1916]—HQs and GHQ either could not read their maps, or could not relate their maps to the shattered ground" (184). When Yu Tsun speaks of the lost labyrinth of his ancestor, he says: "Lo imaginé borrado por arrozales y debajo del agua" (475) ["I imagined it erased by rice fields and underwater"]. *Borrado:* the term is adequate to describe the landscape of the Somme.

Murillo observes that the labyrinth was not known to classical Chinese culture (259), but he does not complement that observation with a reference to the labyrinth that would establish the appropriateness of the image to a story that is about sending a message concerning a place soon to be transformed into a bloody wasteland. Eric J. Leed writes in *No Man's Land:* "The image of the labyrinth appears again and again in reports of combatants not because of its inherent elegance, but because of its obviousness. It was a metaphor that suggested the fragmentary, disintegrated and disjunctive nature of the landscape traversed by the combatants of trench warfare" (78). He then quotes from Charles Carrington's *Subaltern's War,*[31] published in 1929:

> When moving about in the trenches you turn a corner every few yards, which makes it seem like walking in a maze. It is impossible to keep your sense of direction and infinitely trying to proceed at all. . . . When trenches had been fought over the confusion becomes all the greater. Instead of neat parallel trench lines, you made the best use of existing trenches which might run in any direction other than the one you would prefer, until an old battlefield like the Somme became a labyrinth of trenches without any plan. (Carrington 217–18)[32]

The "old battlefield" of the Somme is the very one about which Yu Tsun is trying to send a message to Berlin. The veteran's reference to "a labyrinth of trenches without any plan" suggests that in addition to the allusions to the apocryphal Chinese novel (which could only by a leap of the imagination or the influence of the West refer to the labyrinth in any case, as Murillo has shown), the insistent labyrinth image in the story refers to the battlefields near the town of Albert in France.

Similarly, E. W. Colbrook in *A.B.C. of the Great War* (1919) writes in the entry under "Somme" that "British troops captured the German labyrinth of trenches to the depth of 1,000 yards on a front of seven miles" on 1 July 1916 (192).[33] Both Erich Maria Remarque in *All Quiet on the Western Front* (213, 277) and Henri Barbusse in *Under Fire* (26, 210, 323) describe the experience of getting lost in this maze, and both describe the landscape after the battle in apocalyptic terms. Barbusse writes, for instance: "Without speaking they dash across the maze of the strangely empty trench that seems to have no end" (210) (the word used in the French is *dédale* [*Le Feu* 218]).[34] Yu Tsun is quite precise and vivid when he writes:

Yo poseía el Secreto. El nombre del preciso lugar del nuevo parque de artillería británico sobre el Ancre. Un pájaro rayó el cielo gris y ciegamente lo traduje en un aeroplano y a ese aeroplano en muchos (en el cielo francés) aniquilando el parque de artillería con bombas verticales. (473)

I possessed the Secret. The name of the precise location of the new British artillery park on the Ancre. A bird streaked across the gray sky and blindly I translated it into an airplane and that airplane into many airplanes (in the French sky) wiping out the artillery park with vertical bombs.

One critic has written of this passage that it exemplifies the "infinite possibilities of the imagination . . . a yielding to the irrational, the collapse of the bounds of logic that impede desires from being realized in the imagination" (Koch 185–86). Nothing could be farther from the truth; Yu Tsun writes with the sad knowledge and the astuteness of a talented spy. His reference to what will soon become the battlefield of the Somme is exact and pushes the story much closer to the realistic than to the fantastic variety of narrative.

Another brief passage in the story refers implicitly to the realities of trench warfare. Yu Tsun, on the train to Ashgrove, says:

Recorrí los coches: recuerdo unos labradores, una enlutada, un joven que leía con fervor los *Anales* de Tácito, un soldado herido y feliz. (474)

I walked through the cars: I remember some farmers, a woman in mourning, a young man who was reading with fervor the *Annals* of Tacitus, a soldier who was wounded and happy.

The farmers are the only ones not linked clearly with the progress of the war. The widow, the wounded soldier happy to have been pulled from the trenches, the young student whose choice of reading material[35] is informed with the war fever that turned his entire generation into cannon fodder— their lives are all lived as a function of the war. And Yu Tsun, the one who observes them all, knows it, because his life too has become that of a pawn in a great nightmarish design.

One might be tempted to identify the young student on the train as a self-portrait of Borges, who in 1916 was diligently studying Latin in Geneva only three hundred miles from the trenches at Albert (and closer still to those at Verdun).[36] For Borges's studies were informed by the *Zeitgeist*, as the choice of Tacitus's *Annals* shows; when he learned German, he soon found his way to the powerful war poetry of the expressionists, as is revealed by the poems he chose to translate for the Spanish Ultraist magazine *Cervantes* in 1920.[37] And among his own Ultraist poems there are at least two that refer powerfully to the realities of trench warfare. "Trinchera" (1920) [Trench] reads:

Angustia
En lo último una montaña camina
Hombres color de tierra naufragan en la grieta más baja
El fatalismo unce las almas de aquéllos
que bañaron su pequeña esperanza en las piletas de la noche.
Las bayonetas sueñan con los entreveros nupciales
El mundo se ha perdido y los ojos de los muertos lo buscan
El silencio aúlla en los horizontes hundidos.
(*Poesía juvenil* 59)[38]

Anguish
In the background a mountain walks
Men the color of earth are shipwrecked in the lowest crack
Fatalism anoints the souls of those who bathed their small hope in
    the basins of the night.
The bayonets dream of nuptial encounters
The world has been lost and the eyes of the dead search for it
Silence howls in the sunken horizons.

The erotic element in the encounter with and killing of the enemy, the sense of loss of the world as known previously, the mud, the silence, the proximity of the dead—the picture of life in the trenches is at one with that provided by the whole vast literature (in a great variety of languages) of the Great War.

In fact, even at the moments in "El jardín de senderos" when the discussion between Albert and Yu Tsun is at its most metaphysical, the examples return insistently to the vocabulary of war:

En la obra de Ts'ui Pên, todos los desenlaces ocurren; cada uno es el punto de partida de otras bifurcaciones. Alguna vez, los senderos de ese laberinto convergen: por ejemplo, usted llega a esta casa, pero en uno de los pasados posibles usted es mi enemigo, en otro mi amigo. (478)

In the work of Ts'ui Pên, all possible endings occur; each one is the starting point for other bifurcations. Occasionally, the paths of that labyrinth converge; for instance, you come to this house, but in one of the possible pasts you are my enemy, in another my friend.

El tiempo se bifurca perpetuamente hacia innumerables futuros. En unos de ellos soy su enemigo. (479)

Time forks perpetually into innumerable futures. In some of them I am your enemy.

And the two versions of the epic chapter of Ts'ui Pên's novel hinge on war:

En la primera, un ejército marcha hacia una batalla a través de una montaña desierta; el horror de las piedras y de la sombra le hace menospreciar la vida y logra con facilidad la victoria; en la segunda, el mismo ejército atraviesa un palacio en el que hay una fiesta; la resplandeciente batalla les parece una continuación de la fiesta y logran la victoria. . . . Recuerdo las palabras finales, repetidas en cada redacción como un mandamiento secreto: *Así combatieron los héroes, tranquilo el admirable corazón, violenta la espada, resignados a matar y a morir.* (478, emphasis in original)

In the first, an army is marching toward a battle across a desert mountain; the horror of the stones and of the shadows makes them belittle life and they easily achieve victory; in the second, the same army crosses a palace where a party is being held; the resplendent battle seems to them a continuation of the party and they achieve victory. . . . I remember the final words, repeated in each version like a secret commandment: *Thus the heroes fought, their admirable hearts tranquil, their swords violent, resigned to kill or to die.*

Here, Ts'ui Pên's reflections on military discipline and morale resonate with the much more pessimistic texts that emerged from the experience of World War I.

In his foreword to the Griffith translation of Sun Tzu's *The Art of War* (1963), Liddell Hart writes:

Civilization might have been spared much of the damage suffered in the world wars of this century if the influence of Clausewitz's monumental tomes *On War,* which moulded European military thought in the era preceding the First World War, had been blended with and balanced by a knowledge of Sun Tzu's exposition on "The Art of War." Sun Tzu's realism and moderation form a contrast to Clausewitz's tendency to emphasize the logical ideal and "the absolute," which his disciples caught on to in developing the theory and practice of "total war" beyond all bounds of sense. (v)

Liddell Hart adds that when he first read the book in 1927, "I found many other points that coincided with my own lines of thought, especially his constant emphasis on doing the unexpected and pursuing the indirect approach" (vii), and he quotes with approval Sun Tzu's warning that "there has never been a protracted war from which a country has benefited" (vi).

In *The Real War* (1930), Liddell Hart concedes in the preface: "Some may say that the war depicted here is not 'the real war'—that this is to be discovered in the torn bodies and minds of individuals. It is far from my purpose to ignore or deny this aspect of the truth" (9). But he adds: "The war was . . . waged and decided in the minds of individuals more than in the physical clash of forces" (10). Similarly, Henry de Man intends his book on the war "to show the remaking of a mind during the remaking of the world" (viii).[39] So it is that Yu Tsun recoils from his triumph, experiencing the disillusionment with the war that marks the texts, both poetic and narrative, that were produced during and after the conflict:

Lo demás es irreal, insignificante. Madden irrumpió, me arrestó. He sido condenado a la horca. Abominablemente he vencido: he comunicado a Berlín el secreto nombre de la ciudad que deben atacar. Ayer la bombardearon; lo leí en los mismos periódicos que propusieron a Inglaterra el enigma de que el sabio sinólogo Stephen Albert muriera asesinado por un desconocido, Yu Tsun. El Jefe ha descifrado ese enigma. Sabe que mi problema era indicar (a través del estrépito de la guerra) la ciudad que se llama Albert y que no hallé otro medio que matar a una persona de ese nombre. No sabe (nadie puede saber) mi innumerable contrición y cansancio. (480)[40]

The rest is unreal, insignificant. Madden burst in, arrested me. I have been condemned to the gallows. Abominably I have won: I have communicated to Berlin the secret name of the city they should attack. Yesterday they bombarded it; I read the news in the same newspapers that posed for England the enigma that the learned sinologist Stephen Albert had been killed by an unknown person, Yu Tsun. The chief has deciphered the enigma. He knows that my problem was to indicate (across the noise of war) the city called Albert, and that I found no other means of doing so than killing a person of that name. He does not know (no one can know) my limitless contrition and exhaustion.

Mark Millington has commented:

> The din of the war reenters the story at the very end, at the very moment that the story falls silent. . . . The omission of the reality of war is a kind of negative action, it depends on choice, and the notion of the story's choice highlights its status as a symbolic act, a social and cultural act. . . . The narrative strives to tie up, to bring everything together in resolution, but it turns out that in closing its various strands into convergence it closes out history. . . . The interesting thing is that "El jardín's" own categories can be used to problematize its own position, to reveal that silence, that violence, which the story always poses as inextricably linked to literature and writing. (185)

What Millington elegantly suggests here is that the "silence" in this story is filled with violence, that any attempt to connect body (reality, experience) and imagination (literature, writing) is sustained by repressed violence.

In an interview televised at the end of *Shoah*, Claude Lanzmann's ten-hour documentary on the Nazi death camps, the French director explained that his principal problem was to leave gaps in the film through which the viewer could hear the silence of the dead. In a similar way, "El jardín de senderos que se bifurcan" is a hollow story, a story which alludes insistently to the voices that cannot be heard, the voices of the dead in the battle of the Somme. Borges writes his story in the margin of the most important book published in the 1930s on the Great War, and like Liddell Hart he is conscious that the "real war" cannot be told. As Erich Maria Remarque observes in *All Quiet on the Western Front,* he cannot do more than *allude* to the experience of war.

4

Prague, March 1939: Recovering the Historicity of

"El milagro secreto"

From history I cannot discover what I ought to do, and what I ought to do is what really matters.—Thomas Masaryk, qtd. in Betts 291[1]

The opening of "El milagro secreto" is notable for the precision of its references to place and time: "La noche del catorce de marzo de 1939, en un departamento de la Zeltnergasse de Praga, Jaromir Hladík . . . soñó con un largo ajedrez" (308) [The night of 14 March 1939, in an apartment on Zeltnergasse in Prague, Jaromir Hladík . . . dreamt of a long game of chess]. After the narration of the dream, the first paragraph ends:

> En ese punto, se despertó. Cesaron los estruendos de la lluvia y de los terribles relojes. Un ruido acompasado y unánime, cortado por algunas voces de mando, subía de la Zeltnergasse. Era el amanecer, las blindadas vanguardias del Tercer Reich entraban en Praga. (308)

> At this point he woke up. The sounds of the rain and the terrible clocks ceased. A rhythmic sound in unison, interrupted by occasional shouts of command, came up from Zeltnergasse. It was dawn; the armored vanguard of the Third Reich was entering Prague.

The rest of the story is similarly punctuated with references to 19, 28, and 29 March, and the references to 29 March are even more precise: 8:45 A.M., 9:02 A.M. There are also precise references to places in Prague. These details admit of two contrary interpretations: that they are "datum points" or "reality effects," to use John Sturrock's and Roland Barthes's terms, that serve to create textual verisimilitude (within the system of the text), or that they are there to refer to a reality beyond the text that in turn structures the story. I will be arguing for the latter possibility here. To argue for the former case is too easy and not very interesting, and though skeptics may choose to argue with Treviranus that "la realidad no tiene la menor obligación de ser interesante" (500) [reality does not have the slightest obligation to be interesting], literary interpretation has the obligation to be—at the very least—interesting.

Frequently in Borges's stories, proper names serve as markers pointing toward the author's extremely varied sources. These references almost always reveal a much more complex appropriation of realities beyond the text than has been noted in the criticism. The reason Borges's critics have failed him in this regard is largely due to the tremendous range and rather scattered nature of his erudition. Like the Cervantes in chapter 9 of *Don Quixote* who reads every scrap of paper he finds on the street, the Borges of the 1930s and 1940s—the period of the composition of the columns in *El Hogar* now published as *Textos cautivos,* as well as of the stories in *Ficciones* and *El Aleph*—was a voracious but unsystematic reader, and so his critic must be prepared to look at widely varied sources in the various languages—English, French, Spanish, German, Latin, and Italian—that the writer knew. While the sort of exhaustive analysis of sources that was undertaken by John Livingston Lowes for Coleridge's "Kubla Khan" is daunting and perhaps impossible for the Borges scholar, it is in this direction that I think we must go if we are to discover the "realidad más compleja que la declarada al lector" (219) [more complex reality than the one declared to the reader] that is concealed in the texts of *Ficciones* and *El Aleph*.

In "El milagro secreto," the first clue to the sources Borges used in the composition of the story is provided by the name of the protagonist, Jaromir Hladík, with the surname sporting an acute accent that is anomalous in Spanish and frequently missing or misplaced in the critical writing on the story. Jaromir is the name of a minor character in Gustav Meyrink's *The Golem,* the German-Czech novelist's attempt (heavily influenced by the psychology of his time) at a modern version of the legend of the unintentional creation of a monster by a Prague rabbi. Borges knew Meyrink's work well; he began studying German in Geneva in 1916 soon after the 1915 publication of the novel, and it was to serve him later as the source of the poem "El golem" and perhaps also of the story "Las ruinas circulares." He wrote several essays and notes on Meyrink's work, the most interesting of which is a 1936 review in *El Hogar* of Meyrink's theosophical novel *Der*

Engel vom westlichen Fenster [The Angel in the West Window], a work that he compares unfavorably to *Der Golem* (*Textos cautivos* 35–36).[2]

The surname Hladík does not come from Meyrink, however. It is that of an obscure Czech novelist of the turn of the century, Václav Hladík (1868– 1913), author of an extensive body of work from 1892 to 1912.[3] Count Lützow's article on Bohemian literature in the eleventh edition of the *Encyclopaedia Britannica* (1910) mentions his novel *Evzen Voldan* as "a very striking representation of the life of modern Prague" and adds that "like so many Bohemian authors, Hladík also is a copious dramatic author" (4: 135), a detail consistent with the Borges story. However, Hladík's modest place in more recent accounts of Czech literature is attested to by the mere two sentences he is accorded in Jan Mukařovský's history of Czech literature (3: 422, 566) and the short entry in the dictionary of Czech literature published in Prague in 1964 (Havel and Opelík 153). He is not mentioned at all in Antonin Měštan's history of Czech literature from 1785 to 1985. William E. Harkins in his *Anthology of Czech Literature* treats Hladík in a single sentence: "Václav Hladík (1868–1913) sought to picture a refined Czech upper-class society which never existed" (135); he is not included in the portion of the book that comprises the anthology. Since Hladík's writing is not available in any language other than Czech (which Borges could not read),[4] it seems likely that the source of the name is simply the encyclopedia article.[5]

Borges takes other proper names from a variety of sources. Hladík's mother's maiden name, Jaroslavski, would seem to be based on the first name of the Czech novelist Jaroslav Hašek (1883–1923), author of the famous novel *The Adventures of the Good Soldier Švejk in the World War* (1921–22).[6] The same name appears again as the first name of the protagonist of Hladík's verse drama *Los enemigos* [The Enemies], Jaroslav Kubin; the surname Kubin is that of the Prague artist Alfred Kubin, a friend of Kafka's and of Max Brod's (Brod 61; Mailloux 163, 196). I cannot find sources for two other proper names in the verse drama: the baron of Roemerstadt and Julia de Weidenau.

The street where Hladík lives, Zeltnergasse, was the German name of the major street in central Prague now known as Celetná. It was here at number 3 where the Kafka family lived from 1896 to 1906 (Gruša 18, 34) and where Hermann Kafka's business was located from 1906 to 1912 at number 12; the street is called by its German name in Max Brod's 1937 biography of Kafka (15) but by its Czech name in the article on Prague that Count Lützow wrote for the *Encyclopaedia Britannica*. The other places mentioned in the story—Hradcany Hill, where the Prague Castle is located, and the Clementinum Library—are mentioned in the *Encyclopaedia Britannica* article on

Prague (22: 248–50); the library is described in enthusiastic terms as "very valuable" (22: 249). Also that article gives both the Czech name (Vltava) and the German name (Moldau) for the river that flows through the city (22: 248); Borges uses the German name (also, of course, the one used by Meyrink [for example, 301]).[7]

The use of German names for most of the places in the story is the result of (or promises the effect of) a curious collapse of historical time. During most of the period that Prague and the rest of Bohemia formed part of the Austro-Hungarian Empire, German names were of course part of the stuff of Viennese rule, and up until the end of World War II there was a substantial German-speaking population in Prague and the surrounding area. (The Jews of Prague largely spoke German, as was the case with Kafka, Max Brod, and Franz Werfel.) However, this German-speaking minority, though powerful economically (Mailloux 24), was displaced politically by the rise of majority rule during the republican period of Czechoslovakia from 1918 to 1939, and the German place names were replaced with Czech ones (Mailloux 449).[8] Thus Borges, by using the German names for the street on which Hladík lives and for the river that flows through the city, is harking back to the period before World War I, or conversely is telling the story from the perspective of one of the non-Jewish German speakers who might have sympathized with the annexation of the Sudetenland and the subsequent conquest of Czechoslovakia by the Nazis. Two place names are particularly interesting in this regard: the name of the street where Hladík lives is given its German name because of its association with Kafka, although the Czech name is given in the *Encyclopaedia Britannica* article on Prague (Lützow, 22: 249); the castle hill is given its Czech, not its German, name, evidently because the same source uses it exclusively (22: 248–50).[9]

Beyond these evident markers, though, the story displays a strong relation to Czech culture between the world wars, to that short-lived republic presided over by Thomas Masaryk. If the invasion of Czechoslovakia was one of the crucial events in the outbreak of World War II (which was to begin six months later when Germany invaded Poland), this was partly due to the crushing of a non-German and democratic country. Kafka, Brod, and Werfel formed part of the vibrant cultural life of Prague, though the German-speaking Jews were less important to the national culture than the Czech writers Jaroslav Hašek and Karel Čapek (1890–1938).[10] Čapek, the author of the famous play *R. U. R.,* the dystopian work in which robots made their first appearance, produced a large and varied body of work in the 1920s and 1930s, much of which was swiftly translated into English and German.[11] The English translation of his collection of short prose pieces entitled *Intimate Things,* for instance, went through two printings in October 1935; it includes an observation on maps that seems relevant to "El milagro secreto": "Maps of the world are beautiful things, and full of secret signs. You would like to be everywhere; you would like to live all the lives there are in the world; you would like to know everything and stop at each place, satiated with effort and learning. But you do not manage even to go all over the map of the world and read all the names on it" (29).

The night before his scheduled execution, Hladík dreams that he is in the Clementinum Library, where he enters into conversation with a blind librarian:

> Un lector entró a devolver un atlas. *Este atlas es inútil,* dijo, y se lo dio a Hladík. Este lo abrió al azar. Vio un mapa de la India, vertiginoso. Bruscamente seguro, tocó una de las mínimas letras. Una voz ubicua le dijo: *El tiempo de tu labor ha sido otorgado.* Aquí Hladík se despertó. (511)

> A reader came to return an atlas. *This atlas is useless,* he said, and he gave it to Hladík. The latter opened it at random. He saw a dizzying map of India. Suddenly confident, he touched one of the tiny letters. A ubiquitous voice told him: *The time has been granted for your task.* At this point Hladík woke up.

Borges published a biographical note on Čapek in *El Hogar* on 24 February 1939, two months after Čapek's death in Prague and less than three weeks before the Nazi invasion of that city. In this note he shows thorough familiarity with a wide range of Čapek's work and relates it implicitly to his own project. Čapek, according to Borges, was heavily influenced by William James and John Dewey (as was Borges himself thanks to his father). A journalist, he published a polemical pamphlet the title of which Borges gives as *Crítica de palabras* [Critique of Words], a title highly reminiscent of "Ejecución de tres palabras" [Execution of Three Words] in *Inquisiciones* [Inquisitions], "Palabrería para versos" [Prattle for Verses] and "La adjetivación" [The Use of Adjectives] in *El tamaño de mi esperanza,* and "Indagación de la palabra" [Investigation of the Word] in *El idioma de los argentinos.* His *Makropoulos Affair* of 1921 was, like Shaw's *Back to Methuselah,* a work about "la posibilidad de lograr una extraordinaria longevidad" (*Textos cautivos* 301) [the possibility of achieving an extraordinary degree of longevity], rather like the later Borges story "El inmortal" [The Immortal].[12] Borges notes that Čapek was also the author of a fantastic novel, *La fabricación del Absoluto* [The Factory of the Absolute], and of the dystopian novel *Kratatita* [Kratatite] about a new explosive. He mentions several of

Čapek's plays in addition to the famous *R. U. R.,* including *El azote blanco* [The White Plague], "que fustiga las dictaduras" [that attacks dictatorships], "y el curioso drama *La madre.* Varios personajes de esa obra aparecen después de muertos" (302) [and the curious play *The Mother.* Various characters in that work appear after they have died], a plot element that appears in Hladík's drama *Los enemigos.* The pathetic quality of the note is completed with mention of Čapek's book of conversations with Masaryk, who had resigned as president of the Czechoslovak Republic in 1935 and died in 1937.[13]

The English translation of Čapek's *The Mother* was published in 1939, so Borges in his February 1939 note must have had knowledge of the play from some other source (or advance notice of this edition). In any case, the play merits attention here. The play begins with a note in which Čapek says that its theme was given to him "by the age in which we are living, and the final inspiration by a picture of a widow kneeling on one of today's battlefields" (9). The play revolves around the repeated discovery that modern life and especially modern war are bereft of heroism, yet the mother watches her husband and sons die one after another for what they all (when they return to speak to her after their deaths) acknowledge is a lie.[14] The one character who seems immune to the call of battle is Toby, a bookish young man for whom reading is "like a drug. . . . He loses all sense of reality" (34), yet when the nearby city is attacked and children are killed, his mother finally relents and urges him to join the fight against the foreign invaders (88). The leftist son Peter tells of being executed by a firing squad: "When I stood there with my hands tied and saw those six raw recruits facing me—country lads most likely—I felt sorry for them, I can tell you. I couldn't stand being one of a firing-squad" (53). In another detail that is strikingly similar to the Borges story, the youngest son Toby tells his mother: "Ever since I made up my mind to go [to war], I've been killed heaps of times. I can do it as easily as can be, and you'd be surprised how real it seems" (70). The play, then, has greater similarities to "El milagro secreto" as a whole (rather than to Hladík's *Los enemigos*), though the dead return to the stage in it as in Hladík's play.

Interestingly, although the play was written in Czechoslovakia not long before the Nazi invasion, it does not refer to any specific country, and left and right (represented by the twin brothers Christopher and Peter) are both held up to ridicule. Čapek seems to be following his mentor Masaryk in arguing for a liberal humanist position, yet that position was of course to prove untenable within months of his death (and less than two years after Masaryk's death). In the play the spokesman for the dwindling center is the mother's father, the Old Man, who says: "We looked upon war as if it was something in a story-book. Something that could never really happen to us" (78).[15] The play's message that "it can happen here" was of course painfully clear by the time it appeared in English. The obvious and didactic nature of the play is relieved only by the device of having the dead speak, and that is the element that Hladík makes use of in his play *Los enemigos*.[16]

"El milagro secreto" was first published in *Sur* in February 1943 (no. 101, 13–20) and was preceded in that publication by a series of notes and essays on the war including the 1939 "Ensayo de imparcialidad" [An Attempt at Impartiality] and the bitter note "1941" published in December of that year. It was the seventh of the "ficciones" to appear in *Sur,* following "Pierre Menard" in 1939, "Tlön" and "Las ruinas circulares" [The Circular Ruins] in 1940, "La lotería en Babilonia" [The Lottery of Babylon] and "Examen de la obra de Herbert Quain" [An Examination of the Work of Herbert Quain] in 1941, and "La muerte y la brújula" [Death and the Compass] in 1942.[17] In this company it becomes obvious that "El milagro secreto" is the first story to deal explicitly with current events. "Tlön" and "La lotería" may have veiled political content and "La forma de la espada" may deal explicitly with the Irish revolution of twenty years before, but it is only "El milagro secreto" that takes up an event of very recent history, the full ramifications of which could not yet have been known.

I have not spoken much of the actual invasion of Prague on 15 March 1939.[18] The U.S. diplomat George F. Kennan, who a mere month before had sent Washington a dispatch "on the Jewish problem in the new Czechoslovakia" (42–57), made some "Personal notes, dated March 21, 1939, on the March crisis and the final occupation of Prague by the Germans." Kennan records his encounter with the Czech foreign minister the night before the invasion: "The Foreign Minister . . . appeared punctually and made the rounds of the guests with complete composure—a remarkable performance for a man whose country was known to have just lost one-half of its territory and to stand in imminent danger of losing still more" (84). The notion of politics as performance is highlighted again in Kennan's account of events later the same evening:

> We went to the opera that evening with the Minister. Nazis were demonstrating farther down town, but the streets leading to the opera were quiet. The performance had been intended as a gala one, under the auspices of the President. It turned out to be a performance of the gloomy Slav fairy-tale "Rusalka."[19] The President had called off his at-

tendance only that morning, and we know now that while we watched the opera, he was attending a performance equally fantastic but only too grimly real, in another city. (84)

Kennan goes on to describe events of 15 March: the snow, the disoriented Social Democrats and Jews, the tanks, the women weeping in the street, and the eight o'clock curfew that brought an eerie stillness to downtown Prague: "We were all acutely conscious that in this case the curfew indeed tolled the knell of a long and distinctly tragic day" (87). Though Kennan's account was published many years after the end of the war, it merits the commentary that Borges makes in the 1944 story "Tema del traidor y del héroe" [Theme of the Traitor and the Hero]: "Que la historia hubiera copiado a la historia ya era suficientemente pasmoso; que la historia copie a la literatura es inconcebible" (497) [That history should copy history was already frightening enough; that history should copy literature is inconceivable].

One of the odder aspects of "El milagro secreto" is the historical prescience that Borges expressed in it.[20] The "final solution" was not yet public knowledge,[21] and within a few years Borges would write a curious story about the death camps, "Deutsches Requiem," the story of a camp leader. But Hladík's story is already that of the death of the Jewish people in Central Europe and of the end of Central Europe as an idea. In "Ensayo de imparcialidad," published in *Sur* in October 1939, Borges writes: "Es de fácil comprobación que un efecto inmediato (y aún instantáneo) de esta anhelada guerra, ha sido la extinción o la abolición de todos los procesos intelectuales" (27) [It is easy to establish that an immediate (even instantaneous) effect of this long-desired war has been the extinction or abolition of all intellectual processes], and in several notes during the period just prior to the outbreak of war and just after, he declares his admiration for German culture, an appreciation that leads him to lament the triumph of Nazi savagery over an intellectual civilization.[22] The same note in October 1939 registers his recognition of the dangers for his own country:

> Es posible que una derrota alemana sea la ruina de Alemania; es indiscutible que su victoria sería la ruina y el envilecimiento del orbe. No me refiero al imaginario peligro de una aventura colonial sudamericana; pienso en los imitadores autóctonos, en los *Ueber-menschen* caseros, que el inexorable azar nos depararía. (29)

It is possible that a German defeat may be the ruin of Germany; it is undeniable that its victory would be the ruin and depravity of the entire world. I do not refer to the imaginary danger of a colonial adventure in South America; I am thinking of the local imitators, of the homegrown Supermen, that inexorable chance would provide for us.

The bonds between the dangerous developments in Europe and the dangers at home (so eloquently explored in "La forma de la espada" and "Historia del guerrero y la cautiva") make the setting of Prague in 1939 a logical choice for a story on the rise of fascism, since, after the Anschluss (which is mentioned in the story [508]), that city and that time were the first sites of German expansionism.

In his memoirs, the Czech poet Jaroslav Seifert writes of events that happened to him in 1945:

> Aware of the impossibility of comparing a world-famous genius with a lyrical poet from a small country, still I used to envy Dostoevsky's unique experience: to be sentenced to death, to come to know the moment when one must necessarily leave his life, accept that inexorable fact, and then to be saved and to taste again the security and the sweetness of life, to experience that couple of terrible minutes when time is quickly pulling one towards annihilation, and then to gaze at the broad expanse of time, which lies ahead like a beautiful landscape. What drama must run through a person's mind in those few minutes! What does such a moment mean to someone, especially to a writer, who has the ability to articulate such an experience accurately? (174)

Seifert could have been talking about Hladík. Hladík could have been thinking about Dostoevski. The boundaries between truth and fiction have never been clear, but perhaps in Prague they have been blurrier than in some other places.[23] As Milan Kundera has written: "How is it possible that in Prague Kafka's novels merge with real life while in Paris the same novels are read as the hermetic expression of an author's entirely subjective world?" (106).

In his note in *Sur* at the end of 1941, commenting on the events of that year, Borges writes:

> La noción de un atroz *complot* de Alemania para conquistar y oprimir todos los países del atlas, es (me apresuro a confesarlo) de una irreparable banalidad. Parece una invención de Maurice Leblanc, de Mr. Phillips Oppenheim o de Baldur von Schirach.[24] Es notoriamente

anacrónica: tiene el inconfundible sabor de 1914. Adolece de penuria imaginativa, de gigantismo, de crasa inverosimilitud. . . . Desgraciadamente, la realidad carece de escrúpulos literarios. Se permite todas las libertades, incluso la de coincidir con Maurice Leblanc. . . .

Le vrai peut quelque fois n'être pas vraisemblable;[25] lo inverosímil, lo verdadero, lo indiscutible, es que los directores del Tercer Reich procuran el imperio universal, la conquista del orbe. ("1941" 22)

The notion of an atrocious *plot* by Germany to conquer and oppress all the countries in the globe is (I hasten to confess) of an irreparable banality. It seems like an invention of Maurice Leblanc, of Mr. Phillips Oppenheim, or of Baldur von Schirach. It is obviously anachronistic: it has the unmistakable flavor of 1914. It suffers from poverty of the imagination, from gigantism, from a crass lack of verisimilitude. . . . Unfortunately, reality lacks literary scruples. It permits itself all sorts of liberties, including that of coinciding with Maurice Leblanc. . . .

What is true is sometimes not verisimilar; what is not verisimilar, the truth, the undeniable thing, is that the leaders of the Third Reich aspire to a universal empire, the conquest of the globe.

He ends the note with terrible irony: "Alguien, para frustrar nuestras esperanzas, observa que estamos lejísimos. Le respondo que siempre las colonias distan de la metrópoli; el Congo Belga no es lindero de Bélgica" (22) [Someone, to frustrate our hopes, observes that we are very far away. My answer is that the colonies are always far from the metropolis; the Belgian Congo does not neighbor on Belgium]. It should be stressed that this note was published only fourteen months before "El milagro secreto," and that Borges discusses the war in similar terms in his note on the liberation of Paris, "Anotación al 23 de agosto de 1944" [Note on 23 August 1944], the only one of the political essays mentioned here to be included in the *Obras completas* (727–28).

In all of these writings, then, the nature of the relation between literature and reality is unsure—reality seems literary in the worst sense in the note on 1941, while Hladík's literature is uncannily prescient of the world its author was to die in—but the fact of such a relation is nowhere called into question. When Hladík famously prefers verse "porque impide que los espectadores olviden la irrealidad, que es condición del arte" (510) [because it prevents the audience from forgetting irreality, which is a condition of art], the observation is paradoxical in that it depends for its force on the necessary intrusion of reality into art and vice versa. Why else would a writer struggle to create the distancing mechanisms of literary artifice?

It may be asserted that I have not said very much about "El milagro secreto," that I have talked around it. Just so. Though I do not think it would have seemed this way to readers in 1943, least of all to readers who encountered the story in its first publication in *Sur,* a journal with a strong anti-fascist line,[26] the political urgency that must have informed the story has receded somewhat. The "secret miracle" of the completion of the drama in Hladík's mind is rather more accessible now to the reader of the story than are the Czech circumstances that provide it with verisimilitude. Ortega y Gasset, in a famous sentence frequently parodied by Borges,[27] defined the self thus: "Yo soy yo y mi circumstancia" (1: 322) [I am myself plus my circumstance]; it is Hladík's circumstances I have tried to rescue here.

Often when reading Borges's *Ficciones* and *El Aleph* it is helpful to read Bioy Casares's stories of the same period, because the work of the master stands out in sharper relief in contrast to that of the disciple.[28] In the case of "El milagro secreto," one of Bioy's stories in *La trama celeste* (1948) [The Celestial Plot], his collection of stories most profoundly marked by Borges, brings the historical questions we have examined into sharper focus. "El otro laberinto" [The Other Labyrinth] is a story set not in Prague but in Budapest, and not in 1939 but in 1904. The main character, Anthal Horvath, forges a document that was supposed to have been found on the body of a man who died in mysterious circumstances in Turkish-occupied Buda in 1607. He bases his document on the life of his friend Istvan Banyay, and Banyay falls into the trap of being so fascinated by the 1607 case that he does not notice that the purported document tells a story that closely resembles his own. After Banyay disappears with a photographic copy of the document, Horvath realizes that his forgery has become an element in a fantastic story, since the seventeenth-century Turkish authorities found disturbing the physical aspect of the document, its glossy sheen showing no trace of the ink.

One of the major characters in the story is Professor Liptay, a historian who works at the Hungarian national archive, but who is suspected of being a collaborator with the Austrian authorities by the young Hungarian Patriots. Banyay says of his and Horvath's teacher: "He is a man with a single passion: history. But history, treated by him, is at times illuminated like a fantastic tale, and always like a work of art" (113). Bioy has taken Borges's phrase in "Tlön, Uqbar, Orbis Tertius" about philosophy and theology being branches of fantastic literature (436) and extended it to history, but subordinating the one to the other more completely than Borges himself does. Bioy dutifully fills in the details of the Hungarian backdrop of the story to tell of time travel, but the historical periods visited in the tale interest him less than the fantastic device itself. Thus, it is only near the end of the story (139) that the reader learns that the point of departure is 1904. Up until then it could be any time during the Hapsburg rule of Hungary from Vienna, or perhaps even during the Nazi occupation of Hungary; all that is said early in the story is that the Hungarian patriots hope to kill the "police chief who was arriving from Vienna, insatiable for Hungarian blood" (111), but this could refer to one of the many Austrians who served in the Gestapo and the German army. There is a constellation of historical allusions similar to what we have observed in Borges—the young Magyar patriots of 1904 yearn for a national identity and culture, just as the Hungarians under Ottoman rule in 1607 yearn for freedom to use their national tongue and to create a national identity—but the details lack the persuasive force they have in Borges. The reader has no sense of a "realidad más compleja" than the one made explicit in the story. Indeed, the similarities between the story and the various fictions of time travel discussed in Borges's "La flor de Coleridge," notably H. G. Wells's *The Time Machine* and Henry James's *The Sense of the Past,* suggest that for Bioy the motif of time travel came first, the choice of a Central European setting later. There is no obvious relation between the events of the story and the political history of Hungary during the Nazi and Soviet occupations, while "El milagro secreto," conjured up out of a similar rag pile of historical references, reveals a passionate interest in the fate of Prague, which was taken (quite rightly, as it turned out) by Borges, as by many others, to presage the fate of all of Europe.

In his conversations with Karel Čapek, Thomas Masaryk defines politics as "an attempt to grasp the given moment in the flow of history" (158). The crucial word here is "grasp," which implies the will to interrupt and shape that "flow." There is a great difference between Masaryk's "seizing the day" and Hladík's secret miracle, yet both depend on the idea that we can make use of our time and not let ourselves be time's plaything. They died within two years of each other, these two brave Czechs, the one the architect of a nation, the other the author of an invisible masterpiece.[29] And, though their deaths seem to mark an ending in the history of their nation, the next fifty years of whose history is marked by two foreign occupations, their "attempt to grasp the given moment in the flow of history" has also, in time, been found worthy of imitation.

Ronald Christ asserts: "Thus while many of Borges' stories, like 'The Immortal' and 'Theme of the Traitor and Hero' assume as their point of departure a precise date in history (June, 1929 in the one and January 3, 1944 in the other), they in fact demonstrate the meaninglessness of such dates in light of history's perpetual repetition of itself" (23). "El milagro secreto" is an important challenge to Christ's idea. To read this story starting from the premise that 15 March 1939 signifies nothing is not to read it at all: the power of the story comes in part from a sense of how much is at stake, for Hladík, for his fellow citizens of Prague and of Czechoslovakia, for all the people of Europe. To be sure, the idea of circular time is important in the story because it animates the delirium of the madman in Hladík's play. However, Hladík himself does not share the idea that time is circular: the play ends with the audience's shocked realization that the madman's circular time has been imposed on them, but to realize that is to emerge from the nightmare.

Just as the writing of Karel Čapek (or even that of Franz Kafka)[30] is preoccupied with the rise of fascism, of what one Borges character calls "la historia, encarnada en un insensato" (1065) [history incarnated in a madman], so Hladík's problem in *Los enemigos,* and Borges's problem in "El milagro secreto," are to find ways to escape from a circular nightmare. For the author of that nightmare was Adolf Hitler.

In *Intimate Things,* Karel Čapek writes: "Classical literature is the literature of which we do not expect anything new. That is why we appreciate it so highly, and why we leave it unread. On the other hand we read modern literature as we read newspapers; we want it to tell us something new; as soon as it has told us we throw it aside like yesterday's paper. If we were to let it tell its tale three times over, we might find out what there is in it which is unchanging" (158–59).[31] I hope I have found "something new" to say about "El milagro secreto."

5

Cryptogram and Scripture: Losing Count in

"La escritura del dios"

This we shall write now under the Law of God and Christianity; we shall bring it to light because now the *Popol Vuh,* as it was called, cannot be seen any more, in which was clearly seen the coming from the other side of the sea and the narration of our obscurity, and our life was clearly seen. The original book, written long ago, existed, but its sight is hidden to the searcher and to the thinker.—Recinos, Goetz, and Morley 79–80[1]

The polemic that rages as a series of international cultural establishments celebrate the five hundredth anniversary of the violent encounter of two worlds lends a note of seriousness and a change of focus to a discussion of "La escritura del dios," Borges's only story about the Spanish conquest of the so-called New World.[2] The narrator of the story is a Maya priest, Tzinacán, who has been imprisoned since the conquest of Guatemala (1524–27) by Pedro de Alvarado, and who is trying to figure out the location (and then the meaning) of a magical inscription made by his god at the creation. His prison is half of a dark cylinderlike cell, at the top of which is a small window opened once a day by a guard who lets down a pitcher of water and a platter of meat. The other half of the cylinder is occupied by a jaguar, glimpsed for a moment at noon each day when the window is opened. The story consists of a series of revelations: that the god's script is written on the jaguar, that it is a formula fourteen words long, that once Tzinacán has deciphered it he no longer sees the point of uttering it aloud. The story ends, then, with a great act of renunciation, since if Tzinacán were to utter the magic formula, he would restore the old order and would himself become all-powerful.[3]

In the story almost none of the cultural or historical context is explained;[4] Tzinacán takes for granted the tradition from which he comes and the nature of his calling. He does not of course identify himself as a "Maya," because that designation would not have had a unitary meaning for him in the fractured world of the warring Quiché and Cakchiquel states in highland Guatemala in the early sixteenth century. There is a brief reference near the end of the story to the Aztec emperor Moctezuma II: "Cuarenta sílabas, catorce palabras, y yo, Tzinacán, regiría las tierras que rigió Moctezuma" (599) [Forty syllables, fourteen words, and I, Tzinacán, would rule the lands where Moctezuma ruled]. Some critics have been misled by this reference into thinking that Tzinacán is an Aztec[5] priest (and indeed another reason for the confusion might be his name, which is Nahuatl, not Maya, for "bat").[6] However, there is also an unequivocal reference in the story to the *Popol Vuh* [Book of the Mat or Book of Council], the Quiché scripture that was written down after the conquest of Guatemala in the Roman alphabet, versions of which were the common patrimony[7] of the various Maya-speaking peoples of Guatemala and Mexico:

> Vi el universo y vi los íntimos designios del universo. Vi los orígenes que narra el Libro del Común.[8] Vi las montañas que surgieron del agua, vi los primeros hombres de palo, vi las tinajas que se volvieron contra los hombres, vi los perros que les destrozaron las caras. Vi el dios sin cara que hay detrás de los dioses. Vi infinitos procesos que formaban una sola felicidad y, entendiéndolo todo, alcancé también a entender la escritura del tigre. (599)

> I saw the origins that the Book of Council tells of. I saw the mountains that rose up out of the water, I saw the first men of wood, I saw the jars that turned against men, I saw the dogs that tore at their faces. I saw the faceless god who is behind all the gods. I saw infinite processes that formed a single happiness and, understanding it all, I was also able to understand the writing on the jaguar.

What I propose to do here is to reconstruct what Borges could have known about Maya culture in 1949 when the story was published, to fill out the cultural references in Tzinacán's narrative, and then to speculate on Tzinacán's acceptance of annihilation.

First, it may be helpful to show where Borges got the cultural references that he uses here. Since this is his only story (or text of any kind) on a

Mesoamerican theme,[9] there are few clues, and the search is more challenging than usual. Two friends of Borges had taken an interest in the *Popol Vuh* and the Mesoamerican past. Alfonso Reyes, whose "Visión de Anáhuac" (1917) [Vision of Anáhuac] is a lively re-creation of and meditation on Mexico-Tenochtitlán, wrote *Letras de la Nueva España* [Letters of New Spain] at the request of the minister of education, Jaime Torres Bodet, in 1946, the introduction to which includes a summary and brief discussion of the *Popol Vuh,* characterized by Reyes as

> a labyrinth of cosmogony, theogony and human genesis; creation, not *ex nihilo,* but torn, as with the Greeks, from some preexisting matter; anthropocentrism that unites the twelve cardinal points to the heart of man, according to three concentric layers of heaven, the earth and the underworld; a mixture of religion, in which the priest implores favors, and of magic, in which he commands and enslaves the god by his word; a Kabbalah of sacred numbers; a parallel of the contrast between Aegeans and Hellenes between a belief of the vanquished, popular, chthonic, somewhat persecuted, hidden in caves and full of "nagualismo" (a guardian spirit and metamorphoses into animals), and the official belief of the victors, constituted into a church and ultimately less resistant than the other system of belief to the intrusion of Christianity, as the brave survival of the Lacandon Maya still proves. (12: 287)[10]

Pedro Henríquez Ureña, who was then residing in Argentina after an extended period in Mexico, also discusses the *Popol Vuh,* though much more briefly than does Reyes, in his *Historia de la cultura en la América hispánica* (1947). According to Henríquez Ureña, the Mayas and Quichés[11] had precise notions of astronomy and mathematics and employed a writing system that was evolving from hieroglyphs toward phonetic writing. After the Conquest, the Dominican scholar reports, some of them, "intent on preserving their religious and historical traditions in written form" (15), used the Roman alphabet to record a number of works. Those mentioned by Henríquez Ureña are the *Popol Vuh,* characterized as "the Quiché book about the origins of the world and of humanity," the dramatic work *Rabinal Achí,* the *Anales de los Cakchiqueles,* and the "magical books" called *Chilam Balam* (15). Significantly, most of these works had recently been issued in cheap editions that circulated throughout the Spanish world, published by the new Mexican publishing house Fondo de Cultura Económica, with whose early history and direction both Reyes and Henríquez Ureña were intimately associated.[12] The inaugural volume of the Biblioteca

Americana [American Library] series directed by Henríquez Ureña was Adrián Recinos's translation of the *Popol Vuh* (1947);[13] the eighth volume was Alfredo Barrera Vásquez and Silvia Rendón's edition of the *Libro de los libros de Chilam Balam* (1948) [Book of the Books of Chilam Balam], and the eleventh was Recinos's edition of the *Memorial de Solalá* or *Anales de los cakchiqueles* (1950) [Annals of the Cakchiquels]. Since his story was published in *Sur* in 1949, it would certainly have been possible for Borges to read the first two of these works, and he may have done so to show interest in Henríquez Ureña's project. Certainly these editions of the three works supplied what he needed to write "La escritura del dios." What is impressive about the story is the synthetic and imaginative use of material that to the nonspecialist is rather opaque. Borges, as it were, passed a short course in Maya studies and then went on to use what he had learned to say something new (and as usual he got the details right). It is interesting to find that he is rather more sympathetic to the highland Guatemalan Maya cultures than José Vasconcelos, whose concept of the "cosmic race" does not hold him back from snide attacks on the *Popol Vuh* and the other monuments of indigenous America.[14]

The historical "Tzinacán" was the ruler of the Cakchiquels at Iximché; his Cakchiquel name was Ahpozotzil (meaning "the Bat King" [Kelly 132] or "Keeper of the Bat Mat" [Tedlock 183]).[15] He is mentioned in the *Popol Vuh,* in a discussion of the differences of language and religion between the Quiché and their neighbors and historic enemies, the Cakchiquels. The Recinos translation reads: "Well, the speech of the Cakchiquel is different, because the name of their god was different when they came from there, from Tulán-Zuyva. Tzotzihá Chimalcán was the name of their god, and today they speak a different tongue; and also from their god the families of Ahpozotzil and Ahpoxa, as they are called, took their names" (190). At this point Recinos adds a note that is surely Borges's immediate source: "Ahpozotzil and Ahpoxahil were the names of the king of the Cakchiquel and of his principal assistant and heir. The Spaniards gave the former, who was governing in 1524, the name Sinacán, from the Náhuatl Tzinacán, which also means 'bat'" (190n).

One of "the Spaniards" in question is Bernal Díaz del Castillo, near the end of whose massive *Historia verdadera de la conquista de la Nueva España* we read:

> There they wounded me with an arrow, but the wound was not serious, and then we came to Petapa, and the next day we came to this valley we call "of the Twisted One," where this city of Guatemala is

now located, and then everything was a battle to overcome the natives; and I remember that when we were going down a steep slope the earth began to shake in such a way that many soldiers fell to the ground, because the earthquake lasted a long while; and then we took the road to the place of the former city of Guatemala, where the caciques called Cinacan and Sacachul were, and before entering that city there was a very deep ravine, and in it there were all the squadrons of the Guatemalans who sought to prevent us from passing by, and we made things go so badly for them that we were able to sleep that night in the city. (2: 347–48)

The incident in question took place after the initial conquest of the Quichés in 1524 by Pedro de Alvarado (who was aided by the Cakchiquels, as recorded in the *Anales de los Cakchiqueles*,[16] rather like Cortés was aided earlier by the Tlaxcalans in his fight with the Aztecs in Mexico-Tenochtitlán) and the razing of the Quiché capital Utatlán by Alvarado. Within two years relations between Alvarado and the Cakchiquels had soured to the extent that Ahpozotzil/Tzinacán allied himself with the Quiché leader Sacachul in fighting against the Spaniards. Victoria Bricker comments: "The later date [1526] makes it possible to view the Cakchiquel 'revolt' as the stimulus for the general uprising that apparently occurred in Guatemala in 1526 not only among the Cakchiquel, but also among the Quiche and southern Pokoman. In fact, according to the Spanish view, the general uprising resulted from a conspiracy between Sequechul, the ruler of the Quiche, and Ahpozotzil, the ruler of the Cakchiquel" (35).[17] After this uprising, in turn, Alvarado razed the Cakchiquel capital Iximché and turned to the building of the Spanish city Santiago de Guatemala.[18] The destruction of the pyramid of Qaholom where Tzinacán officiated the sacred rites may be reasonably assumed to have taken place, then, in Iximché in 1526, though clearly some use has been made of the more abundant material about the destruction of Utatlán in 1524.[19]

Tzinacán's god Qaholom is mentioned frequently in the *Popol Vuh,* usually in concert with the female principle Alom. The third sentence of the preamble to the sacred book reads: "And here we shall set forth the revelation, the declaration, and the narration of all that was hidden, the revelation by Tzacol, Bitol, Alom, Qaholom, who are called Hunahpú-Vuch, Hunahpú Utiú, Zaqui-Nimá-Tziís, Tepeu, Gucumatz, u Qux cho, u Qux Paló, Ah Raxá Lac, Ah Raxá Tzel, as they were called" (78). A note by Recinos glosses this rather obscure passage: "These are the names of the divinity, arranged in pairs of creators in accord with the dual conception of the Quiché, Tzacol and Bitol, Creator and Maker. *Alom,* the mother god, she who conceived the sons, from *al,* 'son,' *alán,* 'to give birth.' *Qaholom,* the father god who begat the sons, from *qahol,* 'son of the father,' *qaholah,* 'to beget'" (78n). Later passages where Alom and Qaholom appear include the beginning of the first chapter, where "Alom" and "Qaholom" are together translated as "the Forefathers" by Recinos "to follow the conciseness of the text" (81n; see also 87n). The most interesting passage for our purposes is that in which Alom and Qaholom question the four heroes, Balam-Quitzé, Balam-Acab, Mahucu-tah, and Iqui-Balam,[20] who have just been created (in the fourth creation of the world narrated in the *Popol Vuh*): "Then the Creator and the Maker [that is, Alom and Qaholom] asked them: 'What do you think of your condition? Do you not see? Do you not hear? Are not your speech and manner of walking good? Look, then! Contemplate the world, look [and see] if the mountains and the valleys appear! Try, then, to see!'" (168).

The explicit reference to the *Popol Vuh* in "La escritura del dios" quoted earlier mentions seven separate plot elements of that book, and significantly these elements of sacred scripture become most vivid to Tzinacán when he *sees* them in his *vision:* "Vi" [I saw] he says nine times in five sentences. He sees the following elements of the opening chapters of the *Popol Vuh:*

1. "Vi el universo y vi los íntimos designios del universo." / "Then they planned the creation, and the growth of the trees and the thickets and the birth of life and the creation of man. Thus it was arranged in the darkness and in the night by the Heart of Heaven who is called Huracán" (82).

2. "Vi los orígenes que narra el Libro del Común." / "Great were the descriptions and the account of how all the sky and earth were formed, how it was formed and divided into four parts" (80).

3. "Vi las montañas que surgieron del agua." / "Like the mist, like a cloud, and like a cloud of dust was the creation, when the mountains appeared from the water; and instantly the mountains grew" (83).

4. "Vi los primeros hombres de palo." / "And instantly the figures were made of wood. They looked like men, talked like men, and populated the surface of the earth" (89).[21]

5. "Vi las tinajas que se volvieron contra los hombres." / "And all began to speak: their earthen jars, their griddles, their plates, their pots, their grinding stones, all rose up and struck their faces" (91).

6. "Vi los perros que les destrozaron las caras." / " 'Now you shall feel

the teeth of our mouths; we shall destroy you,' said the dogs, and then, they destroyed their faces" (91).

7. "Vi el dios sin cara que hay detrás de los dioses." / "The face of the sun had not yet appeared, nor that of the moon, nor the stars, and it had not dawned" (94).

The important thing about Tzinacán's vision here is precisely that it is a vision; the emphasis is not on his reading (or his memory of reading) the sacred book, but on the book coming to life. By obeying the creator god's injunction to see, Tzinacán has broken out of an intellectualized stupor; though in prison, he is, as the god instructed, contemplating the world. What is of interest is the result of his meditation.

Borges has Tzinacán reply *avant la lettre* to two important exponents of Western philosophy: René Descartes and José Ortega y Gasset. When Tzinacán finds himself dreaming of being buried alive under an ever growing heap of sand and a voice in the dream tells him that if he wakes up from this dream it will be into yet another dream, he wakes himself up through a sheer act of intellectual will, objecting that there are no dreams inside dreams.[22] This is the idea (which psychoanalysis has not, I believe, sustained) used by Descartes as one of the grounds for certainty for the *cogito* in the *Meditations on First Philosophy* (102). For Tzinacán, however, the "proof" of individual identity is too paltry for words, not worth uttering aloud: the ego, when separated (as Tzinacán has been secluded in his cell) from the world and from time, is not worth saving. His argument with Cartesian thought (and Descartes had not yet been born) turns on an objection to the separation of mind from body, of self from community, of space from time.

Just after the dream sequence, Tzinacán says: "Un hombre se confunde, gradualmente, con la forma de su destino; un hombre es, a la larga, sus circunstancias" (598) [A man is confused, gradually, with the form of his destiny; a man is, eventually, his circumstances]. Here Tzinacán is anticipating Ortega y Gasset's famous formula in the *Meditaciones del Quijote:* "Yo soy yo y mi circunstancia, y si no la salvo a ella no me salvo yo" (322) [I am myself and my circumstance, and if I do not save it I do not save myself]. Borges uses the word "circumstances" in a limited meaning here, in accord with the Latin root, to refer to the things in Tzinacán's cell: the jaguar, the window, his body,[23] the darkness, the stone. The reduction of Tzinacán's physical universe, and his separation from the great continuum of the Long Count, results in a deflation of Ortega's triumphal formula: instead of the implicit imperial gesture of including and incorporating the surrounding world into the self (as in the work of the Spanish philosopher), the Maya priest has had his "circumstances" taken away from him, yet he blesses what remains to him.[24]

Tzinacán's meditation, then, is set against two influential European meditations on identity and existence, but Tzinacán, unlike that other famous imprisoned philosopher, Boethius, finds no consolation in philosophy. Instead, philosophical doubt becomes the ground for mystical experience:

> El éxtasis no repite sus símbolos; hay quien ha visto a Dios en un resplandor, hay quien lo ha percibido en una espada o en los círculos de una rosa. Yo vi una Rueda altísima, que no estaba delante de mis ojos, ni detrás, ni a los lados, sino en todas partes, a un tiempo. Esa Rueda estaba hecha de agua, pero también de fuego, y era (aunque se veía el borde) infinita. Entretejidas, la formaban todas las cosas que serán, que son y que fueron, y yo era una de las hebras de esa trama total, y Pedro de Alvarado, que me dio tormento, era otra. Ahí estaban las causas y los efectos y me bastaba ver esa Rueda para entenderlo todo, sin fin. (598–99)

> Ecstasy does not repeat its symbols; there is one who has seen God in a blinding flash, someone has seen it in a sword or in the circles of a rose. I saw a very tall Wheel, which was not before my eyes, or behind them, or to the side, but everywhere at once. That Wheel was made of water, but also of fire, and it was infinite (although I could see its edge). Interwoven, it was formed of all the things that will be, that are, and that were, and I was one of the threads of that total web, and Pedro de Alvarado, who had me tortured, was another. There were the causes and the effects and it sufficed for me to see that Wheel to understand everything, without limits.

Once again Tzinacán, the Jaguar Priest, is in dialogue with the Old World; his vision is counterposed to that of St. Paul on the road to Damascus (light), of Muhammad (the sword), of the Sufi mystic 'Abd al-Qādir (the rose). The symbol chosen for Tzinacán's vision of divinity may seem problematic, since the Mayas like other New World peoples did not use the wheel and since the wheel is an important symbol in Buddhism.[25] But Borges has not converted Tzinacán to Buddhism here, though there are undoubted Buddhist echoes to his acceptance a bit later of the path of renunciation;[26] the wheel was used in the books of Chilam Balam (books, that is, of the Jaguar Priest) as an image of the great round of time.

According to Miguel León-Portilla (in his *Time and Reality in the Thought of the Maya*): "The Colonial Maya texts which speak of the twenty-year periods or wheels of the *katuns* confirm this peculiar conception of a universe in which the passage of time consists of arrivals, relays, and departures of divine forces. This is shown, for instance, in the 'first prophetic wheel of a circle of *katuns*,' published by Barrera Vásquez and reconstructed from various texts of the *Chilam Balam* books" (51).[27] Here too a detail confirms the accuracy of the design of the story. Within the enmeshed wheels of the various cycles of time in the Long Count calendar, the days were sacred, being themselves gods. When Tzinacán says that the magic formula was a sentence of fourteen words, he confirms his status as Jaguar Priest and the wholeness of his understanding of the physical universe, because fourteen was the number sacred to the jaguar god,[28] again following León-Portilla (who bases his views, in turn, on Barrera Vásquez [193]: "14. *Ix* is a repeated appearance of the jaguar god in his relationship with the earth and the lower world. Its glyph though highly stylized includes spots of the skin of the jaguar" (40).[29] Eric Thompson, in turn, confirms the relation between the jaguar god and the earth: "The jaguar god, corresponding to the Mexican Tepeyollotl, god of the interior of the earth, is an important Maya deity of the surface of the earth or its interior, for the two regions overlap" (*Rise and Fall* 231). Why, then, should Tzinacán reject the gift of the jaguar god, the gift of power over the surface of the earth (and with it, the possibility of avenging himself and his community for the brutality of the Conquest by offering up the heart of Pedro de Alvarado to the god [599])?[30] The answer lies earlier in the story, but first let us examine the Maya conception of the relation between space and time, as expressed in the post-Conquest texts and as reconstructed by archaeologists and field anthropologists.

Thompson has stated the difficulty posed for us by the Maya way of thinking about time and space:

> There are other aspects of the Maya philosophy of time, such as the strange failure to distinguish between past and future in the prophetic chants. What had gone before and what lay ahead were blended in a way that is baffling to our western minds. Mysticism is not now fashionable, and so writers tend to stress the material side of Maya civilization, but surely it is precisely these (to us) strange aberrations of Maya mentality which pose the most interesting questions. (*Rise and Fall* 14)

He adds later in the same book: "Time, in the conception of the Maya, sweeps forward, too, but surviving calculations carry us only a paltry four millennia into the future. Evidently, future time was of less interest than time past, probably because the Maya were much more interested in the past than in the future on account of their belief that history repeats whenever the divine influences are in the same balance" (140). Because of the intricate nature of the Maya calendar, with its "wheels within wheels," a given alignment would not be repeated again for a very long time. Time itself was divine, and the precision with which its passage was calculated (fruit of an advanced knowledge of astronomy and mathematics, as is well known, though this knowledge was apparently not used for more mundane purposes) served the art of divination but, more importantly, reflected an obsession with the thing itself.

This obsession took precedence over all else. León-Portilla explains:

> Isolated from time, space becomes inconceivable. In the absence of time-cycles, there is no life, nothing happens, not even death. The colored regions, divorced from *kinh,* sun-day-time, would become utter darkness devoid of all meaning. The world of the gods would be a mere absence, and the flight of the *katuns* would mark the end of reality. There would be a return to primeval darkness, without the cosmic ceibas, without the sun, the moon, the great star, without human beings, without any meaning whatsoever. (86)

He adds a bit later: "Space and time were inseparable. The spatial universe was an immense stage on which the divine faces and forces were oriented, coming and going in an unbroken order. The Maya sages had found the key to extricate meanings and to foresee the future" (110). Thus, when Tzinacán says early in the story, "He perdido la cifra de los años que yazgo en la tiniebla" (596) [I have lost count of the years I have lain in this darkness], he expresses what for him must be the greatest of tragedies, the most utter humiliation: he has lost track of the Long Count. Though his memory of the *Popol Vuh* and of the arts of divination has not faded, his loss of synchrony signifies his inadequacy to restore the universe. He must be annihilated; the universe must also be annihilated and then created anew.[31]

His tragedy, then, is due in large measure to the darkness of his solitary confinement and to its psychic result—that he has an almost European, almost bourgeois sense of his own individuality: "Cuarenta sílabas, catorce palabras, y *yo, Tzinacán,* regiría las tierras que rigió Moctezuma" (599, emphasis added) [Forty syllables, fourteen words, and *I, Tzinacán,* would rule the lands where Moctezuma ruled].[32] Power over the earth, even though associated with the cult of the jaguar god, even though it may provide the occasion for sweet revenge, is useless without synchrony, without coordination of the ruler, the community, the gods, the earth. "Me sentí perdido" (598) [I felt lost], Tzinacán says, and the expression conveys a Cartesian sense of solitude and autonomy, but he experiences it as loss.

Eric Thompson writes: "Even in the historical fragments which survive in the Colonial transcriptions called the Books of Chilam Balam, there is singularly little stress on the doings of individuals, and that only when individual behaviour affected history" (*Rise and Fall* 168). The Quiché word *tzih* meant, according to Recinos, "word, opinion, history, fate, or destiny" (182n), so the very notion of an individual "affecting history" was somewhat equivocal, since what happened was what was fated to happen. What Tzinacán and other members of the priestly caste, other Jaguar Priests, could do was to discover the design implicit in the unfolding of history:

> The time universe of the Maya is the ever-changing stage on which are felt the aggregate of presences and actions of the various divine forces which coincide in a given period. The Maya strove, by means of their computations, to foresee the nature of these presences and the resultant of their various influences at specified moments. Since *kinh* [time] is essentially cyclic, it is most important to know the past in order to understand the present and predict the future. (León-Portilla, *Time and Reality* 54)[33]

Thus, Tzinacán articulates individuality as loss:

> Quien ha entrevisto el universo, quien ha entrevisto los ardientes designios del universo, no puede pensar en un hombre, en sus triviales dichas o desventuras, aunque ese hombre sea él. Ese hombre *ha sido él* y ahora no le importa. Qué le importa la suerte de aquel otro, qué le importa la nación de aquel otro, si él, ahora es nadie. Por eso no pronuncio la fórmula, por eso dejo que me olviden los días, acostado en la oscuridad. (599, emphasis in original)

> One who has glimpsed the universe, one who has glimpsed the burning designs of the universe, cannot think of a man, of his trivial joys or sorrows, even if that man is himself. That man *has been himself* and does not matter to him any more. What does the fate of that other man matter, what does the fate of the man's nation matter, if he, now, is no one. That is why I do not pronounce the formula, that is why I let the days forget me, stretched out in the darkness.

This almost Buddhist act of renunciation may impress the reader as beautiful, but it is the product of a great human tragedy, one almost completely erased from Tzinacán's account, although, as the quotation here proves, the dimensions of the tragedy are still visible under erasure. "Qué le importa la suerte de aquel otro, *qué le importa la nación de aquel otro*"— Tzinacán is the Jaguar Priest who once officiated the rites in his community and thus bound together time, space, himself, and the community. The name of his sacred book implies this also: it is the "Libro del Común," the Book of Council. Tedlock explains that the literal meaning is "Book of the Mat," and that the mat (also present in Tzinacán's Cakchiquel name, Ahpozotzil, or "Keeper of the Bat Mat") was the symbol of the weaving together of the community and the universe, rather like our word *text*. In solitary confinement, Tzinacán loses track of time; also, and no doubt as part of the same experience of loss, he forgets his community. Even if he had no desire for individual power or glory, he might have uttered the formula to restore his community to its rightful place in the design of the universe, but in forgetting himself he has forgotten them. In the words of the book of Chilam Balam of Tizimin:

> There were rulers:
>   There were lords.
> That's finished—
>   Not now . . .
> Time has passed
>   And unraveled . . .
> That is the word of the *katun*
>   That is coming.
> (Edmonson, *Ancient Future* 161)[34]

6

Going Native: Beyond Civilization and Savagery in

"Historia del guerrero y de la cautiva"

We imperceptibly advance from youth to age without observing the gradual, but
incessant, change of human affairs; and even in our larger experience of history, the
imagination is accustomed, by a perpetual series of causes and effects, to unite the
most distant revolutions. But if the interval between two memorable eras could be
instantly annihilated; if it were possible, after a momentary slumber of two hundred
years, to display the *new* world to the eyes of a spectator who still retained a lively
and recent impression of the *old*, his surprise and his reflections would furnish the
pleasing subject of a philosophical romance.—Gibbon 1: 1199[1]

"Historia del guerrero y de la cautiva" (*Sur*, 1949) is one of Borges's most
curious fictions from history, since it evokes not one but two distinct chains
of historical references: one having to do with the fall of the Roman Empire
to the barbarians, another concerned with the frontier wars of the 1870s in
the Argentine pampas. Much of the interest of the story has to do with the
crossings between these chains of signification, though each preserves an
insuperable difference from the other. This is in fact one of the stories in
which Borges situates himself most clearly at (and as) the site of intersec-
tion between the texts and quietly shows how a new text is imagined and
articulated out of those crossings.

It is a story having to do explicitly with a topos that has been central to
Argentine literature since the publication of Sarmiento's biographical study
of Facundo Quiroga in 1845: *Civilización i barbarie*. Noé Jitrik, in an
important article on the recurrence of polar oppositions in Argentine

literature, observes that "civilization and savagery" is presented to the reader as a dilemma "in the face of which one must choose one of the opposing terms" (244) but that such dualistic thinking is simplistic and antidialectical. The polar oppositions studied by Jitrik—including city/country, official culture/populism, and cosmopolitanism/localism—are founded on terms that are not themselves unified but cracked: "If we examine each sector separately we note that unity does not rule in either sector; new oppositions appear" (228), "overlapping in a way difficult to schematize because it is so varied and so variable, and because of the contamination that frequently confuses the terms" (245). The emptying out of the content of "civilization" and "savagery" while preserving the polar opposition itself in this very brief story by Borges is thus characteristic of a whole literature, but Borges accomplishes here what the Russian formalists called the baring or revealing of the procedures that inform the customary distinction between "civilization" and "savagery," thus allowing it to be rethought and refashioned.

The story opens thus: "En la página 278 del libro *La poesia* (Bari, 1942), Croce, abreviando un texto latino del historiador Pablo el Diácono, narra la suerte y cita el epitafio de Droctulft; éstos me conmovieron singularmente, luego entendí por qué" (557) [On page 278 of his book *Poetry* (Bari, 1942), Croce, summarizing a Latin text by the historian Paul the Deacon, narrates the fate and quotes the epitaph of Droctulft; these moved me in a singular manner; later I understood why]. The passage from Croce comes from the notes to the fourth section of his chapter "La vita della poesia" [The Life of Poetry]; the title of the relevant section of the notes is "Poesia dove si trova" [Poetry Where It Is Found]. The passage reads:

> I enjoyed going around noting, to give an example, that poetry raises its head where it is least expected. There was once in the Church of St. Vitale in Ravenna the epitaph (preserved by Paul the Deacon) of a German named Droctulft, who had abandoned the Lombards to defend that city against his own men. The epitaph in verse contained a statement of gratitude to that man, who had sacrificed the affection for his own relations to his new country ("while loving us, he looked at his own parents with scorn, feeling instead that Ravenna was now his country"). But, in the writing of that couplet, the unknown author becomes prisoner of a lyrical-epic vision of the character, and in a few strokes sketches him in his physical power and in the particular majesty and humanity of the barbarian: "His appearance was frightening but he had a gentle nature, and his long beard fell on his strong chest!"

Since the day I read the *Rerum langobardicarum scriptores* [Historians of the Lombards], this Droctulft entered into the series of poetic figures who live in my memory. (269–70)

Note that Croce emphasizes the importance of his own visual memory in the "poeticization" of Droctulft's epitaph; like other "found poetry," it is not poetic in itself, but memory and reflection make it so. (Borges will repeat this idea, carrying it to unexpected extremes.) The "making" of the found poem is above all a matter of framing the quotation. The "framing" consists both of telling the story of Droctulft and of reporting the effects of the story and epitaph on the reader. Neither narration nor reception is sufficient for the production of "la poesia," but both are necessary for its poetic quality to be perceived.

Borges next gives a brief life and death of Droctulft:

Fue Droctulft un guerrero lombardo que en el asedio de Ravena abandonó a los suyos y murió defendiendo la ciudad que antes había atacado. Los raveneses le dieron sepultura en un templo y compusieron un epitafio en el que manifestaron su gratitud ("contespsit [*sic*] caros, dum nos amat ille, parentes") y el peculiar contraste que se advertía entre la figura atroz de aquel bárbaro y su simplicidad y bondad:

Terribilis visu facies mente benignus,
Longaque robusto pectores [*sic*] barba fuit! (557)

Droctulft was a Lombard warrior in the siege of Ravenna who abandoned his people and died defending the city that he had earlier attacked. The people of Ravenna buried him in the temple and composed an epitaph in which they expressed their gratitude ("he scorned his own parents, so much did he love us") and the strange contrast that could be noted between the frightening aspect of that barbarian and his simplicity and kindness: "His appearance was frightening but he had a gentle nature and his long beard fell on his strong chest."

A footnote to the final quotation reads: "También Gibbon (*Decline and Fall*, XLV) transcribe estos versos" (557n) [Gibbon (*Decline and Fall* XLV) also transcribes these verses]. Gibbon does in fact quote the same two lines in note 48 to the chapter in question, with this comment: "The epitaph of Droctulf [*sic*] (Paul, 1. iii. c. 19) may be applied to many of his countrymen" (2: 403n). Note that Croce does not cite Gibbon as his source but Paulus Diaconus or Paul the Deacon, so only the astonishing memory of Borges could bring the two quotations from Paul the Deacon together (an amazing achievement considering the sheer bulk of Gibbon's *Decline and Fall,* a text all the details of which could only be remembered by a reader like the idiot savant Funes—or Borges, savant but no idiot).

This happens to be one of the moments when it is possible to say quite precisely what Borges read and did not read. Although both Croce and Gibbon cite Paul the Deacon as their source, it is clear that Borges did not consult the medieval author's *History of the Lombards* because there Droctulft is called a "duke," not a common soldier, and Paul states that Droctulft, though fighting initially with the Lombards, was not himself a Lombard but a Swabian, who then chose to join the people of Ravenna in their defense against the Lombards[2]—not as simple or exemplary a story as it appears in Croce's brief narrative. And, instead of the four lines from Droctulft's epitaph as quoted by Croce and then again by Borges, the epitaph in Paul's account is twenty-six lines long.[3]

Though Croce gives Borges the skeletal account he uses of Droctulft's biography, Borges fills out the story with reflections and suppositions. The brief second paragraph of the story is crucial:

> Tal es la historia del destino de Droctulft, bárbaro que murió defendiendo a Roma, o tal es el fragmento de su historia que pudo rescatar Pablo el Diácono. Ni siquiera sé en qué tiempo ocurrió: si al promediar el siglo VI, cuando los longobardos desolaron las llanuras de Italia; si en el VIII, antes de la rendición de Ravena. Imaginemos (éste no es un trabajo histórico) lo primero. (557)

> Such is the story of the fate of Droctulft, a barbarian who died defending Rome, or such is the fragment of his story that Paul the Deacon was able to rescue. I do not even know when it occurred: whether at the beginning of the sixth century, when the Lombards ravaged the plains of Italy; whether in the eighth century, before the surrender of Ravenna. Let us imagine (this is not a work of history) the former.

Despite the final disclaimer, Borges's two suppositions are informed by a careful reading of Gibbon, who records that "during a period of two hundred years [from the sixth to the eighth century] Italy was unequally divided between the kingdom of the Lombards and the exarchate of Ravenna" (2: 400). He quotes Droctulft's epitaph in his general discussion of the Lombard and other barbarian invaders in one place (chapter 45, 2: 403n) and narrates the final surrender of Ravenna to the Lombards in another (chapter 49, 2: 593). Many other details in the next (third) paragraph also derive from Gibbon, mostly from the discussion in chapter 10 of the Germanic barbarians.[4] Thus, Borges characterizes the individual Droctulft, a Swabian in the service of the Lombards, with general information on religion, political structure, character, and geographic setting gleaned from Tacitus and Gibbon about the variety of peoples known as the German barbarians. As Borges says in the story, "Imaginemos, *sub specie aeternitatis,* a Droctulft, no al individuo Droctulft, que sin duda fue único e insondable (todos los individuos lo son), sino al tipo genérico que de él y de otros muchos como él ha hecho la tradición, que es obra del olvido y de la memoria" (557) [Let us imagine, *sub specie aeternitatis,* Droctulft, not the individual Droctulft, who no doubt was unique and fathomless (all individuals are like that), but the generic type that tradition—the work of forgetfulness and of memory—has made of him and of many others like him]. Yet, though Borges claims to be blurring his portrait of Droctulft, the picture of the hero of Ravenna is sharper than that given by Gibbon or Croce:[5] it is much more fully imagined.

The discussion of Droctulft's life and death closes with the fourth paragraph of the story, which reads:

> No fue un traidor (los traidores no suelen inspirar epitafios piadosos); fue un iluminado, un converso. Al cabo de unas cuantas generaciones, los longobardos que culparon al trásfuga procedieron como él; se hicieron italianos, lombardos y acaso alguno de su sangre—Aldiger—pudo engendrar a quienes engendraron al Alighieri. (558)

> He was not a traitor (traitors do not usually inspire pious epitaphs); he was an enlightened one, a convert. In the course of a few generations, the Lombards who blamed the turncoat behaved like he did; they became Italians, and perhaps one of their race—Aldiger—in time engendered those who engendered Aldighieri.

The information on the Lombard derivation of Dante's surname is gleaned from Arthur John Butler's article on Dante in the *Encyclopaedia Britannica:* "Here the German strain appears unmistakably; the name Aldighiero (Aldiger) being purely Teutonic" (7: 811).[6] This discussion, which rests on an assumption of the superiority of the northern races over the southern, had important corollaries in Argentina, and indeed the north/south dichotomy posed here is a subterfuge to draw attention away from another obvious source of the story, this time drawn from the literature of the "meros sudamericanos." For Droctulft's story depends for its dramatic effect in Borges's retelling on its similarity to a famous episode from José Hernández's *El gaucho Martín Fierro* (1872), in which Cruz, one of the gauchos charged with the duty of capturing Fierro, cries out: "¡Cruz no consiente / que se cometa el delito / de matar ansí un valiente!" (1: 1624–26) [Cruz does not consent to the commission of the crime of killing a grave man in this manner!]. But more of that later.

One curious aspect of Droctulft's life that emerges from a reading of Gibbon's chapter 45 is that the categories of "civilization" and "barbarism," so often a concern of his, get rather confused here. The Romans of the late empire are here as elsewhere portrayed as weak, corrupt, degenerate; of the Lombards Gibbon says that "their virtues are all the more laudable, as they were not affected by the hypocrisy of social manners, nor imposed by the rigid constraint of laws and education" (2: 404). Most important for Droctulft's case, according to Gibbon the Lombards were a very malleable people, and once they had set down their swords they soon blended into the Italian population (2: 401), learned the arts of agriculture (2: 402), and worked out what seemed to Gibbon an eminently fair system of law (2: 407). Indeed, the ancient seat of the empire became more "barbarous" than the "barbarian" settlements to the north: "The Campagna of Rome was speedily reduced to the state of a dreary wilderness, in which the land is barren, the waters are impure, and the air is infectious. Curiosity and ambition no longer attracted the nations to the capital of the world; but if chance or necessity directed the steps of a wandering stranger, he contemplated with horror the vacancy and solitude of the city, and might be tempted to ask, where is the senate, and where are the people?" (2: 406–7).[7] The chapter ends with a discussion of Pope Gregory the Great, a figure whose "martial spirit . . . was checked by the scruples of humanity and religion" (2: 412), who held off the fall of Rome by his "mild eloquence and seasonable gifts" (2: 413), and "who commanded the respect of heretics and barbarians" (2: 413). The chapter of Gibbon's *Decline and Fall* that contains the quotation of two lines from Droctulft's epitaph, then, is one telling of the delicate negotiations between the Lombards and the Italians, of the interpenetration of "civilization" and "barbarism." "So rapid was the influence of climate and example, that the Lombards of the fourth generation surveyed with curiosity and affright the portraits of their savage forefathers" (2: 403); the very sentence that is glossed with the note on Droctulft's epitaph tells of the gentle "conquest" of the barbarians by the idea of civilization.

Droctulft's story might be assimilated into some larger notion of progress and civilization, though in Gibbon such an idea does not work very consistently or very long (see Gossman, *Empire Unpossess'd* 25–47) and in this Borges story it works not at all. The progressive model is closely associated in U.S. history with the notion of "manifest destiny," a curious amalgam of theories of racial superiority, social Darwinism, and a nascent imperialism (see Billington 143–67). In Argentina, much the same idea existed in the nineteenth century under the banner of positivism (for example, Sarmiento's *Conflictos y armonías de las razas en América,* 1883 [Conflicts and Harmonies of the Races in America]). David Viñas shows that the consensus of the Argentine intelligentsia, both liberal and conservative, was by the 1870s in favor of the removal or extermination of the pampas Indians (in his *Indios, ejército, y fronteras*). But Borges, despite his military ancestors and his occasional outspoken racism, undercuts the notion of "manifest destiny" by complicating the boundary between "civilization" and "savagery." Though he preserves the notion of transgression, which depends on an opposition between self and other, clean and dirty, sacred and profane (see Stallybrass and White), he subverts the necessary linking of transgression to moral or racial superiority and inferiority, and, interestingly, he does so through the figure of his own paternal grandmother, Fanny Haslam de Borges (1842–1935).[8]

The grandmother's story focuses on Junín, in the northwestern part of the province of Buenos Aires, in the year 1872. Fanny Haslam had come to Argentina about 1870 to join her sister, who had married an engineer named Jorge Suárez ("Autobiographical Essay" 204). The Englishwoman who was "destined" to be Borges's grandmother met Francisco Borges only a year or two before the action of the story:

> It was in Paraná, the capital city of Entre Ríos, that Fanny Haslam met Colonel Francisco Borges. This was in 1870 or 1871, during the siege of the city by the *montoneros,* or gaucho militia, of Ricardo López Jordán. Borges, riding at the head of his regiment, commanded the troops defending the city. Fanny Haslam saw him from the flat roof of her house; that very night a ball was given to celebrate the arrival of the government relief forces. Fanny and the Colonel met, danced, fell in love, and eventually married. ("Autobiographical Essay" 205)

For the next several years Colonel Borges was in command of the frontier region of the north of the province of Buenos Aires and the south of the province of Santa Fe.[9] The grandmother's memory of the encounter with the "cautiva inglesa" is unusually precise as to date: it took place in 1872.[10]

> Alguna vez, entre maravillada y burlona, mi abuela comentó su destino de inglesa desterrada a ese fin del mundo; le dijeron que no era la única

y le señalaron, meses después, una muchacha india que atravesaba lentamente la plaza. Vestía dos mantas coloradas e iba descalza; sus crenchas eran rubias. (558–59)

Once, half amazed, half joking, my grandmother commented on her destiny as an Englishwoman exiled to this end of the earth; they told her that she was not the only one and, months later, pointed out an Indian girl who was slowly crossing the square. She was wearing two red blankets and was barefoot; her bangs were blonde.

The woman hesitates before coming inside: "Todo parecía quedarle chico: las puertas, las paredes, los muebles" (559) [Everything seemed to appear small to her: the doors, the walls, the furniture]. The narrator comments *before* the conversation takes place: "Quizá las dos mujeres por un instante se sintieron hermanas, estaban lejos de su isla querida y en un increíble país" (559) [Perhaps the two women for an instant felt like sisters, being far from their beloved island and in an unbelievable country]. Yet the *cautiva* does not express nostalgia for England or a sense of estrangement on the Argentine plain; the emotional charge of the adjectives describing the two countries, the "isla querida" and the "increíble país," are those attached to Fanny Haslam's story more than to that of the "cautiva."

What the woman does have to say is sufficiently fragmentary that the grandmother and grandson have to fill it out from their imagination and reading:

Haría quince años que no hablaba el idioma natal y no le era fácil recuperarlo. Dijo que era de Yorkshire, que sus padres emigraron a Buenos Aires, que los había perdido en un malón, que la habían llevado los indios y que ahora era mujer de un capitanejo, a quien ya había dado dos hijos y que era muy valiente. Eso lo fue diciendo en un inglés rústico, entreverado de araucano o de pampa, y detrás del relato se vislumbraba una vida feral: los toldos de cuero de caballo, las hogueras de estiércol, los festines de carne chamuscada o de vísceras crudas, las sigilosas marchas al alba; el asalto de los corrales, el alarido y el saqueo, la guerra, el caudaloso arreo de las haciendas por jinetes desnudos, la poligamia, la hediondez y la magia. (559)

It must have been fifteen years that she had not spoken her native tongue and it was not easy for her to recover it. She said she was from Yorkshire, that her parents immigrated to Buenos Aires, that she had lost them in a raid, that the Indians had taken her away, and that now she was the wife of a chief, to whom she had borne two sons and who was very brave. All of this she said in a rustic English interlaced with Araucanian or Pampa, and behind her story could be glimpsed a wild life: the tents of horse hide, the manure fires, the festivals with singed meat or of raw innards, the stealthy marches at dawn, the attack on the corrals, the yelling and sacking, the battle, the taking of the huge herds from the ranches by naked horsemen, the polygamy, the filth and magic.

What the captive woman has to narrate is simple and matter-of-fact: immigration, captivity, marriage, motherhood. The rest is "glimpsed" (that is, imagined) by the grandmother or the grandson, and once again the adjectives "feral," "chamuscada," "crudas," "sigilosas," and "caudaloso" express their fascination with the spectacle of difference, a spectacle summed up at the end of the long sentence with the words "hediondez" and "magia." The unthinkable has happened: "A esa barbarie se había rebajado una inglesa" (559) [An Englishwoman had been debased to that level of savagery]. And yet, when Fanny Haslam tries to persuade her compatriot to remain with her in "civilization," the other woman says no, simply and firmly: she is happy ("feliz") where she is. This is the only time in the story that an adjective of emotion is attributed directly to the captive. She goes back to her family and her "tribe," and the next time she encounters Fanny Haslam they are out in the open plain:

> Mi abuela había salido a cazar; en un rancho, cerca de los bañados, un hombre degollaba una oveja. Como en un sueño, pasó la india a caballo. Se tiró al suelo y bebió la sangre caliente. No sé si lo hizo porque ya no podía obrar de otro modo, o como un desafío y un signo. (559)

> My grandmother had gone out hunting; in a hut, near the marshes a man was slitting the throat of a sheep. As if in a dream, the Indian woman passed by on horseback. She threw herself to the ground and drank the hot blood. I don't know whether she did it because she could no longer act in any other way, or whether it was a challenge or a sign.

Once again, the narrator is fascinated by the savage spectacle but uncertain what the captive intends to express; the grandmother, one assumes, told this last episode with renewed horror. "A esa barbarie se había rebajado una inglesa": the captive woman, destined to be a proper Englishwoman, has "gone native," that horror of horrors among colonizing peoples.

The narrator argues that there was a momentary identification between the two Englishwomen at the instant of their first encounter, and that perhaps later his grandmother saw herself in the other, "también arrebatada y transformada por este continente implacable, un espejo monstruo de su destino" (559) [also carried off and transformed by this relentless continent, a monstrous mirror of her destiny]. Yet the similarities are more than he readily admits: they are both from rural northern England, the captive from Yorkshire (559), the grandmother from Staffordshire, "of Northumbrian stock" ("Autobiographical Essay" 204); the captive has two children, as does Fanny Haslam ("Autobiographical Essay" 205);[11] Francisco Borges was to die in 1874 in the civil war between Mitre and Avellaneda, in the battle of La Verde, fighting for his friend and mentor Bartolomé Mitre (559),[12] while the captive woman's husband would undoubtedly be killed in 1879 in the "Conquest of the Desert." They are even probably about the same age: Fanny Haslam was born in 1842, so she was thirty at the time of the encounter, while the captive woman had come as a young girl to Argentina with her parents and had now spent fifteen years among the Indians. We are left to imagine the captive woman's story, especially what happens to her after the army campaign of 1879: is she one of the captives who are willingly or forcibly "returned to civilization" after the Conquest of the Desert? What happens to her "half-breed" children: is their English blood sufficient to save them from the genocide? What we do know is a little of the rest of the grandmother's story:

> Her husband's death left Fanny Haslam very much on her own. She had two sons to care for and bring up. Undaunted, she opened her home to paying guests, young American women who came to Argentina to teach under an educational program conceived by President Sarmiento when he visited the United States. Borges does not tell this part of his grandmother's story in his "Autobiographical Essay"; nor has he ever mentioned it in his interviews. He prefers to emphasize the less prosaic details of her life, the frontier adventures. But although not picturesque, Fanny Haslam's solid Victorian upbringing saved the day. She managed to keep the family within the bounds of middle-class respectability and saw to it that both her sons had a position in life. The elder followed in his father's footsteps and became a naval officer; Father became a lawyer. (Rodríguez Monegal, *Jorge Luis Borges* 8–9)

Rodríguez Monegal's phrasing is interesting, in light of the grandmother's appearance in a story having to do with frontiers and liminal states: the grandmother keeps the family "within the bounds of middle-class respectability." At least this Englishwoman never demeaned herself to savagery. Fanny Haslam's last words, as reported by her grandson, were: "I am only an old woman dying very, very slowly. There is nothing remarkable or interesting about this" ("Autobiographical Essay" 206).[13] Unlike many of the characters in the grandson's stories, the old woman does not meet up with her destiny at the moment of death; her "manifest destiny" had been revealed more than sixty years before on the frontier. Though perhaps tempted by the savage spectacle offered by the life of her compatriot, she decided to stay "within bounds," and that choice condemns her to a life that is neither remarkable nor interesting.[14]

It should be noted that the family fortunes of the Borges clan would have been very different in another sense had Francisco Borges not gotten himself entangled in the civil war of 1874. No doubt he would have served with his fellow officer Roca in the Conquest of the Desert, and as a "jefe de frontera" he would have been eligible for the grant of 8,000 hectars (Mafud 199).[15] Instead of being the mistress of a great *estancia*, however, Fanny Haslam was condemned to life in the city of Buenos Aires, a city that does not seem to have inspired her to *fervor*.

Be that as it may, the "secret identification" said to exist between the English grandmother and the English captive is a screen for a more important identification, again with the female members of the Borges clan: this time not the grandmother but Borges's mother and sister. The story was published in 1949; on 8 September 1948, Leonor Acevedo Suárez de Borges and Norah Borges, along with Adela and Mariana Grondona and a number of other prominent women, were arrested on Florida Street while singing the Argentine national anthem.[16] Borges's mother was held under house arrest ("kept within the bounds of middle-class respectability"?); Norah Borges, the Grondona sisters, and others spent a month in a prison cell shared with prostitutes (Rodríguez Monegal, *Jorge Luis Borges* 401).[17] Once again, the grandmother's life after 1874 seems rather prosaic in light of the might-have-beens; these other *madres* used femininity as a screen for participation in the public sphere.[18] Francine Masiello has argued that women are associated in the economy of Argentine writing with barbarism, but that by their writing, speech, and action they break out of that subject-position. If Masiello is right about the conflation of femininity and barbarism, then Fanny Haslam is more deeply implicated in the captive's story than she knows. There can be no question of keeping clean, of remaining the proper Englishwoman: her "manifest destiny" has been revealed there in the plains beside the bleeding sheep.

Borges has Fanny Haslam recall not only the incident of the encounter with the captive but the precise year, 1872. Perhaps, given the grandmother's brief marriage and incredibly long widowhood (sixty-one years), every episode of her life with Francisco Borges was perfectly situated in time for her, even as she told her story decades later. In any case, 1872 makes an interesting choice for the setting of the story: it is the year of the publication of *El gaucho Martín Fierro* and of the massacre at Tandil.[19] Of these two events, the second would have seemed particularly important at the time to Fanny Haslam; on New Year's Day, in Tandil, in the southern part of the province of Buenos Aires, seventeen foreigners, including several Englishmen, were killed, most of them with their throats slit, by a group of gauchos:

> A bizarre melange of xenophobia, religious zealotry, superstitious fanaticism, and greed motivated these humble gauchos to embark upon their mission as exterminating angels. Deeper structural causes, including latifundism and legal oppression of the gaucho, also played a role. An anonymous pamphlet published in 1871, entitled *Abusos y ruina de la campaña,* reflected the enmity toward foreigners and rural officials evident in the Tandil affair. (Slatta 172)

Though the episode at Tandil was not repeated elsewhere in the country, Slatta says that numerous rumors of similar incidents circulated elsewhere: "Fear and paranoia gripped the pampa" (173). No wonder Fanny Haslam complains of her "destino de inglesa desterrada a ese fin del mundo" (559).[20]

An event of a very different sort in the same year was the publication by José Hernández of *El gaucho Martín Fierro,* the first part of what Rojas and Lugones would later claim was the Argentine epic poem. The 1872 poem contains the incident previously mentioned of Cruz's changing sides to aid Fierro, an episode that served Borges as the basis for his wonderful story "Biografía de Tadeo Isidoro Cruz (1829–1874)"[21] and which is the subject of repeated commentary in a variety of his essays. In the latter part of the poem, *La vuelta de Martín Fierro,* published in 1879 (the same year as the Conquest of the Desert), Fierro tells of a smallpox epidemic that afflicts the tribe of Indians with whom he and Cruz have taken refuge and of the sacrifice of a foreign captive:

> Había un gringuito cautivo
> que siempre hablaba del barco.
> Y lo augaron en un charco
> por causante de la peste.
> Tenía los ojos celestes
> como potrillito zarco.
> (2: 853–59)

There was a captive foreigner who always spoke of the ship. And they drowned him in a puddle for being the cause of the epidemic. He had light blue eyes like those of a blue-eyed colt.

Borges comments elsewhere on the "austeridad verbal" [verbal austerity] and "patético laconismo" [pathetic laconism] of this episode (*Inquisiciones* 134; *Obras completas en colaboración* 544). The poem goes on to tell of the death of Cruz and the killing of an Indian by Fierro in an attempt to rescue a white captive woman. The captive tells Fierro: "Ese bárbaro inhumano . . . / me amarró luego las manos / con las tripitas de mi hijo" (2: 1113–15) [That inhuman savage tied my hands with the little guts of my son]. After he accompanies her across the frontier to a ranch, he says goodbye: "Me voy, le dije, ande quiera, / aunque me agarre el gobierno, / pues infierno por infierno, / prefiero el de la frontera" (2: 1547–50) [I am leaving, I told her, for wherever, even if the government captures me, because between one hell and another I prefer that of the frontier].

The figure of the "cautiva" is important in a great variety of other Argentine works, starting quite early in colonial times, as Cristina Iglesia has shown. The most famous besides the character in *Martín Fierro* is "La cautiva" of Esteban Echeverría's eponymous poem (1837), which Ricardo Rojas called important for its "incorporation of the Indians into the national literature" (*Los gauchescos*, 2: 471). Iglesia comments on a subtle relation between the Echeverría poem and the Borges story:

> And if in Echeverría's poem a (captive) bound mare has its throat cut by Indians who "thirsty as vampires sip, suck and savor its blood," so Borges's Indian Englishwoman, with long blonde hair and blue eyes, confirms her belonging to the world of the others, her violation beyond remedy, inverting and making her own the gesture of her captors, when she drinks, kneeling on the ground, the blood of a decapitated sheep. . . .
>
> Ambiguous symbol of the frontier between civilization and savagery, of difference and also of contamination, the literary image of the captive woman will function, besides, as a sign of the inversion of a usurpation and domination legalized and ratified on the outskirts of the white world. (82)[22]

The description of the Indians drinking the mare's blood in "La cautiva" is in fact so close to Fanny Haslam's description of the "cautiva inglesa" drinking the blood of the sheep that one cannot but remark on how literary Fanny Haslam's imagination and memory are (in her grandson's account).

As with the fortuitous choice of 1872 for the initial encounter with the "cautiva inglesa" and the imaginative description of her life in the *toldos,* an account heavily indebted to Mansilla's *Excursión a los indios ranqueles* (1870) [Excursion to the Ranquel Indians],[23] so here too Haslam's memory of her experience is heavily colored by her—or her grandson's—reading. The identification of the "cautiva inglesa" with the "damas antiperonistas" mentioned earlier is confirmed by a brief reference in Adela Grondona's memoir of the episode, *El grito sagrado (30 días en la cárcel)* [The Sacred Cry (Thirty Days in Jail)],[24] in which she quotes from a poem about the "madres de la calle Florida":

> "No está cautivo, no, quien no claudica," dice Sara Tomaszewski en el inspirado poem "Las Cautivas," que nos ha dedicado:
> *"Cautivo está quien vive sometido,*
> *y de rodillas al tirano adora."* (43)[25]

> "He who does not give up is not captive," says Sara Tomaszewski in the inspired poem "The Captives" she has dedicated to us: "Captive is he who lives in submission and kneels in adoration to the tyrant."

"Historia del guerrero y de la cautiva" is marked by odd asymmetries. Droctulft crosses from "savagery" to "civilization," the "cautiva" does the opposite; he is a "converso" or "iluminado," she a prisoner; the first half of the story occurs exclusively in a male domain, the second half mostly in a female one. The "philosophical romance" Gibbon proposes to find in a confrontation like this one between *old* and *new* (Old World and New World?) does not take place within either story but out of the crossing of them, from the affirmation that "acaso las historias que he referido son una sola historia. El anverso y el reverso de esta moneda son, para Dios, iguales" (560) [perhaps the stories I have told are only one story. The front and back of this coin are, for God, the same]. The stories are only the same in being structured around the transgression of a frontier, in being about changing sides; the skeptical reader may well remark that perhaps for God the stories are the same but that for us, here and now, the opposition of "civilization" and "savagery," good and evil, clean and dirty do have some significance. "Barbarie," for Sarmiento as for many other romantic writers, had its attraction. "A esa barbarie se había rebajado una inglesa": the story focuses on the transgression of the boundary, not on the direction in which the boundary is transgressed; "civilization" and "savagery" signify not in themselves but by virtue of their opposition to one another.[26]

"Civilization" and "savagery" were strongly contested terms at the time the story was written, thanks to the polarized ideological climate of the years of the presidency of Juan Perón. The liberal opposition—of which Borges was a part—used Sarmiento as a symbol of civilization and attacked the use of Rosas by the Peronists as "savage federalism." At the same time, conservative and Peronist intellectuals—Murena and Fermín Chávez being two of the most prominent—attacked what they saw as the obfuscating use of the term "civilization." Chávez, for instance, says that his book *Civilización y barbarie en la cultura argentina* (1956) is written to combat "the false concept of Civilization which, since 1837, has been imposed by those who for the first time spoke of American Savagery in a negative sense" (11). Some pages later Chávez attacks Borges explicitly for his supposed "belittling of what is original in favor of what is spurious" (41), for his "good Borgesian but not very Argentine" literature (36). "Historia del guerrero y de la cautiva" undoubtedly was infused with these debates about the nature of Argentine culture. Some of Borges's other statements at the time—his speech against Peronist sloganizing, "Déle déle" (1946) [Do It] (*Ficcionario* 223–24), on the occasion of his "promotion" from the Miguel Cané Library to the post of poultry inspector or the virulently anti-Peronist story he wrote with Adolfo Bioy Casares in November 1947, "La fiesta del monstruo" (*Ficcionario* 259–69) [The Monster's Party]—take an active part in those debates.[27] "Historia del guerrero y de la cautiva" was written a bit more than a year after "La fiesta del monstruo," within months of the imprisonment of Norah Borges and the other "madres de la calle Florida." But, instead of entering into the debate about the definition of "civilization" and "savagery," Borges tells a story about defining oneself. And though this act of self-definition necessarily involves choosing sides, for Droctulft as for the captive Englishwoman, the opposite directions they choose suggest that the "destiny" made "manifest" to them is an individual one. Perhaps every such choice need not be seen as a categorical imperative.[28]

The pampa functions in "Historia del guerrero y de la cautiva" (as well as in the famous "Poema conjetural" of a few years before) as a mirror in which the "civilized" character discovers his or her "savage" face.[29] The city, on the other hand, is the place in the story where the "savage mind" discovers the notion of civilization, an association overdetermined by the etymological links between *civitas* and *civilization*, between *urbs* and *urbanity*, between *polis* and *politeness, policy, politics*. If "manifest destiny" preserves its usual connotations in Droctulft's progress from savagery to civilization, its certainty and necessity are undone by the stories of Laprida and the captive Englishwoman. History may be, in Gibbon's words, "little more than the register of the crimes, follies, and misfortunes of mankind" (1: 69), its voice "little more than the organ of hatred or flattery" (1: 237), but it is in history that a person may discover his or her destiny. And though this "destiny" may not be a triumphant one, though it may run against the current of historical change, the discovery itself is sufficient grounds for narrative.

The arms and letters debate, central to such other stories as "Pierre Menard" and "El Sur," is vital to "Historia del guerrero y de la cautiva." For the latter story is really one about vocation: about not choosing the military career of Colonel Francisco Borges, about choosing the profession of letters. Yet, the choice is not so clear, as Fanny Haslam's wavering example shows.

Estela Cédola in her essay on this story asserts that Borges is arguing for an overcoming of antinomies; his task in the story, she says, "consists not so much in repudiating as in trying to understand this figure [of the captive Englishwoman] and her behavior and in demonstrating that antinomies are false. . . . Europe and America are not opposed, but rather there should be a synthesis" (201). She adds: "This is the task of the writer and the function of art: to search for the overcoming of contradictions, to exile [desterrar] cultural Manicheism" (201). Her choice of the metaphor of exile is curious since her book was published not long after the end of a military dictatorship and the return of many political exiles. The real problem is that the critic seems not to have made up her mind: "But this text does not come to a synthesis. . . . It instead limits itself to showing the false antinomies but maintains the tension, perhaps because History has not achieved this synthesis either. Argentina still debates with itself in search of its identity" (201). A story in which Borges sets out clearly enough his political difficulties in 1947–48 is still crucial to questions of national self-definition.

Borges situates himself at the center of this narrative. At the beginning, he tells how Droctulft's story moved him; in the middle, after narrating and commenting on that story, he tells of how he associated it with the story his grandmother told him; at the end, he argues the case for God and the angels. The story seems to have a supplementary force to it (Molloy, *Letras* 82; Balderston, *El precursor velado* 109–11), to beg for a sequel, and that sequel would seem to require some action on the part of the grandmother (and grandson). Yet the action undertaken by them within the text is seemingly passive, limited to the imagining and telling of a story. Given the way the arms and letters debate is framed here, Fanny Haslam and her grandson are marked with the stigma of those who cannot throw caution to the winds, of those who watch from the sidelines. Even the hapless Laprida of "Poema conjetural" [Conjectural Poem] was better off than Fanny Haslam, since he at least finally discovered his "destino sudamericano" [South American destiny] (867). In this story about finding one's destiny, the discovery takes place beyond the categories of "civilization" and "savagery." What is particularly interesting is that though the categories are emptied of value, or at least of their usual value, the stories of Droctulft and the "cautiva inglesa" are staged in the liminal spaces of the frontier and the city wall, spaces that bear the vestiges of archaic power.

But this story is also about the ways in which a person's "manifest destiny" is a work of imagination, and as such it is an oblique homage Borges renders to the woman who more than any other helped form his imagination, helped shape his destiny. Borges often told in his memoirs and interviews of being read to as a young boy by his paternal grandmother, Fanny Haslam de Borges, who was also the one who taught him to read (Rodríguez Monegal 15–16)[30] and whose literary tastes undoubtedly influenced his, since much of his early reading was done with her.[31] And, just as the story of the warrior and the captive suggests that self-definition is a matter of taking stories and making them our own, so one might pause and wonder for a moment about Fanny Haslam as reader. What did she feel— regret, envy, pride, identification?—when she accompanied her grandson in reading "the first novel I ever read through" ("Autobiographical Essay" 209)? For that first novel, *The Adventures of Huckleberry Finn,* refers quite unequivocally to a liminal experience of the kind she experienced on the Argentine frontier in the early 1870s; it closes with the words: "But I reckon I got to light out for the Territory ahead of the rest, because aunt Sally she's going to adopt me and sivilize me and I can't stand it. I been there before" (226).[32]

7

On the Threshold of Otherness: British India in

"El hombre en el umbral"

I have never found one among them [the Orientalists] who could deny that a single shelf of a good European library was worth the whole native literature of India and Arabia.—Macaulay, qtd. in Majumdar 10: 83[1]

"Mr. Gandhi, what do you think of Western civilization?"
"It would be a good idea."[2]

"El hombre en el umbral" brings into sharp focus the issues of colonialism and foreign domination that are present in a less obvious way in such other Borges stories as "El jardín de senderos que se bifurcan" and "El milagro secreto." The choice of venue this time is British India,[3] a choice that is interesting because India was one of the most thorough of the Western experiments in colonialism in the Third World[4] and because its struggle opened the way for the movement to dismantle the British, French, Dutch, and Portuguese empires in Africa and Asia. The story was first published in *La Nación* in 1952, five years after the independence (and partition) of India. Written under the tutelage of Kipling, the story's politics are far removed from the politics of Kipling's narratives of India.[5] In this story Borges and Bioy are situated in some relation to the memory and narrative of colonial rule; the exact nature of that relation is what will be unraveled here.[6]

The story consists of two parts, the second much more extensive than the first. The first is a brief paragraph describing a conversation in Buenos Aires between the narrator,[7] Adolfo Bioy Casares, and Christopher Dewey of the British Council. The second is Dewey's account of his search for a kidnapped British official he calls David Alexander Glencairn, which is divided into three parts: the story of his mission, then the story told him by an old man sitting in a doorway, and a brief final paragraph describing Dewey's encounter with the mad judge and with the body of "Glencairn." I shall discuss the old man's story first, then return to consider the frame narratives situating Dewey, Borges, and Bioy.

The old man in the threshold says: "El hecho aconteció cuando yo era niño. No sé de fechas, pero no había muerto aún Nikal Seyn (Nicholson) ante la muralla de Delhi" (614) [The event occurred when I was a child. I do not know about dates, but Nikal Seyn (Nicholson) had not yet died before the walls of Delhi]. As is usual with Borges, the historical reference is precise. John Nicholson was one of the leading officials in the British colonial administration during the Dalhousie and Canning administrations, known to his fellow officers (because of his cruelty to the native population) as "the autocrat of all the Russias" (Majumdar 10: 348). Hibbert describes him thus:

> Nicholson had arrived in India in July 1839 and had served as a young infantry officer in the Afghan War. Since then, however, most of his time had been spent in civil appointments, principally in the Punjab where he stamped out lawlessness in the districts under his control with the utmost severity, pursuing criminals personally and displaying their severed heads upon his desk. His strange and forceful personality so impressed the natives that numbers of them worshipped him as their spiritual guide and deity, falling down at his feet in reverent submission. (292–93)[8]

Nicholson was active particularly in the Punjab around Amritsar (mentioned in the story) and Ferozpur. Called to Delhi to aid in the crushing of the mutiny of the Indian units of the colonial army in 1857, he died in an attack on the sepoys by the Delhi city wall on 14 September (Dodwell, *Indian Empire* 6: 195)[9] and was later termed "the Hero of the mutiny" (Majumdar 9: 600).

Nicholson was also the proponent of a bill legislating torture in cases of rebellion and had this to say about such remedies:

> As regards torturing the murderers of the women and children: If it be right otherwise, I do not think we should refrain from it, because it is a Native custom. We are told in the Bible that stripes shall be meted out according to faults, and if hanging is sufficient punishment for such

wretches, it is also severe for ordinary mutineers [*sic*]. If I had them in my power to-day, and knew that I were to die tomorrow, I would inflict the most excruciating tortures I could think of on them with a perfectly easy conscience. (Majumdar 9: 600)[10]

Yet the anonymous *Encyclopaedia Britannica* article on Nicholson describes him both as a "severe ruler" and as "eminently just," quotes Lord Roberts as saying that he was "the *beau idéal* of a soldier and a gentleman," and reports that "the natives worshipped him as a god under the title of Nikalsain." One of his officers is quoted at length as saying:

He was a man cast in a giant mould, with massive chest and powerful limbs, and an expression ardent and commanding, with a dash of roughness; features of stern beauty, a long black beard, and a deep sonorous voice. There was something of immense strength, talent and resolution in his whole frame and manner, and a power of ruling men on high occasions which no one could escape noticing. His imperial air, which never left him, and which would have been thought arrogant in one of less imposing mien, sometimes gave offence to the more unbending of his countrymen, but made him almost worshipped by the pliant Asiatics. (19: 657)[11]

In Kipling's *Kim,* the Ressaldar, who was loyal to the Crown during the Mutiny in 1857 and fought against his own people, sings the "song of Nikal Seyn before Delhi—the old song" (93): "Wail by long-drawn wail he unfolded the story of Nikal Seyn (Nicholson)—the song that men sing in the Punjab to this day. . . . *'Ahi! Nikal Seyn is dead—he died before Delhi! Lances of North take vengeance for Nikal Seyn'*" (93).[12]

The reference to Nicholson in the Borges story is more than a casual one, since the picture of the domineering British official painted by the old man in the threshold closely resembles that of the cruel sadist, his desk decorated with the severed heads of his victims, reported in some of the accounts. The physical description of "Glencairn" in the story reads:

Una sola vez lo vieron mis ojos, pero no olvidaré el cabello muy negro, los pómulos salientes, la ávida nariz y la boca, los anchos hombros, la fuerte osatura de viking. (612)

Only once did my eyes see him, but I will never forget his raven black hair, prominent cheekbones, avid nose and mouth, broad shoulders, strong Viking bone structure.

This closely matches the description given of Nicholson in the encyclopedia article, as does the story of the "peace" established by the stern ruler:

> El mero anuncio de su advenimiento bastó para apaciguar la ciudad. Ello no impidió que decretara diversas medidas enérgicas. Unos años pasaron. La ciudad y el distrito estaban en paz; *sikhs* y musulmanes habían depuesto las antiguas discordias y de pronto Glencairn desapareció. (612)

> The mere announcement of his coming sufficed to pacify the city. This fact did not prevent him from decreeing various decisive measures. Some years passed. The city and the district were at peace; Sikhs and Moslems had laid down their ancient discords and all of a sudden Glencairn disappeared.

> On the annexation of Punjab he [Nicholson] was appointed deputy commissioner of Bannu. There he became a kind of legendary hero, and many tales are told of his stern justice, his tireless activity and his commanding personality. In the course of five years he reduced the most turbulent district on the frontier to such a state of quietude that no crime was committed or even attempted during his last year of office, a condition of things never known before or since. (*Encyclopaedia Britannica* 19: 657)

Even the question of the "pliant Asiatics" worshipping Nicholson as a god is somewhat more equivocal in the old man's story of the judge whom Dewey calls "Glencairn":

> Cuando se pregonó que la reina iba a mandar un hombre que ejecutaría en este país la ley de Inglaterra, los menos malos se alegraron, porque sintieron que la ley es mejor que el desorden. Llegó el cristiano y no tardó en prevaricar y oprimir. . . . No lo culpamos, al principio; la justicia que administraba no era conocida de nadie y los aparentes atropellos del nuevo juez correspondían acaso a válidas y arcanas razones. *Todo tendrá justificación en su libro,* queríamos pensar, pero su afinidad con todos los malos jueces del mundo era demasiado notoria, y al fin hubimos de admitir que era simplemente un malvado. Llegó a ser un tirano y la pobre gente (para vengarse de la errónea esperanza que alguna vez pusieron en él) dio en jugar con la idea de secuestrarlo y someterlo a juicio. (614)

When it was announced that the queen was going to send a man who would carry out the law of England in this land, the least recalcitrant were happy because they felt that law is better than disorder. The Christian arrived and was not long in acting corruptly and oppressively. . . . We did not blame him at first; the justice he administered was not familiar to any of us, and the apparent excesses of the new judge were perhaps due to valid (if arcane) reasons. *Everything must be justified in his book,* we wanted to believe, but his affinity with all the evil judges in the world was too obvious, and we finally had to admit that he was simply a scoundrel. He turned into a tyrant, and the poor people (to avenge the mistaken hope they had once deposited in him) began playing with the idea of kidnapping him and bringing him to justice.

Thus the devotion that Nicholson inspired in the "pliant Asiatics"—according to the British sources—is revealed in the old man's story as the vain hope that the subject people feel until they meet their man.

Furthermore, Nicholson's main area of activity was focused on the city of Amritsar, and according to Dewey the story of Glencairn took place in the Punjab (616), though he initially equivocates and says condescendingly: "La exacta geografía de los hechos que voy a referir importa muy poco. Además, ¿qué precisión guardan en Buenos Aires los nombres de Amritsar o de Udh?" (612) [The exact geography of the events I am going to tell matters very little. Besides, what exactitude can the names of Amritsar or Oudh have in Buenos Aires?]. Of course the difference between Amritsar in the Punjab and the native state of Oudh or Avadh (now Uttar Pradesh) matters a great deal, not least in the fact that there is repeated reference in the story to the unpeaceful coexistence in the city of Sikhs, Moslems, and Hindus, which would be true of Amritsar but not, say, of Lucknow in Oudh.[13]

The "A or B" structure is used again a bit later in the story when Dewey doubts whether the old man can be a reliable informant about something that happened only recently (in the period between the world wars): "*Nuevas de la Rebelión o de Akbar podría dar este hombre* (pensé) *pero no de Glencairn.* Lo que me dijo confirmó esta sospecha" (613) [*This man could give news of the Mutiny or of Akbar* (I thought) *but not of Glencairn.* What he said confirmed this suspicion]. The old man of course could have lived through the events of the 1857 Mutiny (and the cruel repression that followed), but the second possibility is offered as a red herring: the old man could hardly offer testimony about Akbar, the great Mogul ruler of India from 1556 to 1605.[14] (Unless, however, the old man is "ageless," as implied in the stereotypical description: "Los muchos años lo habían reducido y pulido como las aguas a una piedra o las generaciones de los hombres a una sentencia" [613] [The many years had reduced and polished him like the waters a stone or the human generations a saying]).[15] This time, though, the "A or B" structure, in which B is an obvious red herring, shows Dewey the dupe of his own stereotype: the event that the old man narrates happened not in his childhood during the Mutiny, nor in the distant past; it is happening right here, right now, and everyone knows it but Dewey.[16]

"Amritsar" is one clue to the contemporaneity of the story. Though the city played an important role in the history of the Mutiny of 1857, it was equally important in the history of the twentieth-century movement toward independence, a movement unexpectedly reinvigorated with the passage of the Rowlatt Acts of March 1919. It was at Amritsar, on 13 April 1919, that British troops massacred a peaceful Indian crowd in a square called Jallianwalla Bagh, an event that Sir Valentine Chirol called "that black day in the annals of British India" (qtd. in Fischer 179). Louis Fischer remarks: "For Gandhi it was a turning point. Indians never forgot it" (179),[17] and even Philip Mason, usually an apologist for British rule, acknowledges: "After Amritsar, the whole situation was changed. Government had been carried out with the consent of the governed. That consent was now changed to mistrust" (288). Though the dates of Dewey's residence in India are not given in the story except in general terms ("entre las dos guerras" [612] [between the two wars]), even that lack of precision indicates that he visited Amritsar after the massacre at Jallianwalla Bagh. If he reads "Amritsar" in the book of history as referring exclusively to the events of the Mutiny (or to Nicholson), he is indeed a poor observer (or reader) of the history of his own time.[18]

Dewey is also distracted as an observer by his assumption that India is a land of the spirit where politics has no place. Thus, he observes after coming to the house where "Glencairn" is being tried that "en el último patio se celebraba no sé qué fiesta musulmana" (613) [in the last patio I know not what Moslem festival was being celebrated]; the "no sé qué" is interesting, since it acknowledges his ignorance of Moslem religious customs yet also reveals his mistaken idea that the "fiesta" taking place inside is a religious one. In fact, he interrupts his telling of the old man's story several times to inform his listeners of the comings and goings in the house: first, "unas mujeres . . . entraban en la casa" (614) [some women . . . were entering the house], then "unas personas . . . se iban de la fiesta" (615) [some people . . . were leaving the festival], and then finally, and most tellingly, after the old man has finished his story:

> Una turba hecha de hombres y mujeres de todas las naciones del Punjab se desbordó, rezando y cantando, sobre nosotros y casi nos barrió. (616)

> A crowd composed of men and women of all the nations of the Punjab overflowed, praying and singing, pushing against and almost trampling us.

The old man has already said that people of all the faiths of the region were involved in the trial:

> Alcoranistas, doctores de la ley, *sikhs* que llevan el nombre de leones y que adoran a un Dios, hindúes que adoran muchedumbres de dioses, monjes de Mahavira que enseñan que la forma del universo es la de un hombre con las piernas abiertas, adoradores del fuego y judíos negros, integraron el tribunal, pero el último fallo fue encomendado al arbitrio de un loco. (614–15)

> Scholars of the Koran, doctors of law, Sikhs who bear the name of lions and who worship a single God, Hindus who worship a multitude of gods, monks of Mahavira who teach that the universe has the form of a man with his legs crossed, fire-worshippers and black Jews made up the tribunal, but the final judgment was left to the determination of a madman.

Dewey, then, is duped by his own certainties of the roles played by the colonizers and the colonized; he cannot tell a religious festival of whatever creed from a trial and execution. He is a victim of what Francis Hutchins has called the "ideology of permanence": "The certainty of a permanent Empire in these years, however, seemed to increase in proportion to its fragility, and to serve for many people as a defense and retreat from reason long after the course of events had proved its impossibility" (xii).

In *El género gauchesco: Un tratado sobre la patria* [The Gauchesque Genre: A Treatise on the Fatherland], Josefina Ludmer has discussed the conflict in the gauchesque works in Argentine literature between two laws: the written law of the nation-state and the oral law of the gaucho community (227–36). A similar conflict is set up in this story, between the "justice" of the British Raj (which is presented as unjust, arbitrary, and cruel) and the "justice" of the people's court.[19] What is interesting in the latter instance is the recourse to a judge who is literally insane. The subterfuge depends on a knowledge of the British system of justice, which will not punish an insane man for casting judgment (or for carrying out the death sentence, since the madman serves both as judge and as executioner). Yet it also plays in an astute way with the colonizers' stereotypes of the Indian people as childlike, irrational, and more than a little bit mad.

The notion of a law so universal and so transparent that it would be obvious even to a madman implies also that the community shares notions of right and wrong and can communicate them (even to an inquiring British official). First, then, the colonized community must find unity, even if it is the temporary unity of the oppressed against the colonial power; thus, even Dewey sees representatives of "todas las naciones del Punjab" at what he first took to be a Moslem religious festival.[20] Second, the old man must discover a "pedagogy of the oppressed," a way of communicating this universal sense of right and wrong to his obtuse British interlocutor. The narrative strategy he adopts has almost a fairy tale structure at first: "El hecho aconteció cuando yo era niño. No sé de fechas. . . . El tiempo que se fue queda en la memoria; sin duda soy capaz de recuperar lo que entonces pasó" (614) [The event took place when I was a child. I know nothing about dates. . . . The time that has gone remains in memory; no doubt I am capable of recovering what happened then]. Later, though, he makes clear that his story, though archetypal in structure, has gone from generals to particulars: "En esta ciudad lo juzgaron: en una casa como todas, como ésta. Una casa no puede diferir de otra: lo que importa es saber si está edificada en el infierno o en el cielo" (615) [In this city they judged him, in a house like all the others, like this one. One house cannot differ from another; what matters is knowing whether it is built in hell or in heaven]. Moral absolutes thus reestablished (on a universal level, and therefore no longer as the property of the colonial power), he ends his story and the body is revealed. Thus the story closes with a mute writ of habeas corpus: "You shall have the body," he seems to be telling Dewey, "but take the story with it."

Of course the narrative devices employed in the story are familiar to readers of the *Arabian Nights*. Thus, the nesting of narratives through what Todorov calls "hommes-récits" [story-men] and the spinning out of the story until some action can be accomplished behind the scenes (in this case, the execution of "Glencairn") are typical "Oriental" stratagems. Even more important, though, is the British stereotype of Indian "guile," a stereotype that played an important role in the misunderstandings between the two peoples (Nandy 77, 110, 112, and passim). This "guile," which Nandy prefers to call "a fluid open self-definition" (112), was part of a literary stereotype used in characterizations of Indians by Stevenson (in *The Master of Ballantrae,* in which the Indian servant does not let on for most of the novel that he speaks English), Kipling,[21] and many others. Interestingly, the same concept was often used to characterize Gandhi, whom Nandy finds often compared to Charlie Chaplin (104),[22] though Nandy prefers to point to what he calls Gandhi's "political and psychological shrewdness" (49). (Orwell asserts much the same thing when he says of Gandhi that "inside the saint, or near-saint, there was a very shrewd, able person" [463].)

An old man clad in traditional garb sitting in a doorway, who possesses sufficient guile to delay and educate his British listener with a story (or with a reinterpretation of history), and whose story tells of a subject people's discovery of the evil of the foreign invaders and of the stratagems employed to reassert traditional judicial and ethical authority: the description closely matches that given by exasperated British officials who dealt with Gandhi. Winston Churchill's comment is the most famous, on "the nauseating and humiliating spectacle of this one-time Inner Temple lawyer, now seditious fakir, striding half-naked up the steps of the Viceroy's palace, there to negotiate and to parley on equal terms with the representative of the King-Emperor" (qtd. in Fischer 277). That Gandhi would never have condoned the execution of a British official, however corrupt, or have entrusted the case to the judgment of a madman, does not prevent defenders of the British Raj from seeing his nonviolence as a subterfuge or something worse. Thus Percival Griffiths writes:

> We are not concerned with the history of that sterile [noncooperation] movement, nor with the terrorist activity which naturally grew out of it. It is doubtful if non-co-operation or its successor, civil disobedience, advanced self-government by a single day. On the other hand, it engendered a racial bitterness, which has fortunately disappeared since the transfer of power, and a disregard of law and order which has left an enduring mark on the youth of India. (83; see also 73)

Thus, the "man in the threshold," despite his obvious differences from Gandhi, functions in the story as the projection of British paranoid self-doubt (Nandy 100) in the face of the self-rule movement, a condition born of what we could call (after Hutchins) the "disillusion with permanence."

One of the tasks that British education set itself in India was the implantation of a Western idea of a linear progression in history. Chatterjee has studied the impact of this model on the thought of Bankimchandra Chattopadhyay (1838–1894), an important Bengali man of letters. Bankimchandra's task, according to Chatterjee, was to separate myth from history (59), to foster the "knowledge of its own history" that for him was national consciousness (58), to create pride through historical writing (82; see also Nandy 23).[23] Chatterjee sees Gandhi's critique of modern civilization as extending to this progressive ideology and its obsession with history (86, 93–94, 97), while Nandy asserts that Gandhi "rejected history and affirmed the primacy of myths over historical chronicles" (55). Nandy sees a conflict between two different models for thinking about the relation between past and present: "If for the West the present was a special case of an unfolding history, for Gandhi as a representative of traditional India history was a special case of an all-embracing permanent present, waiting to be interpreted and reinterpreted" (57). Of course the extent to which Gandhi was a "representative of traditional India" is open to debate, but what is significant for "El hombre en el umbral" is the willingness of militants for self-rule to use the "all-embracing permanent present" of Mother India[24] to mobilize the subject people and to frustrate and ultimately drive out the occupying power.[25]

To return to Dewey's first description of the old man:

> A mis pies, inmóvil como una cosa, se acurrucaba en el umbral un hombre muy viejo. Diré como era, porque es parte esencial de la historia. Los muchos años lo habían reducido y pulido como las aguas a una piedra o las generaciones de los hombres a una sentencia. (613)[26]

> At my feet, motionless as an object, a very old man was curled up in the threshold. I will describe what he looked like because it is an essential part of the story [historia]. The many years had reduced and polished him like the waters a stone or the human generations a saying.

Dewey's problem here is a conflict of paradigms. His Western concept of history (and this description is, he says, "parte esencial de la historia," with all the resonances of that last word) cannot cope with this figure from the "all-embracing perpetual present" except as someone who is outside of human history as it is taught in the British schools. So Dewey sees the old man as a figure from the world of myth, as a representative of "traditional" (ageless, eternal, ahistorical) India. But because he needs to have it one way or the other, he is not prepared for the truth, which is that the old man has something to tell him about "Glencairn," his own mission, himself, and the present time.[27]

Now to return to the first paragraph of the story, which serves as a sort of narrative frame. It reads:

> Bioy Casares trajo de Londres un curioso puñal de hoja triangular y empuñadura en forma de H; nuestro amigo Christopher Dewey, del Consejo Británico, dijo que tales armas eran de uso común en el Indostán. Ese dictamen lo alentó a mencionar que había trabajado en aquel país, entre las dos guerras. (*Ultra Auroram et Gangen,* recuerdo que dijo en latín, equivocando un verso de Juvenal.) De las historias que esa noche contó, me atrevo a reconstruir la que sigue. Mi texto será fiel: líbreme Alá de la tentación de añadir breves rasgos circunstanciales o de agravar, con interpolaciones de Kipling, el cariz exótico del relato. Este, por lo demás, tiene un antiguo y simple sabor que sería una lástima perder, acaso el de las Mil y unas noches. (612)

> Bioy Casares came back from London with a strange dagger with a triangular blade and a handle in the shape of an H; our friend Christopher Dewey of the British Council said that arms like that were common in Hindustan. This declaration encouraged him to mention that he had worked in that country in the period between the wars. (*Ultra Auroram et Gangen* [Beyond the Dawn and the Ganges] I remember he said in Latin, misquoting a line from Juvenal.) Of the stories he told that night, I will venture to reconstruct the one that follows. My text will be faithful: may Allah save me from the temptation to add brief circumstantial details or to exaggerate the exotic character of the tale with interpolations from Kipling. The tale, besides, had an ancient and simple flavor that it would be a shame to lose, perhaps that of the *Arabian Nights*.

Dewey's error in quotation of a line from Juvenal's tenth satire is most interesting. In the initial reported conversation with Borges and Bioy, the sight of the dagger leads him to memories of Hindustan and then to Juvenal. By an association of ideas here, Dewey's ability to identify the dagger authorizes his memories, among them the quotation, yet the error in the quotation threatens to unravel his authority, as the narrator quietly notes. The original passage in Juvenal reads:

> Omnibus in terris, quae sunt a Gadibus usque
> Auroram et Gangen, pauci dinoscere possunt

vera bona atque illis multum diversa, remota
erroris nebula. quid enim ratione timemus
aut cupimus? quid tam dextro pede concipis, ut te
conatus non paeniteat votique peracti? (10.1–5)

In every land, from furthest west (Cádiz) to furthest east (the Ganges),
few only can discern true blessings from their counterfeits, clear from
all mist of error. For what do we with reason fear, covet with reason?
What do you undertake with foot so right, with a start so lucky, but
you rue your attempt and the success of your desire? (Mayor trans. 2:
65)

Dewey remembers the verse as referring to travel beyond [ultra] the
bounds of the known world, whereas Juvenal refers instead to the known
world within marked limits (Cádiz in the west, the Ganges or the place of
dawn in the east). "Usque" here means "as far as" or "up to" those thresholds. Within the world as he knew it, Juvenal sees the realm of error and
self-deception; the whole of this satire is concerned with those who err
when they overreach, whether as warriors, as rulers, as scholars, or in hopes
of good health or good fortune. As one example of such an overreacher
Juvenal cites Alexander, who, though he did not reach the Ganges, reached
the Indus, but in the process lost all:

Unus Pellaeo iuveni non sufficit orbis,
aestuat infelix angusto limite mundi,
ut Gyari clusus scopulis parvaque Seripho;
cum tamen a figulis munitam intraverit urbem,
sarcophago contentus erit. mors sola fatetur,
quantula sint hominum corpuscula. (10.168–73)

For Pella's youth one globe is all too small; he chafes, poor soul, in the
narrow bounds of the universe, as though pent in Gyara and tiny
Seriphus; yet, let him once set foot in Babylon that city of brick, and a
stone coffin will satisfy his every want: death and death alone betrays
the nothingness of men's puny frames, what dwarfs our bodies are.
(Mayor trans. 2: 118)

Alexander's example is recalled in the story in association with David
Alexander Glencairn. Dewey comments: "Los dos nombres convienen;
porque fueron de reyes que gobernaron con un cetro de hierro" (612) [The
two names are appropriate because they were those of kings who ruled with
scepters of iron]. Going beyond the narrow limits of one's world is rash and

dangerous, then, as the new empire-builders discover in the story. The "manifest destiny" that Juvenal speaks of is of being content with one's own lot, with one's own world:

> 'Nil ergo optabunt homines?' si consilium vis,
> permittes ipsis expender numinibus, quid
> conveniat nobis rebusque sit utile nostris. (10.346–48)

> Is nothing then to be sought by our vows? If you wish my counsel, leave the gods themselves to decide what is meet for us, what can promote our welfare. (Mayor trans. 2: 172)

Dewey's lapsus, then, is linked with his having overreached himself and with the excessive and rash nature of the British adventure in India.

Where does that leave Dewey's interlocutors? Bioy is present here simply as intermediary, as traveler and collector, and of course in light of the theme of the story it is interesting that he should have just returned not from India but from London, that great emporium of objects from the colonies.[28] Borges is there only to correct Dewey's Latin and to record one of his many stories in written form, or so he says. In fact, though, he turns the tables on Dewey, since he reveals himself as the superior Latinist, despite the fact that he was largely self-educated and did not have access to the British tradition of the classical education.[29] Similarly, his pledge not to change Dewey's story by adding "circumstantial details"[30] or cribbing from Kipling gives away his conviction that Dewey is guilty of both offenses.[31]

Dewey tells Borges and Bioy a tale cribbed from Kipling. He was not really ever there (in the sense that his perceptions were so clouded by his preconceptions that he could not see around him), as Borges slyly points out when he corrects the quotation from Juvenal. But even subtler is the implication of the story, which though cribbed from Kipling is most unlike that author's work in its politics.[32] For the story that Dewey relates—or that "Dewey" is used as a mouthpiece to relate—is one that tells of the end of British colonialism in India, as surely as that colonialism ended in the Gandhian campaigns of the 1920s and particularly during the Salt March (see Fischer 274 and Nandy 62–63 on Gandhi's breaking out of the colonial mind). And though the tale is told through stereotypes ("circumstantial details")—the dutiful British soldier, the sly old Muslim, the tyrannical British officer—the old man's "guile" is not contemptible as so often in Kipling; it is not the justification for colonial rule but the means of undoing that rule. "Quit India," it says in all clarity. The old man may look to Dewey like that "naked fakir" that Churchill saw in Gandhi, but he is the one who is controlling the narrative.

Yet, oddly enough, this move too was anticipated by Kipling. In "On the City Wall," the British narrator addresses his audience after he has been duped by his beloved, the prostitute Lalun, and her friends into rescuing the disguised political prisoner Khem Singh: "Of course you can guess what happened? I was not so clever. When the news went abroad that Khem Singh had escaped from the Fort, I did not, since I was then living this story, not writing it, connect myself, or Lalun, or the fat gentleman of the gold *pince-nez,* with his disappearance" (329). Dewey is less than nothing, though: he neither lives the story nor writes it. He is a witness too dim to see what is happening before his very eyes, too steeped in prejudice to see things for what they are. Yet years later in Buenos Aires he still has an air of superiority about him ("¿qué precisión guardan en Buenos Aires los nombres de Amritsar o de Udh?"), an air quite undeserved as it turns out. For once again, speaking to Borges (who knows quite well the distance from Amritsar to Oudh), he does not know to whom, or about what, he is speaking.

In "On the City Wall," Kipling argues that Indians will never be capable of self-rule (4: 305) and makes fun of British sympathizers with the self-rule movement: "Overmuch tenderness of this kind has bred a strong belief among many natives that the native is capable of administering the country, and many devout Englishmen believe this also, because the theory is stated in beautiful English with all the latest political color" (4: 306). Here the rewriting of the political message in Borges's version is clearest.[33] The stereotypes that Dewey uses to process his experience in India—or his reading of India, if, as I suspect, he was never really there—include notions of Indian spirituality, detachment, and timelessness, and these lead him to accept the authority of the old man in the threshold, at the same time that he convinces himself that the old man is telling him a tale of long ago, of the Mutiny or of the Mogul invasion. That is to say, the old man knows how to use British stereotypes of India against Britain, and at the same time to educate the earnest young British official in the iniquities of British rule. What Josefina Ludmer has called "las tretas del débil" [the snares of the weak] in her essay on Sor Juana Inés de la Cruz describes the process that is happening here.[34]

Of course that same process marks the frame tale. Borges, by correcting Dewey's Latin, does not merely establish himself as the better Latinist. He discredits Dewey as a narrator and more subtly shows that Dewey's "experience" of India is in every way derivative: Dewey was no more in India than Borges or Bioy were, and his Argentine friends at least have the advantage of postcolonial detachment from the British Raj (and perhaps identification up to a certain point with the colonized subjects). The conversation in Buenos Aires restates the one in the uncertain Indian city, and once again Dewey is denied all authority.

One other element of the story that becomes clearer when it is compared with "On the City Wall" is the extent to which Borges has suppressed domesticity. The encounter between the British soldier and the representative of the self-rule movement in the Kipling story is mediated through the prostitute Lalun, her servant Nasiban, and several other characters; indeed the story is cast initially as a love intrigue. In the Borges story all mediation (and in this particular rewriting that means particularly all female mediation) is excluded from the face-to-face encounter between Dewey and the old man. Dewey is distracted by what he assumes is a religious festival going on inside the final patio, just as the narrator of "On the City Wall" is distracted by the love intrigue, but Dewey's distraction is still the stuff of public history, given the extraordinary degree of fusion between the religious and the political in the most dramatic years of what Chatterjee calls "the Gandhian intervention in the politics of the nation" (155).[35]

The contrast with Borges's earlier story/essay of India, "El acercamiento a Almotásim" (1936) [The Approach to Al-Mutasim], is instructive. "Almotásim" is assembled out of the same materials as "El hombre en el umbral": readings of Kipling and Burton, of Eastern religious texts (especially here of Farīd od-Dīn 'Attār's *Conference of the Birds*), and of the British press. Yet "Almotásim" is a story wholly concerned with Eastern mysticism, whereas "El hombre en el umbral" uses the religious elements to make way for the political revelation. One sentence is particularly interesting in "Almotásim":

> Algún inquisidor ha enumerado ciertas analogías de la primera escena de la novela con el relato de Kipling *On the City Wall;* Bahadur las admite, pero alega que sería muy anormal que dos pinturas de la décima noche de muharram no coincidieran. (418)

> Some inquisitor has enumerated certain analogies between the first scene of the novel and Kipling's story "On the City Wall"; Bahadur recognizes them but alleges that it would be very strange if two portraits of the tenth night of Muharram did not coincide.

"On the City Wall" has a much closer relation to "El hombre en el umbral" than to "Almotásim," precisely because of the political intrigue, and indeed

"El hombre en el umbral" is fashioned as a sort of reply to the Kipling story, a reply in which the subaltern is given voice.

In one sense, though, Borges is already up to the same tricks in 1936 that he uses to greater effect in 1952. He calls attention to the origin of Almotásim's name, which is that of one of the Abbasid caliphs (417), a maneuver that has the effect of calling attention to Bahadur's own name: Bahadur Shah II ruled Delhi at the time of the Mutiny, while "the Company Bahadur" was the first name used for British "paramountcy" or colonial rule in India (Spear 203–14). Similarly, the reference to the tenth day of Muharram may refer tangentially to the battle of Arcot, fought on that day in 1751, a battle in which the British established themselves over the French as the prime colonial power in India (Mason 27). But the historical references in "Almotásim", if that is what they are, do not connect with each other in a rich thematic web. Between 1936 and 1952 much happened, both in the development of Borges's ideas about the representation of reality and in that world outside of his fiction: India and Pakistan were independent, Gandhi was dead at the hand of an assassin, and those facts, too, were "parte esencial de la historia."

In "On the City Wall," the Westernized Indian Wali Dad says to the narrator: "India has gossiped for centuries—always standing in the bazars until the soldiers go by. Therefore—you are here today instead of starving in your own country, and I am not a Muhammadan—I am a Product—a Demnition Product. That also I owe to you and yours: that I cannot make an end to my sentence without quoting from your authors" (4: 310–11).[36] Thus, quotation—or interpolation, as Borges calls it in the first paragraph of "El hombre en el umbral"—is the mark of colonial language par excellence,[37] and yet consciousness of this vicious habit may be a first step toward breaking out of the colonized mind.

Significantly, Wali Dad, Kipling's Westernized colonial who becomes "converted" back to Islam by the religious and political excitement associated with the particular feast of Muharram when Khem Singh escapes from prison, is described for the last time near the end of the story: "On returning to Lalun's door I stumbled over a man at the threshold. He was sobbing hysterically, and his arms flapped like the wings of a goose. It was Wali Dad, Agnostic and Unbeliever, shoeless, turbanless, and frothing at the mouth, the flesh on his chest bruised and bleeding from the vehemence with which he had smitten himself. A broken torch-handle lay by his side, and his quivering lips murmured, '*Ya Hasan! Ya Hussain*' as I stooped over him"

(4: 336). A moment later the narrator sees "a man . . . bending over a corpse" in the square by the mosque (4: 336). When Borges rewrites this story in "Hombre en el umbral," the "man at the threshold"[38] recovers his dignity, and the corpse in the patio is British. He might have said with Wali Dad, "I cannot make an end to my sentence without quoting from your authors,"[39] but the quotation in this case marks the distance from the world of the original.

8

Behind Closed Doors: The Guayaquil Meeting

and the Silences of History

In a subsequent letter Bolívar informs this same Santander of these other events: "General San Martín told me, some hours before he embarked, that the lawyers of Quito wanted to form a state independent from Colombia with these provinces. I replied to him that I was satisfied with the spirit of the people of Quito and did not have the slightest fear; he replied that he was advising me of that so that I might take appropriate measures, insisting greatly on the *need to keep the men of letters under control.*"—Lecuna, *Crónica razonada* 3: 206 (emphasis added)

"Guayaquil": the brief title takes for granted that the reader will know that the story is concerned with the only encounter between Simón Bolívar and José de San Martín. And that the enigma that animates the narrative has to do with what transpired in the private meeting between the Liberator of Colombia and the Protector of Peru for four hours on 27 July 1822 at which no witnesses were present. And that the silence[1] of the two principals about the private meeting has provoked a huge amount of writing by historians and a whole series of furious polemics as a number of controversial (and some allegedly forged) documents have come to light.

Gerhard Masur has written: "The meeting at Guayaquil is probably the most discussed topic in South American history. The controversial literature dealing with this problem constitutes a veritable ocean of passion and ink" (526). Indeed, the scandal provoked by the two heroes' silence shows no signs of going away. Emilio Carilla tucked this judicious comment into a footnote of a paper on San Martín published in the proceedings of a conference (presided over by Juan Domingo and Eva Perón)[2] to commemorate the centenary of San Martín's death in 1850: "It is not strange that one should take note of this rivalry, carried on unfortunately to this day by the biographers of these two great Americans. Even if one could hardly avoid mentioning the one when speaking of the other, the reputation of one does not require ruining that of the other" (468n).[3] Carilla eludes the controversy by barely mentioning Bolívar, but almost all of the other accounts are furiously partisan, none perhaps more so than the most important: Bartolomé Mitre's biography of San Martín and Vicente Lecuna's vast writings on Bolívar.[4]

Borges, in this 1970 story from *El informe de Brodie,* cleverly displaces the rivalry from the two heroes of the independence wars onto the two historians who are contending for the privilege of going to Sulaco to transcribe a hitherto unknown letter by Bolívar.[5] The other clever touch is the claim that the letter was found in the archives of the historian Don José Avellanos of Sulaco, author of *History of Fifty Years of Misrule,* who is one of the main characters in Conrad's only novel of South America, *Nostromo* (1904). History and fiction are thus inextricably entwined and contaminate each other—the historicity of the accounts of the meeting being marked by partisan forgery, the fictionality of the story (and of the Conrad novel) being undercut by the attention in them to historical events.[6] The scandal that history and fiction constitute for one another is the center of the narrative here, and the category of "narrative" itself is threatened by the centrality in this event of silence.[7]

The narrator of the story, like Hladík in "El milagro secreto" and Dahlmann in "El Sur," has many elements of authorial self-parody.[8] Borges of course prided himself on his illustrious ancestors from the time of the independence wars, including Francisco Narciso Laprida, the president of the Congress of Tucumán in 1816 (and the subject of "Poema conjetural" [Conjectural Poem], to be discussed briefly in chapter 9), and Colonel Isidoro Suárez, who fought under Bolívar in the penultimate battle of the war of liberation (at Junín in Peru in August 1824) and was later termed "el héroe de Junín" [the hero of Junín].[9] In the story, Zimerman refers to the decisive cavalry charge led at Junín by Colonel Suárez, though he calls the hero "Juárez," apparently in order to allow his rival to correct him (1064).

A minor change in the story from its first publication in *El informe de Brodie* (1970) to the text as it appeared in the so-called *Obras completas* (1974) alerts the reader to someone's desire to disguise—however slightly—the model for the rival historian. In the 1970 version he is Eduardo Zimerman, a Czech Jew who immigrated to Argentina in the 1930s and now teaches at the Universidad del Sur (located in Bahía Blanca, at the southern extreme of the province of Buenos Aires);[10] in the 1974 version his surname is now spelled Zimmermann. By 1974 the similarity of the name to that of Jacobo Timerman, then director of the newspaper *La Opinión* (where Borges had published the Spanish version of his autobiographical essay), was uncomfortable, perhaps for Borges, perhaps for the editor of the volume, Carlos Frías. Timerman, a prominent Jewish immigrant to Argentina from the Ukraine, was an important player in the complex Argentine political scene in the period from the Cordobazo to the fall of Isabelita, and the picture given of Zimerman/Zimmermann in the story accords only too easily with the vicious portraits of Timerman by his enemies.[11] In a political world that was ever more sharply polarized, the portrayal of Timerman/Zimerman bears uneasy testimony to the idea in the story that there is no objective or impartial truth. All historical accounts are partial or "biased" (expressions of some partisan position), as Zimerman[12] himself points out (1065).[13]

Earlier, in my reading of "El jardín de senderos que se bifurcan," I called attention to an error by the editor of Yu Tsun's account who replaces late June 1916 with late July 1916, thereby revealing an abysmal ignorance of the history of the preparations for the battle of the Somme; the narrator of "El hombre en el umbral" similarly notes a minute error in Christopher Dewey's quotation from Juvenal and thereby helps cast Dewey as an unreliable narrator. In "Guayaquil" an astonishing error by the narrator reveals the extent to which he is motivated by an irrational hatred of his Jewish rival. The error occurs in the description of the documents that are the cause of the rivalry:

> Para que mi relato se entienda, tendré que recordar brevemente la curiosa aventura de ciertas cartas de Bolívar, que fueron exhumadas del archivo del doctor Avellanos, cuya *Historia de cincuenta años de des-gobierno,* que se creyó perdida en circunstancias que son del dominio público, fue descubierta y publicada en 1939 por su nieto el doctor Ricardo Avellanos. A juzgar por las referencias que he recogido en diversas publicaciones, estas cartas no ofrecen mayor interés, salvo una fechada en Cartagena el 13 de agosto de 1822, en que el Libertador refiere detalles de su entrevista con el general San Martín. Inútil destacar el valor de este documento en el que Bolívar ha revelado, siquiera parcialmente, lo sucedido en Guayaquil. (1062)

In order for my tale to be understood, I will have to recount briefly the curious adventure of some of Bolívar's letters, discovered in the archive of Dr. Avellanos, whose *History of Fifty Years of Misrule* was believed lost in circumstances that are in the public domain but was discovered and published in 1939 by his grandson Dr. Ricardo Avellanos. To judge from the references I have gathered from various publications, these letters offer little of interest except for one written in Cartagena on 13 August 1822, in which the Liberator recounts details of his encounter with General San Martín. It is useless to insist too much on the value of this document in which Bolívar has revealed, even if only partially, what happened in Guayaquil.

In the following paragraph the narrator says of Zimerman: "De su labor, sin duda benemérita, sólo he podido examinar una vindicación de la república semítica de Cartago, que la posteridad juzga a través de los historiadores romanos, sus enemigos" (1063) [Of his no doubt worthy labor, I have only been able to examine a defense of the Semitic republic of Carthage, which posterity judges through the accounts of the Roman historians, its enemy]. The meeting between Bolívar and San Martín took place on 26–27 July 1822 in Guayaquil, on the Pacific coast of South America; it would be quite impossible for Bolívar to be in Cartagena, on the Caribbean coast, by the date given, two weeks later. Going by sea to Panama, then overland, then by boat again to Cartagena was out of the question because in 1822 Spain still held the isthmus of Panama (and would be unlikely to let the Liberator pass), while the overland journey from the coast of Ecuador through the mountains and then down the Magdalena River in Colombia would have taken much longer than two weeks in those days. In fact, on 13 August Bolívar was still in Guayaquil, and it was there—and on the date in question—that he wrote a letter to General Santander[14] (Lecuna, *Cartas del Libertador* 3: 68–71). He stayed until 1 September, when he left Guayaquil for Cuenca (Lecuna, *Catálogo* 3: 360). Our narrator's error is pathetic, as he himself calls his account in the second paragraph of the story;[15] his hatred for his Semitic rival (an expert on the Phoenician city-state of Carthage) so inflames his mind that he confuses the geography of his own hemisphere (changing the location of Cartagena from the Caribbean to the Pacific and confusing Cartagena with Guayaquil).

Carthage/Cartagena: the minimal pair stands for a number of others: Old World/New World, Europe/Argentina, Rome/Carthage, San Martín/ Bolívar. (In a famous page of *Facundo,* Sarmiento contrasts San Martín, the European-trained general to Bolívar, an expert at what Sarmiento could not yet have called guerrilla warfare.)[16] Zimerman is disturbing to the narrator because he is a European intruder in the hemisphere, but an intruder whose presence is not a novelty: long before his arrival, Cartagena was already named in honor of Carthage (and of the Phoenician settlement in Spain, Cartago). The fight against the "godos"[17] has to be fought all over again. Even the rivalry of Rome and Carthage is unexpectedly revived in this struggle between the Creole and the Jewish historian. The battles of history are never over, even if one of the rival historians finally cries out: "Mon siège est fait" (1067) [My siege is done].[18]

The most important difference between the two historians in the story has to do with their conception of their profession. In justification of his having been designated for the task of going to Sulaco to decipher the manuscript, the narrator says of himself: "Esta misión corona, con una suerte de dichosa fatalidad, la labor de toda mi vida, la labor que de algún modo llevo en la sangre" (1065) [This mission crowns, with a sword of happy fatality, my whole life's labor, the labor which in some ways I bear in my blood]. Zimerman replies:

> En la sangre. Usted es el genuino historiador. Su gente anduvo por los campos de América y libró las grandes batallas, mientras la mía, oscura, apenas emergía del ghetto. Usted lleva la historia en la sangre, según sus elocuentes palabras; a usted le basta oir con atención esa voz recóndita. Yo, en cambio, debo transferirme a Sulaco y descifrar papeles y papeles acaso apócrifos. Créame, doctor, que lo envidio. (1065)

> In your blood. You are the true historian. Your people wandered over the battlegrounds of America and served in the great battles, while my obscure people barely were emerging from the ghetto. You bear history in your blood, according to your eloquent words; for you it suffices to listen with attention to that hidden voice. I, on the other hand, must travel to Sulaco and decipher papers, perhaps apocryphal papers. Believe me, doctor, I envy you.

Earlier, in my discussion of "Pierre Menard" in chapter 2, I observed that in Menard's *Quixote* the debate about "arms and letters" is transformed into a debate between pacifist intellectuals and militarist intellectuals. Here, the same debate is transmuted into a struggle between genealogy and graphology, or dynastic history and textual history. The shade of Dr. Pierre Menard presides over the discussion of the marks of pen on paper here (and the related war between the Academia de la Historia in Caracas and the Academia Nacional de la Historia in Buenos Aires over the Colombres Mármol papers). Not unlike the traditional knife fight between gauchos in the River Plate and in southern Brazil, the goal here is to mark the face of the opponent or to mark the other's text,[19] for even a textual historian or graphologist like Eduardo Zimerman views the contest as a test of wills. Zimerman himself says—of the meeting between Bolívar and San Martín—"Acaso las palabras que cambiaron fueron triviales. Dos hombres se enfrentaron en Guayaquil; si uno se impuso, fue por su mayor voluntad, no por juegos dialécticos" (1066) [Perhaps the words they exchanged were trivial. Two men faced each other in Guayaquil; if one triumphed, it was because of his greater power of will, not because of dialectical moves].

Before providing the "explanation" just quoted (heavily—and explicitly—indebted to Schopenhauer, as will be discussed shortly), Zimerman sums up the critical debates about the Guayaquil meeting:

> Algunos conjeturan que San Martín cayó en una celada; otros, como Sarmiento, que era un militar europeo, extraviado en un continente que nunca comprendió; otros, por lo general argentinos, le atribuyeron un acto de abnegación; otros, de fatiga. Hay quienes hablan de la orden secreta de no sé qué logia masónica. (1066)

> Some conjecture that San Martín fell into a trap; others, like Sarmiento, that he was a European military man, lost in a continent he never understood; others, usually Argentines, attribute to him an act of abnegation; others, of fatigue. There are even some who speak of the secret order of some Masonic lodge or other.

This sentence is a succinct summary of the debates among the historians from Mitre ("una celada") and Sarmiento ("un militar europeo") to Ricardo Rojas ("un acto de abnegación"), Vicente Lecuna ("fatiga"), and Pérez Amuchástegui ("logia masónica").[20]

For Mitre, the "Guayaquil question" was an open one in that both Colombia and Peru had valid claims to Ecuador, at least until Bolívar solved the question the way Alexander "solved" the problem of the Gordian knot—by occupying Guayaquil with his army (4: 417–38). Mitre describes the Guayaquil meeting as a tragic pantomime:

> The stage is the brightly illuminated arc of the equator in the New World, with its horizon on the ocean and its huge chains of mountains in perspective, its ever green palm trees and its burning volcanos. The protagonists are the arbiters of a new political world. The world sharpens its ears and hears nothing. One of the protagonists disap-

pears silently from the scene, covering his retreat with empty words. The other silently takes his place. The mystery lasts twenty years, without either of the interlocutors revealing what had happened in the meeting. At last, part of the veil is withdrawn, and it is possible to see, by combining the written or spoken words with the actions of the time, and the antecedents with their consequences, that the mystery merely consisted in the failure of the meeting itself. (4: 444–45)

The document mentioned by Mitre that came to light twenty years after the Guayaquil meeting was a letter from San Martín to Bolívar from Lima, dated 29 August 1822, published in French translation by a merchant sea captain, G. Lafond de Lurcy, in his *Voyages autour du monde et voyages célèbres.—Voyages dans les deux Amériques* [Travels around the World and Famous Voyages.—Travels in the Two Americas], published in 1844 (4: 478n). Mitre describes this letter as San Martín's "political testament" and translates it from French back to the alleged "original" Spanish, an operation worthy of Pierre Menard (but outdone here by my translation of a translation of a translation):

I will write to you, not only with the frankness, but also with what the highest interests of the New World demand.

The results of our meeting have not been what I hoped for to bring a speedy end to the war. Unfortunately, I am privately convinced, either that you did not believe that my offer to serve under you with the forces at my command was sincere, or that my person is embarrassing to you. The reasons you reported to me, that your delicate character would never permit you to command me, and that, even should you so resolve, you were sure that the congress of Colombia would not authorize your absence from the territory of the republic, have not appeared very plausible to me. The first reason refutes itself. As for the second, I am persuaded that if you expressed your desire, it would be received with unanimous approval, since it is a matter of finishing with this campaign, by means of your cooperation and that of your army, the struggle that we have undertaken and in which we are engaged, and that they would be cognizant of the honor that putting an end to it would bring to you and to the republic over which you preside.

Do not deceive yourself, general. The news that you have about the royalist forces is mistaken. They consist in Lower and Upper Peru of more than 19,000 veterans, and can be reunited within two months. The patriotic army, decimated by illness, cannot put but 8,500 in the field, mostly recruits. General Santa Cruz's division (which fought at

Pichincha), the casualties of which have not been replaced despite his requests, has experienced considerable losses in its long and painful march on land and will not be of use in this campaign. The 1,400 Colombians you are sending will be needed to maintain the garrison at Callao and to preserve order in Lima. Consequently, without the support of the army you command, the operation that is being prepared via ports in between will not provide the advantages that should be expected if substantial forces do not attract the attention of the enemy from other directions, and thus the struggle will be prolonged indefinitely. I say indefinitely because I am personally convinced that despite the vicissitudes of the present, the independence of America is irrevocable; but the prolonging of the war will cause the ruin of its peoples, and it is a sacred duty of the men to whom their destinies are entrusted to keep such afflictions from them.

Finally, my general, my decision is irrevocably taken. I have convoked the first congress of Peru, and the day after it is installed I shall embark for Chile, convinced that my presence is the only obstacle that impedes your coming to Peru with the army you command. For me it would have been the greatest happiness to finish the war of independence under the orders of a general to whom America owes its freedom. Destiny has resolved otherwise, and it is necessary to accept it!

I do not doubt that after my departure from Peru, the government that is established there will request your active cooperation, and I think you cannot deny such a fair request.

I have spoken to you with frankness, my general; but the feelings that this letter expresses will remain buried in the deepest silence; should they become known, the enemies of our freedom can find a way to harm it, and the intriguers and ambitious ones to cause discord. (4: 478–80)

This letter, usually known as the "Lafond letter" in honor of the merchant seaman who published it, is the source of the most bitter polemic in the historiography of nineteenth-century Spanish America. Published in San Martín's lifetime, and commented upon by Sarmiento in his address to the French academy of history in 1847 in presence of San Martín,[21] it is said to be a copy of a letter sent by San Martín to Bolívar, but the original, which should (according to this version) be in the Bolívar archives in Caracas, is absent. Vicente Lecuna, who for many years was the director of the Bolívar archives and the editor of the Bolívar papers, has written thousands of (rather repetitive) pages on why the letter must be fraudulent.[22] His explanation for the apparent acquiescence of San Martín in its publication (and his presence at Sarmiento's talk in Paris on the Guayaquil meeting) is that San Martín mulled over his humiliation in the New World and—from the Old—tried to rewrite history, to say what he wished he had said at the time. In his posthumous three-volume *Catálogo de errores y calumnias en la historia de Bolívar* [Catalog of Mistakes and Slanders in the History of Bolívar] (1956), Lecuna calls the letter the product of San Martín's "slow mental fabrication" (2: 202) and says that "the apocryphal document shows every sign of having been forged to deceive posterity" (2: 215), making it clear that he holds San Martín responsible for what he is calling a forgery.[23] He later quotes with approval the following statement by the Chilean historian Irarrázaval Larraín, who accuses San Martín (more directly than Lecuna himself) of having forged the Lafond letter:

> He began, then, in his years of sedentary life, to mull over how, since he could no longer change the event, he could surround it with signs of generosity and nobility that would justify or, even more, exalt the most inexcusable step of his career. . . .
>
> Slowly his reflections began taking shape in such a way that he took concrete steps to find the instrument he judged most appropriate: a communication addressed to the other protagonist at Guayaquil that would make full reference to the points that *should* have been treated at a meeting conceived of in this way. And thus life was breathed into a hypothetical letter from San Martín to Bolívar to which he assigned the date of 29 August 1822. (qtd. in Lecuna, *Catálogo* 2: 350)[24]

In the *Catálogo* Lecuna also feels it necessary to answer Julio César Raffo de la Reta's *Guayaquil: Fragmento de una conferencia* [Guayaquil: Fragment of a Meeting], in which the author tacitly accuses Lecuna himself of having destroyed the original of the Lafond letter: "The author begins with a hypothesis that is offensive to us: he supposes that the original of the Lafond letter could be or should be in the Bolívar Archive and asks: 'did it disappear from that archive by being lost, destroyed, or removed in a premeditated way?' We have not reached the cultural level of other countries. We have still not learned to falsify historical documents, nor to remove them from the archives" (2: 281). The reference here is not only to the Lafond letter but also to a trove of seven more letters about the Guayaquil meeting, first published in 1940 in *San Martín y Bolívar en la Entrevista de Guayaquil, a la luz de nuevos documentos definitivos* [San Martín and Bolívar at the Guayaquil Meeting, in Light of New Definitive Documents], signed by the former Argentine ambassador to Peru, Eduardo L. Colombres Mármol,[25] but apparently ghostwritten by Rómulo D. Carbia (Irarrázaval Larraín, qtd. in Lecuna, *Catálogo* 2: 356).[26] Lecuna waxes eloquent in referring to this "series of apocryphal documents invented expressly to exalt the glory of General San Martín at the expense of our heroes. An ineffective and clumsy attempt, because sooner or later the truth imposes itself" (3: 4).[27] He systematically demolishes the new letters (which include letters from Bolívar to San Martín, San Martín to Bolívar, Bolívar to Santander, Bolívar to Sucre, and San Martín to La Serna), commenting: "All this confusion and deception are due to the fact that it is impossible to falsify historical events when these have been established by an infinite number of authentic documents, and for this reason its place in the unfolding of events is unalterable" (3: 15).[28] The Chilean historian Irarrázaval Larraín, an ally of Lecuna's in the battles over the Lafond and Colombres Mármol letters, says of their adversaries: "The exposition and development of their respective theses can serve as an example to explain how *fictions* acquire the shape that allow them to be taken for *history*" (qtd. in Lecuna 2: 324, emphasis added).

In the story, the narrator says that the minister arranges for an interview between Zimerman and the narrator[29] "para evitar el espectáculo ingrato de dos universidades en desacuerdo" (1063) [to avoid the unpleasant spectacle of two universities in disaccord]. Borges's irony (delightful to all those who have survived the battles of academic politics) is no doubt based on the climax of the struggle over the Lafond and Colombres Mármol letters. Lecuna, hardly an impartial source, tells it this way:

> For its part the National Academy of History in Buenos Aires, without reason or proof, has reached an agreement, with the force of dogma, declaring that the apocryphal Lafond letter is authentic, and to be taken as the basis for Argentine and American history,[30] while our Academy of History, based on a study documented by Dr. Cristóbal L. Mendoza, has declared it false and mendacious in all of its parts, because it is that not only in its thesis, but also in the affirmations on which it sustains itself, all perfectly mistaken as we have shown with undeniable facts and documents. (*Catálogo* 2: 315)[31]

Of course, the reader's likely conclusion after reading the charges and countercharges is to doubt whether there are such things as "undeniable documents."[32]

Borges spins his story out of this skepticism, since the focus of the historians' task with regard to the Avellanos letter will be not so much the publication as the authentication or refutation of it. But, as this brief account of the controversies that have been provoked by the Lafond and Colombres Mármol letters has shown, any "authentication" or "refutation" of the Avellanos letter would necessarily involve taking sides in the larger controversies surrounding the Guayaquil meeting.

Zimerman is the first to raise the question of the new document's authenticity:

> Que sean de puño y letra de Bolívar . . . no significa que toda la verdad esté en ellas. Bolívar puede haber querido engañar a su corresponsal o, simplemente, puede haberse engañado. Usted, un historiador, un meditativo, sabe mejor que yo que el misterio está en nosotros, no en las palabras. (1066)

> Even if they are in Bolívar's own hand . . . that does not mean that they contain the whole truth. Bolívar may have wanted to deceive his correspondent or, simply, may himself have been deceived. You, as a historian and thinker, know better than I that the mystery is in us, not in the words.

He also makes clear that the person who publishes the document cannot be the one to refute it:

> En materia bolivariana (perdón, sanmartiniana) su posición de usted, querido maestro, es harto conocida. *Votre siège est fait.* No he deletreado aún la pertinente carta de Bolívar, pero es inevitable o razonable conjeturar que Bolívar la escribió para justificarse. En todo caso, la cacareada epístola nos revelará lo que podríamos llamar el sector Bolívar, no el sector San Martín. Una vez publicada, habrá que sopesarla, examinarla, pasarla por el cedazo crítico y, si es preciso, refutarla. Nadie más indicado para ese dictamen final que usted, con su lupa. ¡El escalpelo, el bisturí, si el rigor científico los exige! (1065)

> In matters respecting Bolívar (excuse me, San Martín) your position, my dear master, is well known. *Your siege is done.* I have not yet deciphered the pertinent letter by Bolívar, but it is inevitable or reasonable to conjecture that Bolívar wrote it to justify himself. In any case, the famous epistle will reveal more to us about what we might call the Bolívar sector, not the San Martín sector. Once it is published, it will be necessary to weigh it, examine it, pass it through the critical sieve, and, if necessary, refute it. There is no one more qualified to make this final judgment than you with your magnifying glass. The scalpel, the surgical knife, if scientific rigor so demands!

Zimerman adds that the name of the historian who publishes the document will be linked forever to the document itself (as the Lafond letter is linked to the name of Lafond), and that the narrator's position as a partisan of the "San Martín sector" will be compromised by that linkage.

But the last line of the story tells us that the narrator will not, in fact, be the one to refute the document: "Presiento que ya no escribiré más. *Mon siège est fait*" (1067) [I foresee that I shall not write any more. My siege is done]. The narrator, like San Martín, chooses silence (or, more exactly, *says* that he will choose silence).[33]

The archive where the Bolívar letters are found (only one of which, according to the reports the narrator has heard, refers to the Guayaquil meeting) is that of Don José Avellanos, the historian of Costaguana who dies in the midst of the civil war that ends in the creation of an independent Occidental State in *Nostromo*. The sentence that describes the archive merits attention:

> Para que mi relato se entienda, tendré que recordar brevemente la curiosa aventura de ciertas cartas de Bolívar, que fueron exhumadas del archivo del doctor Avellanos, cuya *Historia de cincuenta años de des-gobierno,* que se creyó perdida en circunstancias que son del dominio público, fue descubierta y publicada en 1939 por su nieto el doctor Ricardo Avellanos. (1062)

> In order for my tale to be understood, I will have to recount briefly the curious adventure of some of Bolívar's letters, discovered in the archive of Dr. Avellanos, whose *History of Fifty Years of Misrule* was believed lost in circumstances that are in the public domain, but was discovered and published in 1939 by his grandson Dr. Ricardo Avellanos.

The syntax here entangles the fate of the Bolívar letters—not previously known, so hardly "in the public domain"—with that of the manuscript of *Fifty Years of Misrule,* the Avellanos history of the first half-century of independent Costaguana (and, of course, confuses a document referring to a "real" historical event with one referring to "historical events" that are "in the public domain" thanks only to the Conrad novel). Conrad, of course, was there first; in the "Author's Note," written in first-person narration referring directly to his own experience and prior publications, he mentions "my venerated friend, the late Don José Avellanos, Minister to the Courts of England and Spain, etc., etc., [and] his impartial and eloquent 'History of Fifty Years of Misrule.'" He adds: "That work was never published—the reader will discover why—and I am in fact the only person in the world possessed of its contents" (x). The first reference in the novel itself is to "his manuscript of a historical work on Costaguana . . . which, at present, he thought it was not prudent (even if it were possible) 'to give to the world' " (112). There are a series of other references to the manuscript (140, 142, 182, 185). Finally Martin Decoud, the firebrand of the independence movement and editor of Avellanos's newspaper *Porvenir,* sees—once the war has broken out—the loose sheets of Avellanos's book, "which we have begun printing on the presses of the *Porvenir,* littering the Plaza, floating in the gutters, fired out as wads for trabucos loaded with handfuls of type, blown in the wind, trampled in the mud." He adds: "I have seen pages floating upon the very waters of the harbour" (235). The precise wording in the Conrad novel, then, does not say that the *manuscript* was lost ("en circunstancias que son del dominio público") but only that the loose sheets from the unfinished first printing were scattered in the midst of a further episode of political chaos and misrule.

Nostromo is a novel caught between "reality" and "unreality."[34] Thus, a "bizarre sense of unreality" afflicts Decoud when he is left on the little island in the Sulaco harbor with the boatload of silver (302). The contrary "sense of reality" is introduced especially through the Anglo-Saxon characters—Gould, the administrator of the mine, Captain Mitchell, the supervisor of the port for the steamship company, and Dr. Monygham, the head of medical services for the mine and later the inspector of state hospitals (481). Of particular note is the tour that Captain Mitchell gives his visitors in the penultimate chapter of the novel—a tour of the historic places of Sulaco, with emphasis on the recent revolution. The curious "sense of unreality" in the novel is produced above all by the principle of combination: there are frequent references to Latin American realities, but they end up canceling one another out by their sheer quantity and variety. Thus, for instance, there are descriptions of knife fights and *pulperías* obviously drawn from Sarmiento's picture of the life of the gauchos in the first section of *Facundo* (385, 405)[35] and odd mixtures of cultural features from different parts of the continent. The people of Costaguana (like people in the River Plate countries and southern Brazil) drink Paraguayan tea or yerba maté (104); the local cowboys are called "llaneros" like the cowboys of Venezuela and Colombia (388), yet even the *llaneros* drink maté (397); there are Mexican serapes (125, 258) and "nopal hedges" (359); the Occidental flag bears the colors of the Brazilian flag, green and yellow (384); the inhabitants use River Plate slang ("China girls," that is, *chinas,* for mestizas [24]); and a description of the former dictator, Guzman Bento, is based on accounts of Dr. Francia, the supreme dictator of Paraguay.[36] There is even a reminiscence of Porfirio Díaz's famous description of Mexico ("so far from God, so close to the United States") in a Sulaco saying that "God is very high above" while the U.S.-owned silver mine is all too near (206).

The description of Sulaco in the Borges story—"No veré la cumbre del Higuerota duplicarse en las aguas del Golfo Plácido" (1062) [I shall not see the summit of Higuerota reflected in the waters of the Placid Gulf]—calls attention to the region's most striking geographical feature: the great snow-clad mountain rising above the town and the bay, a mountain "that seemed a colossal embodiment of silence" (27). Sulaco and the surrounding province are drawn from two important port cities of the northern part of South America, Santa Marta (Colombia) and Guayaquil (Ecuador). Higuerota is a combination of Chimborazo, the highest mountain in Ecuador, and the Sierra Nevada de Santa Marta, while the country is described in terms that suggest both Colombia and Ecuador, with an inland capital (here called "Santa Marta," to confuse things all the more) that could be Quito or Bogotá. The historical event narrated in the novel—the secession of the "Occidental Province" from Costaguana—is based on the separation of Ecuador from "Gran Colombia" in 1830, the rumblings of which were already being felt in 1822 when the intellectuals of Quito and Guayaquil (about whom San Martín warns Bolívar in the passage I have used as the epigraph for this chapter) tried to take advantage of the chaos of the end of the independence struggle by carving out an independent state for themselves between the larger states dominated by the great figures of the two liberators.[37] Indeed many of the accounts coincide in finding the immediate cause of the Guayaquil meeting in the anxiety the two liberators experienced because of these early stirrings of Ecuadoran independence.

But Santa Marta, the Colombian port near the Sierra Nevada and the Guajira desert (so familiar to readers of García Márquez's short fiction), is also important in the description of Sulaco, not least because it was near the hacienda where Bolívar died in 1830.[38] And Bolívar—cited once in the novel[39]—is to some extent the model for Martin Decoud. Most important, though, is the following discussion of the genesis of the novel in Conrad's "Author's Note": "As a matter of fact in 1875 or '6, when very young, in the West Indies or rather in the Gulf of Mexico, for my contacts with land were short, few, and fleeting, I heard the story of some man who was supposed to have stolen single-handed a whole lighter-full of silver, somewhere on the Tierra Firme during the troubles of a revolution" (vii–viii). "Some man" here is no less than Simón Bolívar, for one of the more enigmatic events of the Liberator's career was his flight from Caracas in 1814 into the eastern part of Venezuela, and subsequent embarkation at the Caribbean port of

Cumaná, with a treasure trove of almost 28,000 ounces of silver taken from the churches of Caracas (Madariaga, *Bolívar* 1: 457–65).[40] Conrad (in the preface to *Nostromo*) says of the incident of the boat full of silver:

> It's either true or untrue; and in any case it has no value in itself. To invent a circumstantial account of the robbery did not appeal to me. . . . It was only when it dawned upon me that the purloiner of the treasure need not necessarily be a confirmed rogue, that he could be even a man of character, an actor and possibly a victim in the changing scenes of a revolution, it was only then that I had the first vision of a twilight country which was to become the province of Sulaco, with its high shadowy Sierra and its misty Campo for mute witnesses of events flowing from the passions of men short-sighted in good and evil. (ix)

"It's either true or untrue; and in any case it has no value in itself": Conrad's reflection on the insignificance of historical fact per se shows that he, like the two historians in the Borges story, was a devoted reader of Schopenhauer's *The World as Will and Representation*.[41]

On examining his rival's library, Zimerman comments:

> Ah, Schopenhauer, que siempre descreyó de la historia. . . . Esa misma edición, al cuidado de Grisebach, la tuve en Praga, y creí envejecer en la amistad de esos volúmenes manuables, pero precisamente la historia, encarnada en un insensato, me arrojó de esa casa y de esa ciudad. (1064)

> Ah, Schopenhauer, who always disbelieved in history. . . . That same edition, edited by Grisebach, is the one I had in Prague, and I thought I would grow old in the company of those handy volumes, but it was precisely history, incarnated in a madman, that threw me from that house and that city.

Schopenhauer's skepticism about history is most strongly expressed in chapter 38 of the supplements to his *World*, entitled "On History."[42] Against Hegelian "universal history" and "philosophy of history," Schopenhauer asserts that history is the insignificant collection of minutiae or particulars and that it lacks all traces of a universal design. He writes:

> History is therefore the more interesting the more special it is, but also the less trustworthy; and thus it approximates in all respects to a work of fiction. . . . Now in so far as history always has for its object only the particular, the individual fact, and regards this as the exclusively real, it

is the direct opposite and counterpart of philosophy, which considers things from the most universal point of view, and has the universal as its express object. (2: 441)

He adds, "The material of history . . . is the individual thing in its individuality and contingency; this thing exists once, and then exists no more for ever" (2: 442), and says that because it consists of an atomized collection of insignificant facts, history is "untruthful" (2: 444). By "fiction" and "untruth," though, he does not mean deliberate lying but simply a lack of significance or truthfulness.[43] Though he calls history the "long, heavy, and confused dream of mankind" (2: 443),[44] he concedes that such a dream or memory may have a function: "*What the faculty of reason is to the individual, history is to the human race.* . . . Only through history does a nation become completely conscious of itself. Accordingly, history is to be regarded as the rational self-consciousness of the human race" (2: 445, emphasis in original). And as the instrument of a human community's self-consciousness, history becomes useful when recorded:

> Now what *language* is for the reasoning faculty of individuals, as an indispensable condition for its use, *writing* is for the reasoning faculty of the whole race which is indicated here; for only with writing does the actual existence of this faculty of reason begin, just as the existence of the individual's reason first begins with language. Thus writing serves to restore to unity the consciousness of the human race, which is incessantly interrupted by death, and is accordingly piecemeal and fragmentary. (2: 445–46)

For Schopenhauer, then, the "truth" of history matters less than its function as the "memory of the human race," and such a memory can be erected as well on "fiction" as on "fact." The "making" of history is an act of will, its writing an act of representation.[45] Hence Zimerman's formulation in the story: "Dos hombres se enfrentaron en Guayaquil; si uno se impuso, fue por su mayor voluntad, no por juegos dialécticos" (1066) [Two men faced each other in Guayaquil; if one triumphed, it was because of his greater power of will, not because of dialectical moves].[46] And hence, too, San Martín's silence and the narrator's decision to withdraw from the field: "Presiento que ya no escribiré más. *Mon siège est fait*" (1067) [I foresee that I shall not write any more. My siege is done].

"Guayaquil" is Borges's most explicit reflection on the relations between the writing of history and the writing of fiction, and though he caricatures both historians (most mercilessly the one who more closely resembles himself), his attention to the details of the Guayaquil controversy suggests that the puzzle of what really happened behind those closed doors engaged his imagination no less than it engaged that of several generations of historians. The story shows him skeptical of historical "truth" but fascinated with problems of historiographical "verification." He could say with Pierre Menard that for him historical truth was not so much what happened as what we judge to have happened, or with William James that: "The truth of an idea is not a stagnant property inherent in it. Truth *happens* to an idea. It *becomes* true, is *made* true by events. Its verity *is* in fact an event, a process: the process namely of its verifying itself, its veri-*fication*. Its validity is the process of its valid-*ation*" (*Essays in Pragmatism* 161, emphasis in original). What we make of the "fact" of San Martín's withdrawal from the field (or the self-conscious imitation of that act in the narrator of the story's announcement that henceforth he will be silent) depends, however, on a prior element of the story, the exact nature of which is still unknown. What Bolívar and San Martín said to each other during their private meeting— what we imagine they said to each other—shapes the rest of the event; without certain knowledge of their conversation, the stories that lead up to San Martín's withdrawal are infinite in variety and possibility. It is as if Stephen Albert and Jaromir Hladík were right in their sense of many "possible worlds": imagination (fiction) blasts open historical causality.

9

Conclusion

This profound kinship between the quasi past of fiction and the "unrealized" potentialities of the historical past explains, perhaps, why . . . the liberation of fiction from the constraints of history is not the last word concerning the freedom of fiction. It is only the Cartesian moment: the free choice in the kingdom of the imaginary. But is not fiction's rapport with the quasi past the source of more subtle constraints which indicate the Spinozist moment of freedom—interior necessity? Free *from* the exterior constraint of documentary proof, must not the creator still make himself [*sic*] free *for*—on behalf of—the quasi past?—Ricoeur, "Narrated Time" 354

History is better defined as an ongoing tension between stories that have been told and stories that might have been told.—Hunt, "History as Gesture" 103

Arguably the greatest of Borges's poems, "Poema conjetural" [Conjectural Poem], is a reflection on the conditions of possibility of historical action:

> Yo que anhelé ser otro, ser un hombre
> de sentencias, de libros, de dictámenes,
> a cielo abierto yaceré entre ciénagas;
> pero me endiosa el pecho inexplicable
> un júbilo secreto. Al fin me encuentro
> con mi destino sudamericano. (866)

> I who desired to be someone else, to be a man of sayings, of books, of decrees, will lie among swamps beneath the open sky; but a secret joy

transports my inexplicable heart. At last I meet my South American destiny.

The poem is a dramatic monologue obviously patterned after those of Robert Browning. It begins with a note: "El doctor Francisco Laprida, asesinado el día 22 de setiembre de 1829 por los montoneros de Aldao, piensa antes de morir" [Dr. Francisco Laprida, murdered on 22 September 1829 by the guerrillas of Aldao, thinks before his death]. Once again, as in "El milagro secreto," "Historia del guerrero y de la cautiva," and "La escritura del dios," the revelation that the destiny of the individual is made manifest in that of the group, a revelation *sub specie aeternitatis,* is carefully situated in historical time. Laprida—historical figure and ancestor—reflects on how his destiny fits into the destiny of his race; his reflection necessarily mirrors that of his sister's great-grandson, the author of the poem. "En el espejo de esta noche alcanzo / mi insospechado rostro eterno" (868) [In the mirror of this night I grasp my unsuspected eternal face]: Laprida's self-discovery is situated in, and outside of, time.

Leoncio Gianello, in his history of the Congress of Tucumán, says of Laprida: "A friend of San Martín's, he was, like the rest of the Cuyo deputies, an instrument of San Martín's politics, to which he subscribed fully. Without a doubt Laprida and Godoy are the two most representative deputies of San Martín's message and orientation. His ideas on independence were well-defined and he contributed decisively to the declaration of 9 July 1816, which he would sign as president of that historic session" (48). Gianello provides the following capsule biography in a footnote:

Laprida participated in important debates in Congress. He supported a republican form of government. On 4 March 1818 he ceased being a member of the body. In San Juan he had a distinguished public career: a government minister during the rule of Dr. Salvador María del Carril, a deputy in the San Juan legislature, deputy for San Juan at another of the great assemblies of the country: the National Congress of 1824–27, of which he was president during the initial period of the Congress. He was one of the principal spokesmen for a form of government consolidated in a single regime. When the Congress was dissolved he returned to San Juan. He participated in the civil struggles on the Unitarian side. At Mendoza he enlisted as a corporal in the civilian battalion. On 22 September 1829, when his battalion was at the horse farm of Pilar, during a truce period, the truce was violated by Aldao; the troops were surprised and Laprida (who was trying to flee) was taken prisoner and killed. The story that his corpse was mutilated and displayed at the entrance to the Mendoza city hall has not been confirmed. Damián Hudston, an eyewitness to the combat or surprise attack on Pilar, says that Laprida's body was never found. (48n)[1]

He was forty-two years old. Sarmiento—in *Recuerdos de provincia*—gives a dramatic account of an encounter he had with Laprida shortly before the latter's death,[2] while his *Vida de Aldao* gives a vivid picture of Laprida's antagonist.[3] Sarmiento comments in *Facundo:* "San Juan had been, up until that time [1831], sufficiently rich in civilized men, that it gave the famous Congress of Tucumán a president of the abilities and distinction of Dr. Laprida, who later died murdered by the Aldaos" (72).

Julie Jones, in her discussion of the poem in an article on Borges and Browning, notes that the poem "takes place at a specific historical moment" (213) to a specific individual, but she holds that "Laprida looks to the universal, embodied in literature, to come to terms with his individual situation; that is, the particular has meaning only in relation to the general" (214). My view is that this generalizing from a particular situation may indeed describe Laprida's point of view, but that it is rash to assume that his point of view is representative of a whole, or as Jones puts it, "of the collective unconscious of his race" (214). Even the notion of a "manifest destiny" is tailored to the individual speaker of the poem (and one imagines Laprida—like Sarmiento—on the battlefield dressed in frock coat and top hat, perhaps equipped like Sarmiento with a raincoat):[4] Laprida speaks of "my South American destiny," not of "the South American destiny" or "the destiny of the South American" or "the destiny of South America." If Sarmiento's treatment of civilization and savagery maintains the notion of a collective destiny (to which individual destinies must submit as a categorical imperative), Borges's treatment of Laprida undermines the adequacy of the polar opposition to represent the "realities on the ground." And though Laprida frames the problem as one of a fateful choice between civilization and savagery, between arms and letters, his own place in those webs of signification is confused. He is the man of letters who discovers his destiny on the battlefield, and whose elegant penmanship proves unequal to the knife play of his opponents. He discovers in death that his casting of himself in the role of "man of letters" has been his undoing: the "profession of letters" and the "profession of arms" are not two mutually exclusive options, since each implies the other. Sarmiento's motto, "On ne tue point les idées" (*Facundo* 4–5) [Ideas can never be killed],[5] cannot be Laprida's consolation—or salvation—here.

"Poema conjetural" was written against the background of the rise of

Perón, and the denigration of the despised Others—"gauchos," "bárbaros"—masks the speaker's fascination (and partial identification) with them.[6] Laprida expresses something like eagerness for his moment of truth: "me endiosa el pecho inexplicable / un júbilo secreto" [a secret joy transports my inexplicable heart], "El círculo / se va a cerrar. Yo aguardo que así sea" [The circle is going to close. I am waiting for that to happen]. And just as the poem describes a mirroring—of Laprida in Borges, of Borges in Laprida—so the poet may be expressing his eagerness to enter the "public sphere" of national debate or his recognition that literature is never "au-dessus de la mêlée."[7] "Ya el primer golpe, / ya el duro hierro que me raja el pecho, / el íntimo cuchillo en la garganta" [Already the first blow, already the hard iron ripping my chest, the intimate knife on my throat]: "Words, words, but they hold the horror of the world" (Remarque 132).

In the introduction to *Epistemology of the Closet,* Eve Kosofsky Sedgwick writes: "A point of this book is *not to know* how far its insights and projects are generalizable, not to be able to say in advance where the semantic specificity of these issues gives over to (or: itself structures?) the syntax of a 'broader' or more abstractable critical project" (12, emphasis in original). So to conclude I would like to reflect on the implications—as well as on the limits—of my project here.

After the research for this book, I am tempted to say with Funes, "Mi memoria, señor, es como vaciadero de basuras" (488) [My memory, sir, is like a garbage heap], but I do not really think so. What I have done, very slowly, quite imperfectly, with a sense of my own inadequacies to the task, is to replicate the intellectual operations of a man of incredible genius, the sort of genius that startles one at every turn. The extraordinary patchwork that is Borges's stories is a work of collage beyond anything that the Dadaists and surrealists could have imagined, but one controlled always by intelligence and will. Who else would have thought to put the brave words that Padraic Pearse spoke during the British court-martial in Dublin in 1916 into the mouth of a Chinese spy captured in the English midlands in that very year? Who else would rewrite a Kipling story, respecting the general outline but turning the politics inside out? Who else could create a work of such complexity that it cannot be read twice in the same way, yet at the same time a work of such conciseness and elegance? One cannot but feel grateful to the spaciousness of that intellect. "Tlön será un laberinto, pero es un laberinto urdido por hombres, un laberinto destinado a que lo descifren los hombres" (443) [Tlön will be a labyrinth, but it is a labyrinth created by human beings, a labyrinth destined to be deciphered by human beings].

At the same time, I think my research reveals how fully human Borges was, how much engaged in the world. The argument often made about his participation in Argentine politics, particularly his nasty turn to the right in reaction to a Peronism that he could only see as a homegrown fascism, should not obscure the fact that earlier in his career—and for that matter, also at the very end of his life, after the Malvinas war—his sympathies were those of a post-Enlightenment liberal intellectual, with the inborn limitations of the breed but without the nastiness for which he was later (and quite properly) reproached.[8] It is important to read the stories from *Ficciones* and *El Aleph* in light of the essays, reviews, and other occasional writings of the time during which they were written. Borges had the misfortune to become a celebrity late in his life and played the game with his usual irony and feigned innocence, but he did not, I think, realize that his chance remarks spread as far and as quickly as they did or understand that they could have an awful "proyección ulterior" utterly unlike the carefully chosen details in his fiction.[9] But to argue—as Alazraki does—that Borges's work "is a prodigious artifice, an iridescent language, a self-contained work severed from historic reality" (*Borges and the Kabbalah* 187) is to neglect the ways in which his work implies a textual reality "más compleja que la declarada al lector" and requires a "reader who exists in the real world" (Hutcheon 11).[10] Already in 1923, in the preface to *Fervor de Buenos Aires,* Borges writes: "Todos somos unos; pocos difieren nuestras naderías, y tanto influyen en las almas las circunstancias, que es casi una casualidad esto de ser tú el leyente y yo el escribidor—el desconfiado y fervoroso escribidor—de mis versos" (n. pag.) [We are all one: our nothingnesses differ very little, and circumstances so influence our souls, that it is almost chance that you should be the reader and I the writer—the uncertain and fervent writer—of my verses];[11] the emptying out of the concept of "self" heightens the importance of circumstance, of context.

Are the readings I have made of the stories studied here arbitrary? Could someone do this sort of reading and come out with totally different results? Sonia Mattalía Alonso and Juan Miguel Company Román, in a provocative article on what they term the impossibility of the real in Borges, seem to think so: "As Pierre Macherey says, Borges, instead of tracing the large structural lines of the story, merely suggests the possibility of doing so. And generally speaking this possibility remains postponed when it is not rejected altogether. *Borges indicates a story: not only the one he could write, but also the one that others could have written*" (134, emphasis in original). The authors do not explore, however, a sense in which Borges's stories could indeed have been written by others; since they are constructed from webs of references to historical reality, these webs necessarily overlap with those found in other texts: historical documents, works of historiography, other historical fictions. The particular design "found" woven into the historical carpet will of course differ from other accounts, as each of those accounts will differ from the others. So, in "Guayaquil," despite the seemingly infinite malleability of the historical material, readers who begin from an assumption of the possibility of the real (and not its impossibility, as in Mattalía and Company) will have a desire to know what happened that day in July 1822, and that desire will animate the text in new and fruitful ways. As Slavoj Žižek has suggested, "The real that serves as support of our symbolic reality must appear to be *found* and not *produced*" (*Looking Awry* 32); were it not so, the things of the world would in fact be *hrönir,* the world would indeed be Tlön.

Was Borges conscious of the political or ideological implications of the stories I have studied here? Not necessarily. But that does not mean that we need to allow the metaphysical elements in the stories to make us think that the other implications are not present or do not matter.

Unlike Robbe-Grillet and Kafka, who blur or erase the context that some critics have reconstructed, reality is present in all of its painful detail in Borges; not the author but the critics have erased the historical and political references. (Of course the author may have collaborated in the process in the many interviews he gave at the end of his life—decades after the composition of most of the stories considered here—but we need not fall for these snares.)

Thus, when some critics complain that the historical situations of the kind mentioned here are mere pretexts not to be taken seriously, they are confessing that they have chosen not to take them seriously. John Sturrock says of the initial reference to Liddell Hart in "El jardín de senderos que se bifurcan," "I have not checked this quotation because it does not matter in the least whether it is accurate; Borges needs a datum point and he has provided himself with one" (191): whether or not the quotation matters in the story can of course only be determined by an examination of it. Similarly, when Jean Franco writes that Borges removes causality from history (69), or when R. K. Britton argues that Borges transmutes "history into literature and thence into myth" (612), the conclusion they reach depends on the acceptance of the dubious premise that a contextual reading of Borges is impossible. In all of these assessments, history is fragmented, providing Borges with loose elements on which to found his fictions, and by implication history is subordinated to literature. What I have been suggesting here is in fact quite the opposite: that history often becomes in Borges that "more complex reality" the existence of which is implied—and required—by the literary text.

Indeed, Borges's conception of history is not as close to that of Hayden White, for whom history is discourse,[12] as to that of Fredric Jameson, for whom history is not narrative or textual, but an Other only partially recoverable to us in textual form.[13] History inhabits Borges's literature in much the same way as the final tiger of his poem is always just beyond expression: the other tiger is the one "que no está en el verso" [that is not in the verse]. So too the definition of beauty at the end of the essay "La muralla y los libros" [The Wall and the Books] suggests that it is "la inminencia de una revelación, que no se produce" [the imminence of a revelation that does not occur]. To cite Žižek again (for his definition of "reality" is not far from Borges's definition of "beauty"): "Reality itself is nothing but an embodiment of a certain blockage in the process of symbolization. For reality to exist, something must be left unspoken" (*Looking Awry* 45). Or later in the same book: "The real resists symbolization, but it is at the same time its retroactive product" (143).

Why should Borges have chosen to play with the historical record in the stories I have studied here (and in many others that could be read in analogous ways)? The answer lies, I think, in the constraints that history provides, constraints within which human lives may seem unbounded, but the reader, looking back, knows better. Borges plays in his fictions with narrowly constricted space and time yet suggests that even there (as in the Aleph) there is infinite possibility. But though the possibilities may seem infinite at a given moment, only one of the possibilities will be realized, as is demonstrated with such terrifying precision in "El jardín de senderos que se bifurcan." Because the historical record is public, the curious reader can go back and recover the context that is often only barely implicit in the stories. The stories will be opened up by this process, the sense of infinite possibility restored, but the reader will also grasp the tragic dimension of the story that actually emerged from that interplay of chance and necessity.[14]

What I have been doing here will no doubt seem arbitrary or mischievous to some. Indeed I would not be upset by such an assessment. Yet, as Borges eloquently argues in "La supersticiosa ética del lector" [The Superstitious Ethic of the Reader], only transgressive readings can rescue our classics from the universe of dead letters. Since Borges is a notoriously self-conscious writer, it is hard to write about him without repeating what is already present in his texts (without "incurring in a tautology," to echo Pierre Menard). The free (some would say crazy) use I make of the historical and political references most definitely breaks us out of the vicious hermeneutic circle, moving us from mere "explications de texte" toward the study of textual implications.

Notes

1 Introduction: History, Politics, and Literature in Borges

1 Unless otherwise indicated, quotations from Borges are from the 1974 Emecé edition of the so-called *Obras completas*. I have supplied quotations from Borges in both the original and my own translations. Other quotations are given in English translation only (unless some feature of the original merits attention), and all translations are mine unless otherwise noted.

2 For a concise discussion of the relation between Borges and the fiction of Azuela, Barrios, and others, see Donald Shaw's essay on *Ficciones* in Swanson, *Landmarks in Modern Latin American Fiction*. See also Carlos Alonso's book on the regionalist novel, which opens with a discussion of Borges (1–6).

3 The collection edited by Juan Fló contains a number of texts charging Borges with escapism. An early discussion of this charge is to be found in Rodríguez Monegal's *El juicio de los parricidas,* though the ground has shifted a lot since Monegal's defense of Borges against the angry young men of the journal *Contorno* (Adolfo Prieto, Noé Jitrik, Tulio Halperín Donghi, David Viñas, and others). For a good overview of the period, see William Katra's book on *Contorno,* as well as two crucial essays by members of the *Contorno* group: Adolfo Prieto's *Borges y la nueva generación* (1954) and Noé Jitrik's much later "Sentimientos complejos sobre Borges" (1987). See also Blas Matamoro, *Jorge Luis Borges o el juego trascendente,* and Pedro Orgambide, *Borges y su pensamiento político,* as well as the final pages of Alazraki's *Borges and the Kabbalah*. Another recent piece, notable for the fervor of the argument against Borges's supposed "contradicción de la historia," is Blas Matamoro's "Historia de Borges," especially 136ff.

4 Molloy's discussion of the *vaivén* is related to her important discussion of the *hiato* or *grieta* (*Letras,* especially 163–90). Molloy's concept of the narrative gap is rather more literal and pragmatic than Wolfgang Iser's almost metaphysical concept of the gap as

"those very points at which the reader can enter the text, forming his [sic] own connections and conceptions and so creating the configurative meaning of what he [sic] is reading" (*Implied Reader* 40). Despite the frequency of the use of the concept of "gap" in Iser's work, neither here nor in his subsequent *The Act of Reading* does he give a more precise definition of what he means by the term or how some other reader is to locate these gaps in a text. Molloy, in contrast, refers to very concrete details. She notes, for instance, that the first reference to the fantastic literature of Uqbar refers to the imaginary regions of Mlejnas and Tlön and observes that this passing reference to Mlejnas, never further elaborated in the text, tantalizes the reader in part by contrast to the dizzying complexities of the later references to Tlön (*Letras* 170).

5 Perhaps I should also cite Roberto González Echevarría for his insistence that "Tlön" is "corrosively aware of the mimetic pact between Latin American narrative and the anthropological mediation" (*Myth and Archive* 162), though his designating it as Borges's regionalist novel (161) strains even my credulity.

6 James Irby in his admirable essay on "Tlön" cites Derrida's famous formulation from the *Grammatology*, "Il n'y pas de hors-texte." It should be obvious that I do not start from this premise. For a discussion of the implications of Derrida's affirmation, see Timothy Yates.

7 Some of them are, to be sure. So far, at least, no one has turned up a copy of the *First Encyclopaedia of Tlön*. But the frequency of these inventions is much less than people like Ferrer assume. For instance, Ferrer writes: "George Loring Frost is a clear case of an apocryphal author" (179), but, unfortunately for Professor Ferrer, this is not the case, and the same can be said of many other affirmations in his book.

8 An issue that I shall not pursue here is Borges's relation to idealist philosophy. For the argument that Borges's position be considered in relation to Berkeley and Hume, see Marina Martín. I am more in sympathy with Carla Cordua, who argues that Borges was not a metaphysician and, hence, that for him "the philosophical element, first isolated from its context and then treated not as a concept but as a thing or as a singular existing situation, is thus removed from its medium, separated from the function it had in that medium, and converted into an opaque sign, suggestive but in the final analysis undecipherable" (637). Juan Fló makes a similar point in his introductory essay to *Contra Borges* (46–47), as does Jaime Rest (74–75).

9 A more subtle approach to the question of reality in Borges's fiction may be found in Sonia Mattalía Alonso and Juan Miguel Company Román's article "Lo real como imposible en Borges" [The Real as Impossible in Borges], which argues, using Barthes and Lacan, that reference to a reality beyond the text is central but that such reference is "always already" alienated, fictive, textual. They write: "Reality is a mirror, but it is also a simulacrum. It would be superfluous to cite here the innumerable *superficial reality effects* [*efectos de superficie realista*]—facts, dates, historical events—with which Borges sprinkles his stories. The author seems to enter fully into the famous clutter of literary realism, using his whole rhetorical arsenal, his whole wealth of verisimilitudes. But the final result is not an integral image of the world, a fearless mirror of certainty which wanders along the edge of the road, as Stendhal wanted. It more closely resembles an interrogation than a certainty" (134). While I am in general accord with the import of this observation, I hope to show here that Mattalía and Company's account of the "reality effects" in Borges is well intentioned but superficial, and that a fuller account of the "reality effects" must be constructed through a contextualized rereading of the texts. My readings of the seven

stories considered here are very different from their reading of "Ulrica" in the approach to
the referents.

10 A number of other candidates suggested themselves: "Tlön, Uqbar, Orbis Tertius," "La
forma de la espada" [The Shape of the Sword], "Tema del traidor y del héroe" [Theme of
the Traitor and the Hero], and "La muerte y la brújula" [Death and the Compass] from
Ficciones; "El inmortal" [The Immortal], "Los teólogos" [The Theologians], "La otra
muerte" [The Other Death], "Deutsches Requiem," and "La busca de Averroes" [Aver-
roes's Search] from *El Aleph;* and "Avelino Arredondo" from *El libro de arena* [The Book
of Sand]. The final choices were dictated above all by a desire for variety in the historical
events discussed. Translations of the stories are available in *Labyrinths* ("The Garden of
Forking Paths," "Pierre Menard," "The Secret Miracle," "Story of the Warrior and the
Captive," and "The God's Script"), *The Aleph and Other Stories* ("The Man on the
Threshold"), and *Doctor Brodie's Report* ("Guayaquil").

11 For commentaries on this essay, see Molloy, *Letras* 105–20; Fló 26–28; Eduardo González
17–48; and Balderston, *El precursor velado* 27–35.

12 See Kaplan on "Tlön" and *Urne Buriall.*

13 The strongest statement to date on the need to contextualize Borges's writings in the act
of interpretation is Davi Arrigucci's essay on "Biografía de Tadeo Isidoro Cruz ("Da fama
e da infâmia"). See also Balderston, "The Mark of the Knife."

14 For discussions that parallel my argument about the presence of the Great War in Borges
here, see Wendy Steiner on *The Waste Land* and Sidra Stich on surrealist art.

15 On the "historical imagination," see Collingwood's *The Idea of History* 231–49. The
concept is also central to Carlyle's ideas on historiography.

16 Cf. also the title of *Historia de la eternidad,* which plays with the paradox of considering
history and eternity (or abstraction) at the same time.

17 In the same section of *The World as Will and Representation,* Schopenhauer writes: "What
history relates is in fact only the long, heavy and confused dream of mankind" (2: 443).
This line is recalled by Borges at the end of "El tiempo y J. W. Dunne" [Time and J. W.
Dunne]: "(Ya Schopenhauer escribió que la vida y los sueños eran hojas de un mismo
libro, y que leerlas en orden es vivir; hojearlas, soñar)" (649) [(Schopenhauer already
wrote that life and dreams are pages of the same book, and that reading them in order is
living; leafing around in them, dreaming)]. I will have more to say about Schopenhauer
in chapter 8 on "Guayaquil."

18 See chapter 2 on "Pierre Menard."

19 More about Valéry in chapter 2.

20 I think Borges is often closer to other Valéry texts than he is to those involving Monsieur
Teste. Monsieur Teste, and his friend and biographer, are so disinterested in "events" that
it could be said that the interest of the "Soirée" and the "Promenade" for students of
narrative is that nothing happens in them. This is quite different from Borges.

21 Similarly, in the essay on Shaw: "El libro no es un ente incomunicado: es una relación, es
un eje de innumerables relaciones. Una literatura difiere de otra, ulterior o anterior,
menos por el texto que por la manera de ser leída: si me fuera otorgado leer cualquier
página actual—ésta, por ejemplo—como la leerán el año dos mil, yo sabría cómo será la
literatura del año dos mil" (747) [A book is not an inert being: it is a relation, an axis of
innumerable relations. One literature differs from another later or earlier literature less in
its texts than in the ways in which these are read: if I were granted the possibility of

reading any current page—this one, for example—as it will be read in the year 2000, I would already know what the literature of the year 2000 would be like]. This reconstruction of the universe from a textual fragment (similar to the archaeological metaphor used in "Pierre Menard" [450]) is as true of historiography as it is of literary criticism.

22 This is also true of the stories. In the new concordance to Borges's stories, the word "historia" appears (in its various senses) 56 times in *Ficciones*, 47 times in *El Aleph*, 31 times in *El informe de Brodie* (most often in "Guayaquil"), and 24 times in *El libro de arena* (mostly in the 1955 story "El congreso"). See Isbister and Standish 3:1170–74.

23 Cf. also the reference to the same Carlyle essay on history (actually published in 1830) in "Del culto de los libros" (716) [The Cult of Books]. For a brief commentary on the Carlyle essay, see my essay on Carlyle and Roa Bastos.

24 Another reference to Schopenhauer's ideas on history is in the essay on Hawthorne: "La mente que una vez los soñó volverá a soñarlos; mientras le mente siga soñando, nada se habrá perdido. La convicción de esta verdad, que parece fantástica, hizo que Schopenhauer, en su libro *Parerga und Paralipomena,* comparara la historia a un calidoscopio, en el que cambian las figuras, no los pedacitos de vidrio, a una eterna y confusa tragicomedia en la que cambian los papeles y máscaras, pero no los actores. Esa misma intuición de que el universo es una proyección de nuestra alma y de que la historia universal está en cada hombre, hizo escribir a Emerson el poema que se titula *History*" (679) [The mind that once dreams them will dream them again; as long as that mind keeps dreaming, nothing will be lost. The conviction that this, which seems fantastic, was the truth, made Schopenhauer, in his book *Parerga und Paralipomena,* compare history to a kaleidoscope, in which the figures change but not the little pieces of glass, or to a confused endless tragicomedy in which roles and masks change but not the actors. This same intuition that the universe is the projection of our soul and that universal history is in each person made Emerson write the poem entitled "History"]. The relevant passage in Schopenhauer is an attack on popular enthusiasm for history by "those who want to learn something without undergoing the effort required by the real branches of knowledge which tax and engross the intellect"; "whoever, like myself, cannot help always seeing the same thing in all history, just as at every turn of the kaleidoscope we always see the same things under different configurations, cannot share that passionate interest, although he will not find fault therewith" (*Parerga* 2: 445).

25 For a collection of Borges's observations on history, see Agheana 165–68. Unfortunately, like nearly everything else in Agheana's "reasoned thematic dictionary" of Borges, Agheana's own formulations are appalling. Here is a sample: "Borges distinguishes two types of history: live history, and past history" (165); "The history of facts is dead history. The operative principle of history is chronology, which Borges finds quite misleading" (165–66); "In virtually all the attempts at elucidating the subject of history there is mention of God" (167). For a further collection of Borges's comments on history, taken from articles and interviews in the popular press, see Stortini 110–11.

26 See Jameson's lucid essay "Imaginary and Symbolic in Lacan" in *The Ideologies of Theory,* especially the following: "It is not terribly difficult to say what is meant by the Real in Lacan. It is simply History itself; and if for psychoanalysis the history in question here is obviously enough the history of the subject, the resonance of the word suggests that a confrontation between this particular materialism and the historical materialism of Marx can no longer be postponed" (1: 104). See also the brilliant works of Slavoj Žižek, *The*

Sublime Object of Ideology and *Looking Awry,* which further explore the question of the real in Lacanian thought.

27   On the larger problem of reference, see Strawson, "On Referring," and Whiteside and Issacharoff, *On Referring in Literature.* Also see Descombes, "The Quandaries of the Referent."

28   The example given in "La postulación de la realidad" of a "circumstantial detail" is a soup pot, mentioned in Larreta's *La gloria de don Ramiro,* "con candado para defenderlo de la voracidad de los pajes" [with a lock on it to defend its contents from the voracity of the pages] (19; qtd. in Borges, *Obras completas* 220). Borges calls this a "memorabilísimo rasgo . . . tan insinuativo de la miseria decente, de la retahíla de criados, del caserón lleno de escaleras y vueltas y de distintas luces" (220) [a very memorable trait . . . so suggestive of the decent misery, the series of servants, the mansion full of staircases and turns and of different degrees of light].

29   In a recent article, Ana María Barrenechea has discussed the repeated description of the old men in the two stories, though her conclusion is rather bland: "Such repetition-with-variants is often vague and circumstantial, yet this fact may make it all the more revealing of Borges's transformational modus operandi" ("On the Diverse Intonation" 19). Another account of Borges's practice of rewriting his own texts, Michel Lafon's *Borges ou la réécriture* [Borges or Rewriting], also notes that these "rewritings" are an important characteristic of his writing but looks almost not at all at the changing contexts in which the variants are inserted. Lafon's project is also radically different from mine here because he hardly ever looks at Borges's sources, a rather curious omission in a book on intertextuality.

30   Another example: the number *fourteen* appears prominently in "La casa de Asterión" [The House of Asterión], where it signifies "infinity" (569n), and in "La escritura del dios," where it signifies the jaguar god in his aspect as ruler of the surface of the earth (León-Portilla, *Time and Reality* 40). For a *reductio ad absurdum* of the usual critical method of searching for repetitions in Borges, see Ferrer 129–32; a three-page comparison of "La casa de Asterión" and "La escritura del dios" yields the startling revelation that fourteen equals fourteen. I will have much more to say about "La escritura del dios" in chapter 5.

31   For a challenging contextual reading of Robbe-Grillet's *La Jalousie,* see Jacques Leenhardt's *Lecture politique du roman* and Jameson's review-essay, "Modernism and Its Repressed; or, Robbe-Grillet as Anti-Colonialist" (*Ideologies of Theory* 1:167–80). On Kafka, see the essays collected by Mark Anderson (*Reading Kafka*). On Beckett, see Theodor Adorno's *Aesthetic Theory* (especially 45–47, 194–96, 220–21, 333, 354, 444). On Eliot, see Wendy Steiner's "Collage or Miracle: Historicism in a Deconstructed World"; I am grateful to María Rosa Menocal for having pointed out the parallels between Steiner's project in this article and my project here.

32   Besides White, Gossman, Barthes, Collingwood, Jameson, de Certeau, Gearhart, and the others mentioned along the way, I have consulted the following authors on the relations between literature and history and related issues: Dominick LaCapra, Paul Ricoeur, Georg Lukács, Michael Riffaterre, Richard James Blackburn, Sande Cohen, Albert Cook, Robert D'Amico, Mark Poster, and Paul Veyne. I have also consulted the volumes edited by Lynn Hunt; Aram Veeser; Jerome McGann; Barbara Kruger and Phil Mariani; Carlos Altamirano and Beatriz Sarlo; Derek Attridge, Geoff Bennington, and Robert Young;

Philippe Desan, Priscilla Parkhurst Ferguson, and Wendy Griswold; and Mike Gane. On the literature/history relation in Latin America, see also the volumes edited by Roberto González Echevarría (*Historia y ficción en la narrativa latino americana*) and myself (*The Historical Novel in Latin America*).

33 Cf. the phrase in "El pudor de la historia" quoted earlier on how easy it is to create such episodes.

2 Menard and His Contemporaries: The Arms and Letters Debate

1 Frow goes on to say: "The point is surely that, once we have disposed of the red herring of authorship, what is at stake is the historicity of a single, verbally self-identical text; what the parable suggests is that 'textual "identity" under changing conditions becomes "difference."' . . . Let me propose, schematically, that every text is marked by a multiple temporality: the time of its production . . . and the times of its reception. . . . The force of this is to build into Marxist theory a fuller conception of the historicity of the text, accounting not merely for its pastness but also for its productive interaction with historically distinct systems" (171).

2 I am well aware of the limitations to the usefulness of "generational" schemes in organizing literary history or structuring critical interpretation (see Soufas 3–31). However, in the case of Pierre Menard, about whom so little is known, a mapping out of the period or context in which Menard operated seems helpful—if only to trace the "simpatías y diferencias" that we can discover between Menard and his fellows.

3 Benda comments on his relations with the journal and with Paulhan and Gide in *La Jeunesse d'un clerc* (314–15).

4 Gérard Genette in an amusing passage in *Palimpsestes* has reconstructed part of Menard's version of the Valéry poem, with the comment: "As with the atomic bomb, it is enough to know that someone has done it to know that the thing is possible" (254). See Chadwick on the metrical scheme of the Valéry poem (49).

5 Valéry explains in one of his diary entries that he introduced the Zeno stanza into the poem "to give this ode the particular character of the meditation-song of an intellectual man, a *culture addict*" (*Monsieur Teste* 151). Anselm Haverkamp comments: "By quoting Zénon, Valéry describes in the repetition of the paradox the paradoxical repetition of second reading that in the act of reading always overshoots the text. The repeated appeal to Zénon thus simulates the continuity of tradition as the very apparent movement that Zénon had rejected: 'Zénon!'; 'Cruel Zénon!' allegorically, 'Zénon d'Elée!' academically (st. 21). Just as Zénon saw continuous motion refuted in repetition, so living movement is postponed in reading. Repeating commonplaces of contemporary discourse, the poem caricatures the futility of the repeated reflections in antique anamnesis and Christian anagogy. Thus it is a pensive pause before the decisive step into life, a step in which the author, in the end, is ahead of the reader" (177–78). It is easy to see the relevance of these observations to Menard's "repetition" of *Don Quixote*.

6 I mention Sorel here although he cannot strictly speaking be considered of the same generation as Benda, Valéry, and Menard. He will be central to my later argument, however.

7 I disagree to some extent with Sylvia Molloy on this point, as she has argued that the "visible bibliography" of Menard's works cannot be made to cohere into a single whole

(*Letras* 54–56). Though this is true enough, it is hard to see how Valéry's essay "Education et instruction des troupes" (1897) [Troop Education and Training] or his "Eléments d'économie politique pure" (1896) [Elements of Pure Political Economy] cohere with "Narcisse parle" (1891) [Narcissus Speaks] or "La Soirée avec Monsieur Teste" (1896) [An Evening with Monsieur Teste]. What is surprising is not the range of topics surveyed by Menard or Valéry in the years before the Great War but the extent to which this was no longer possible by the time of the writing of Menard's obituary in 1939.

8 Carilla, unable to consult the Dresden edition, guesses wrong about which fragment is referred to. The fragment he chooses (from some other edition of Novalis) reads: "It happens in love as in Philosophy: it is (it is supposed to be) everything for each person. It could be said that love is the self—the ideal of every aspiration" (*Jorge Luis Borges* 27).

9 Borges was perhaps one of the first Spanish-speaking writers to take notice of *Ulysses,* and his translation of the last page of the novel has been compared favorably to a variety of more recent translations (Schwartz 143–55).

10 The narrator, of course, not the author. Ferrer forgets this elementary distinction when he observes, apropos of the reference to "Nîmes, 1901" (the place and date of one of Menard's publications in the bibliography): "That Nîmes . . . is as false as that which dates the story at the end. After his accident in 1938, Borges did not leave Buenos Aires. P. Ménard [*sic*] 'a symbolist from Nîmes' proves Borges = P. Ménard [*sic*]" (125n).

11 The original version of the text published in *Sur* in 1939 lacks the final reference to Nîmes. The other significant difference from the text as it appears in *Ficciones* is that in place of the famous reference to palimpsests (in the third paragraph from the end), immediately after the phrase describing Menard's destruction of his drafts ("cuidó que no le sobrevivieran" [he was careful not to let them survive him]), there is the following sentence: "Me dijo, inolvidablemente: *En vida nos toleran los amigos*—c'est leur métier—*pero que un muerto siga requiriendo atenciones . . .*" (16) [He said to me, unforgettably: "While we are alive our friends tolerate us—that is their function—but for a dead man to continue requiring attention . . ."].

12 William James did indeed assert that history is the mother of truth: "The truth of an idea is not a stagnant property inherent in it. Truth *happens* to an idea. It *becomes* true, is *made* true by events. Its verity *is* in fact an event, a process: the process namely of its verifying itself, its veri-*fication.* Its validity is the process of its valid-*ation*" (*Essays in Pragmatism* 161, emphasis in original).

13 In this discussion, I would like to quote directly from Menard's *Quixote.* However, since that book has unfortunately not been preserved (except for twenty-nine words from the ninth chapter), it will be necessary to reconstruct the text from that of Cervantes's *El ingenioso hidalgo don Quijote de la Mancha,* following the archaeological metaphor proposed in the story (450).

14 *Sur,* where "Pierre Menard, autor del Quixote" appeared in 1939, was of course strongly identified with pacifism. See King 60–62.

15 That is, secular pacifism, not dependent solely on religious belief, and often influenced by pragmatism.

16 It should be noted that these essays by Rolland were first published in the *Journal de Genève* in 1914 and 1915, so it is easy to imagine young Borges reading them while they still had the power to scandalize. In a 1937 note on Rolland in *El Hogar,* Borges recalls "una serie de articulos en el 'Journal de Genève'" (*Textos cautivos* 151) [a series of articles in the *Journal de Genève*]. Borges, like Julien Benda, was later to reject Rolland for his sentimen-

talism; the note in *El Hogar* is a model of "el arte de injuriar" [the art of invective], as when Borges writes: "La gloria de Rolland parece muy firme. En la República Argentina lo suelen admirar los admiradores de Joaquín V. González; en el Mar Caribe, los de Martí; en Norteamérica, los de Hendrik Willem Van Loon. En Francia misma no le faltará jamás el apoyo de Bélgica y de Suiza" (150) [Rolland's glory seems very secure. In Argentina he tends to be admired by the admirers of Joaquín V. González; in the Caribbean, by those of José Martí; in the United States, by those of Hendrik Willem Van Loon. In France herself the support of Belgium and Switzerland is never lacking]. (Borges also makes the charge of sentimentalism against Erich Maria Remarque's pacifist novel *Im Westens nicht neues,* published a decade after the end of the war.)

17   I refer to this Remarque novel, which Borges read but did not like, several times in chapter 3 on "El jardín de senderos que se bifurcan." For Borges's disparaging remarks on this book, see *Obras completas* 185 and *Obras completas en colaboración* 492.

18   The original British title was *Principles of Social Reconstruction* (1916).

19   Charvet writes: "The war of 1914 . . . at the outset at least . . . gave a great impetus to Nietzschean influence: life to be lived at a level of intense experience, the search for the deepest sources of energy and power in human nature as a basis, *inter alia,* of new moral values, heroism. The generation that went to war in 1914 was deeply imbued with these ideas and had found their most brilliant expression in the writings of Barrès" (155). Cf. Gibson on the period before the war: "The underlying mood of the nation was essentially anti-intellectual, chauvinistic, and increasingly bellicose. The writers who most accurately expressed this mood and, indeed, helped to incite it were those who, in spite of repeated defeats for the nationalist cause from the Boulanger fiasco onwards, continued to affirm their faith in the Church and the Army and consistently urged their youthful readers to seek in war the surest proof of their manhood. In this respect, the most representative and influential writer of the age was Maurice Barrès" (55). This critic notes, however, that during the war the "bellicose mood was sustained in France, as in each of the other warring nations, by writers too old to fight" such as Barrès (60), and that the most representative writing of the postwar period expressed the "mood of militant pacifism" (68).

20   See Klaus Theweleit's excellent study, *Male Fantasies,* which shows the virulent misogyny and homophobia of the Freikorps writers. Of particular interest is the (con)fusion of the hatred of nurses, Communist women, male homosexuals, pacifists, and Jews.

21   On Lewis, see Fredric Jameson's *Fables of Aggression.* Of particular interest here is Lewis's initial enthusiasm for Hitler, later tempered by skepticism; this is the same pattern one can find in Pessoa and Valéry's feelings about fascist dictators, and apparently also in Menard, especially if the ending of *Don Quixote,* with its renunciation of the profession of arms, is taken into account.

22   Beatriz Sarlo has pointed out in her wonderful study of Buenos Aires in the 1920s and 1930s that Benda was part of the group of anti-fascist writers who attended a 1937 conference in Spain organized by Neruda and others, and that he met a number of Argentine delegates there. She notes that *Sur* at this point invoked Benda's seeming argument of 1927 against the engagement of the intellectual in politics at the same time that Benda himself had transmuted that argument into something quite different (135). For the text of Benda's speech at the writer's conference, see Aznar Soler and Schneider (3: 15–19); the same volume also contains Benda's diary of his ten days in Spain (3: 271–75). In "Le clerc et le politique" (1935) Benda writes: "The mysticism of the left honors

justice and truth. It is beautiful. The mysticism of the right—at least of the right of today—honors force, subordinates truth to the interests of society, resigns itself to 'inevitable' injustice. It is ugly" (*Précisions* 23).

23 One such exponent of an argument for militarism and against pacifism is contained in the "essay on militarism" near the end of a book on the Great War, *Subaltern's War* by Charles Carrington. Carrington makes an interesting admission of the underlying pacifist sentiments in *Don Quixote,* despite the knight's defense of the profession of arms: "That great part of European literature produced under the shadow of the Wars of Religion is infused by this reaction against war, which forms the subject of Don Quixote, and explains the meaning of 'Julius Caesar,' even of 'Henry V,' which is by no means a jingo play. This does not imply that the particular brand of anti-militarism fashionable at the present day can be deduced from Shakespeare or Cervantes, but only that these writers were lovers of peace because they had seen war" (198).

24 But compare this later thought: "The creative impulses in different men are essentially harmonious, since what one man creates cannot be a hindrance to what another is wishing to create. It is the possessive impulses that involve conflict" (259).

25 Russell's concept of "Truth militant" is quite close to Gandhi's ideal of Satyagraha.

26 Cf. Jennings: "Throughout *Réflexions sur la violence* he constantly attacked what he alternatively described as 'the little science' or 'the intellectualist philosophy,' the view that man should act only according to the dictates of his reason, for its inability to understand human motivation" (135).

27 The scholarship on Sorel does not for the most part justify this last assertion of Russell's. Sorel was apparently willing to publish in monarchist publications without adopting the monarchist creed (Jennings 146–52).

28 "Sorel attacked the [Republican] bloc in general and Jaurès in particular. He denounced the 'socialist fanatics' of pacifism and anticlericalism. He did not take issue with an antimilitarism directed against the army as the instrument of a reactionary state, but antimilitarism was not to be confounded with a vulgar and unrealistic pacifism or antipatriotism" (Roth 19).

29 This is hardly a reasonable line of defense, since Valéry abandoned the "traditional eulogy" in his own inaugural address in the French Academy, in which he attacked his predecessor, Anatole France (*Oeuvres* 1: 728–37).

30 His speech on Pétain, "Réponse au remerciement du maréchal Pétain à l'Académie française" [Response to the Thanks of Marshal Pétain to the French Academy], is included in the Pléiade edition (*Oeuvres* 1: 1098–1128). Liddell Hart's account of Pétain's conduct of the defense of Verdun is less favorable to the marshal; he ascribes the success of the French defense to "two great pieces of luck . . . the fortunate destruction of all the German 17-in. howitzers by the French long-range guns, and the blowing up of the great German artillery park near Spincourt, which held 450,000 heavy shell, unwisely kept fused" (*Real War* [1930] 240).

31 Benda, in an acid note on Valéry first published in 1947, "Le cas Valéry: un poète de cour" [The Case of Valéry: A Court Poet], discusses a hymn to Pétain that Valéry published in 1944. He calls attention to the poet's reactionary nature and his hatred for justice and comments: "In the last instance the hymn to the Marshal seems to me to be representative of an essential trait of its author's psychology: the desire to obtain favor from state power" (*Les Cahiers d'un clerc* 239–40).

32 See note 13.

33 Quevedo (in "La hora de todos") also attacks the invention of artillery for having taken away something from the nobility of war, though interestingly he casts the invention of artillery as part of a technological struggle between arms and letters: "Little by little artillery was invented to attack the lives of those who were safe at a distance, lessening the importance of stone masonry walls and giving more victories to the good shot than to the brave man. However, later still the printing press was invented against artillery, lead against lead, ink against powder, canons against cannons" (205).

34 Cf. Horowitz on Sorel's "mock heroic approach to violence": "Sorel was captivated by the legendary Homeric conception of war to such an extent that even modern conflict is made to appear as a logical extension of good manners and dignified breeding. The ghastly features of scientific warfare were, it is true, far from reaching the refined stage of our atomic epoch, but nonetheless the contours of future warfare were clearly etched, even at the turn of the century. Explorations in chemical warfare, aerial bombardments, mechanized battalions were quite well known fifty years ago. Yet Sorel preferred to think in terms of the Greek myths. 'Everything in war is carried out without hatred and without the spirit of revenge.' The sacrifices that war entails at both individual and institutional levels were justified by its cleansing effect on the body politic in general" (123).

35 Cf. Benda: "Nietzsche proclaims that 'every superior culture is built up on cruelty,' a doctrine which is explicitly proclaimed in many places by Barrès, author of *Du sang, de la volupté et de la mort*. Nevertheless, the cult of cruelty, which may also be thought necessary 'to succeed,' has remained limited to a few particularly artistic sensibilities, at least in France" (*Betrayal* 115). Cf. Charvet: "Whether as the egotist of the early works, or the traditionalist and fervent Nietzschean nationalist of later years, the neo-romantic moralist [Barrès] was provided a code of values that exactly fitted a generation" (127).

36 See, for example, this reflection on the disappearance of the blank spaces on the map ("But down there [*là-bas*] there are no more unknown lands, nothing but repetitions of our Europe") in which Barrès—like Conrad later—suggests that "darkness" can still be "made visible" or invented at the fringes of "our" world: "There is no more solitude; there are no more lives that we can invent out of whole cloth. . . . To give some flavor to our overly banal, over-used feelings, we have but one recourse, that of mixing them together: like Spain, to compose for ourselves an intense and contrasting life" (*Du sang* 182).

37 Christopher L. Miller, in his article on French Orientalism in Hollier's *A New History of French Literature,* notes that the route followed by Chateaubriand and later pilgrims was "clockwise around the Mediterranean, to Greece, Turkey, Lebanon, Jerusalem, Egypt, Tunis, and home through Spain" (701), and that Hugo's preface to *Les Orientales* lists the author's Oriental reveries as "Hebraic, Turkish, Greek, Persian, Arab, even Spanish" (700). Oddly enough, Edward Said does not mention the role played by Spain in notions of the Orient in his important book *Orientalism.* Barrès begins the essay "A la pointe extrême d'Europe" [At the Far Edge of Europe] with the words: "To break one's boredom, Spain is a great resource. I know of no other country where life has so much flavor. Spain wakes man from the goodness deadened by modern bureaucracy. There, finally, one can glimpse the fact that human feelings are not limited to two or three strong sensations (love, grief, the assize courts) which are all that are left in our Parisian civilization. Spain is an Africa: she stirs up a sort of fury in the soul like that caused by a chile pepper in the mouth" (*Du sang* 175).

38 It is interesting that the narrator should juxtapose Barrès and Larreta. The French

nationalist and the Argentine ambassador to France were friends, having met in Toledo in 1903. Molloy comments: "A thoroughly strange experience, that which brought together two foreigners in Spain, both searching for their dead, and both somewhat baffled in their quest" (*Diffusion* 22). After this experience, Larreta wrote *La Lampe d'argile* (in French), not published until 1918, while Barrès wrote *Greco, ou le secret de Tolède* (1912). Larreta describes their encounter in Toledo in his prefatory letter in *La Lampe d'argile,* dedicated to Barrès (5–12); he notes that he took a later trip with Barrès—to the French trenches in the Lorraine (10–12). Larreta's best-known work, *La gloria de don Ramiro* (1908), was published in French translation in 1910 (Molloy, *Diffusion* 268).

39   There is reference in the story (446) to a local writer whose work often deals with exotic lands and who—like Menard—appropriates *Don Quixote* and makes it his own: Alphonse Daudet, born in Nîmes in 1840. Menard was a contemporary of Daudet's son Léon, born in 1868, a writer for *L'Action française.*

40   Cf. the narrator's comment on the two versions of *Don Quixote:* "El texto de Cervantes y el de Menard son verbalmente idénticos, pero el segundo es casi infinitamente más rico. (Más ambiguo, dirán sus detractores; pero la ambigüedad es una riqueza.)" (449) [Cervantes's text and Menard's are verbally identical, but the second is almost infinitely richer. (More ambiguous, his detractors will say; but ambiguity is an asset.)].

41   Before, that is, there were intellectuals who thought of themselves as a class or caste or social category; see Brombert 31–33; Schalk 6; and Debray 21–24.

42   Larreta was Argentine ambassador to France during World War I; the Borello article on him in the *Historia de la literatura argentina* includes a photograph of Larreta inspecting the French trenches (3: 61).

43   Oddly, there is no reference to this second European trip in the "Autobiographical Essay," and the account of the first trip (1914–21) includes visits to places that were visited only on the second one. The autobiographical account of the first trip ends: "We returned to Buenos Aires on the *Reina Victoria Eugenia* toward the end of March, 1921. It came to me as a surprise, after living in so many European cities—after so many memories of Geneva, Zurich, Nîmes, Córdoba, and Lisbon—to find that my native town had grown" (223–24). Córdoba and Lisbon were only visited on the second trip according to other accounts; I assume that this was also the case with Nîmes. This is not the only point at which the "Autobiographical Essay" is unreliable; see Rodríguez Monegal, *Jorge Luis Borges,* for numerous other examples (e.g., 160, 161, 163, 255, 257).

44   An interest in graphology marked all of Menard's generation, thanks to the importance of forgery in the Dreyfus affair. See Jeffrey Mehlman, especially the following: "Proust's reference to the 'science' of handwriting points to the fact that the Dreyfus Affair was from the outset obsessed with issues of writing. . . . Writing was for Bertillon [the chief prosecution witness in the first trial] a vanguard 'structuralist' struggle against those 'graphologists' intent on interpreting handwriting as the *expression* of human identity. Against them, in 1897, he posited that identity to be construable in no other terms than *as* the idiosyncrasies of script. What makes his case of particular interest to literary history—and links it more provocatively to that of Freud—is that his endeavors turned into a laboratory for perfecting techniques of textual superimposition" (826). Though Menard does not cite Bertillon in his book on graphology, his *Quixote* benefits from these "techniques of textual superimposition."

45   Rodríguez Monegal (*Jorge Luis Borges* 123) asserts that Pierre Menard is based on the French writer Louis Ménard (1822–1901). This is a good guess, but he has the wrong

member of the family. Our Pierre Menard must be the son or grandson of Louis Ménard, because he has the latter's autographed copies of books by Landry and Barbey d'Aurevilly (II, 31). It should be noted that the accent in the surname is used inconsistently throughout the book.

46 "Writing is the graphic inscription of involuntary gestures in which one can determine in a precise and objective way the following qualities: energy, extension, form, rhythm. All of our gestures always translate our stages of mind. Graphology thus stands on a solid, even a scientific, foundation" (7). The writers whose influence on his "graphology" Menard acknowledges are William James, Lange, Janet, Grasset, and Freud (7).

47 Here a footnote appears in Menard's text, providing a translation of Freud's letter: "'To my knowledge, no one has looked for a bridge between psychoanalysis and graphology. With my highest esteem. Yours: Freud.' Translation of a letter from Freud to Dr. Pierre Menard. Vienna, 20 March 1928" (111n).

48 According to Menard, the Marquis de Sade's handwriting proves that he was not as cruel as his reputation would lead us to believe (129).

49 The arms and letters question will come up again in chapter 4 on "El milagro secreto" and chapter 8 on "Guayaquil." The next chapter considers a story set in 1916, so the matter of the Great War will be central to my argument.

3   The "Labyrinth of Trenches without Any Plan" in "El jardín de senderos que se bifurcan"

1 The Nazis made a still more terrible use of such postcards, sent home from the death camps.

2 A recent example of such a reading, celebratory of Stephen Albert's "multiple worlds" and dismissive of Yu Tsun's successful mission, is Floyd Merrell's discussion of the story in *Unthinking Thinking: Jorge Luis Borges, Mathematics, and the New Physics* (177–82). Slavoj Žižek is rather more interesting in his comments on an analogous problem of "possible worlds." In a discussion of the possible endings of *Casablanca*, he says: "The only answer is, of course, that the experience of a linear 'organic' flow of events is an illusion (albeit a necessary one) that masks the fact that it is the ending that *retroactively* confers the consistency of an organic whole on the preceding events. What is masked is the radical contingency of the enchainment of narration, the fact that, at every point, things might have turned out otherwise" (*Looking Awry* 69). Žižek's observations are more useful than Merrell's in understanding the ways in which Borges creates narrative tension and suspense by playing the beginning ("Todo episodio, en un cuidadoso relato, es de proyección ulterior" [231] [Every episode in a careful story is of subsequent importance]) against the end.

3 I have already written of the importance of the theme of war in the story in an article in *Perspectives on Contemporary Literature*.

4 In his review of Edward Kasner and James Newman's *Mathematics and the Imagination*, Borges writes: "Revisando la biblioteca, veo con admiración que las obras que más he releído y abrumado de notas manuscritas son el *Diccionario de la filosofía* de Mauthner, la *Historia biográfica de la filosofía* de Lewes, la *Historia de la guerra de 1914–1918* de Liddell Hart, la *Vida de Samuel Johnson* de Boswell y la psicología de Gustav Spiller: *The Mind of Man*, 1902. A ese heterogéneo catálogo (que no excluye obras que tal vez son meras costumbres, como la de G. H. Lewes) preveo que los años agregarán este libro amení-

simo" (276) [Looking over my library, I see with surprise that the works that I have reread the most and covered with handwritten notes are Mauthner's *Dictionary of Philosophy,* Lewes's *Biographical History of Philosophy,* Liddell Hart's *History of the World War 1914–1918,* Boswell's *Life of Johnson,* and Gustav Spiller's work on psychology, *The Mind of Man* (1902). This heterogeneous catalogue (which includes works that are no more than mere habits of mine, like the book by G. H. Lewes) will no doubt be supplemented in years to come by this charming book]. This review was published in *Sur* in October 1940, only a year before the publication of the story.

5 Another apparent error is the page number in Liddell Hart. In fact, the earliest published version of the story—in December 1941—has page 252, not 242 (*El jardín de senderos que se bifurcan* 107). Page 252 corresponds with the passage in question only in the first, British edition of *The Real War* (1930). The 1931 U.S. edition of the same book has the reference on page 234; the 1934 British edition of Liddell Hart's *History of the World War, 1914–1918* refers to the rains on page 315; and the 1935 U.S. edition of the *History* also contains the reference on page 315. To confuse matters further, most editions of *Ficciones* refer to page 22 of Liddell Hart, not to 242 or 252.

6 This is the term Kipling uses in *Kim* for the British espionage service in colonial India, a service into which the young hero is initiated in the course of the novel. The "real life" model for the espionage subplot in *Kim* was the life of Richard Francis Burton, as discussed by Edward Rice in his recent biography of Burton (e.g., 5–6, 29–33).

7 The same episode is of course referred to famously in Borges's "Magias parciales del Quijote" (668–69). Although most familiar editions of the *Arabian Nights* (Galland, Burton, and Lane, for instance) do not contain the "regressus" that Borges describes, the German translation of Enno Littmann (commented on at length by Borges in *Discusión*) does indeed contain such a "regressus," and a footnote by Littmann calls attention to it: "This is a separate version of part of the preamble of the entire work; see volume 1, pages 19–22" (4: 365).

8 Note the German interest in the British preparations and the early use of aerial espionage: "On 24th June, wherever you moved along the front you saw lines of the enemy's sausage balloons. In them were highly expert photographers, who snapped the flash of our guns from many angles, while observers noted down all manner of information both for the gunners and the higher command" (Thomas 52). In his discussion of the British bombardment of the German trenches in the last week of June, Liddell Hart holds that the massive bombardment was a tactical error because it removed all elements of surprise (*Real War* [1930] 252). Travers concurs in his recent discussion of the battle of the Somme (e.g., 136, 152) and comments: "What happened at the Somme was really the application of prewar styles of thinking and operating to a technical reality that could not be so easily or quickly mastered" (190).

9 Compare Liddell Hart: "From now onwards the British were to take up the main burden of the western front campaign, and because of this fact alone July 1, 1916, is a landmark in the history of the war" (*Real War* [1930] 248).

10 Frank and Vosburg in their article on the story (534n) note that Wheelock thought that Albert was a city in England, while Stabb placed it in Belgium.

11 See also Murillo 160 and Balderston, "'El jardín de senderos que se bifurcan': un cuento de la guerra" 93–94.

12 For a history of the reception of Sun Tzu in the West, see Griffith's appendix to his translation of *The Art of War.*

13   The product of Tsingtao that is best known now in the West is related to the German occupation—Tsingtao beer.

14   Note the presence of "missionaries" in the narrative that serves as an excuse for German colonialist intervention in northeastern China. The missionary-spy connection that I will allude to later is, alas, too well known to dwell upon here.

15   For an early work of propaganda on the virtues of German colonization in Kiaochow, see Franzius (especially 92–97).

16   Schrecker gives his source on the Deutsche-Chinesische Hochschule as Wilhelm Schrameier, *Kiautschou: seine Entwicklung und Bedeutung* [Kiautschou: Its Development and Importance] 56. The reference in question actually appears on 49–50. See particularly the charming discussion of the school's philosophy: "What is more, it is the most essential core of German culture to offer something to Chinese culture and to stand by their side. China's and German's interests go hand in hand" (50). See also Hans Stange's 1937 article "Die deutsch-chinesischen Beziehungen in Kultur und Wissenschaft" [The German-Chinese Relation in Culture and Science], especially 65–66. The school is also mentioned in Liang's *The Sino-German Connection* (9). As Paul Fussell says, Borges "sometimes gives the impression of knowing everything" (183).

17   The invocation of Goethe as representative of Germany but also of the idea of humanity was practiced not only by the Chinese spy in the story but also by Romain Rolland at the beginning of one of the most controversial books of the war period, *Au-dessus de la mêlée*. In the 1914 letter to Gerhart Hauptmann that opens the book, Rolland says: "Even now, at this hour, I recall the example of the example and the words of *our* Goethe—for he belongs to the whole of humanity—repudiating all national hatreds and preserving the calmness of his soul on those heights '*where we feel the happiness and the misfortunes of other peoples as our own*'" (*Above the Battle* 19, emphasis in original). In his second book of essays on the war, Rolland again refers to the embattled notion of humanity when he evokes the martyrs of the "Human International"—Jean Jaurès, Karl Liebknecht, Rosa Luxemburg, Kurt Eisner, and Gustav Landauer (*Forerunners* 5). In both books there are frequent references to Goethe.

18   Less than two months, that is, if we emend the text to June instead of July (and less than three months if the emendation is not accepted).

19   For more details on the "German Conspiracy," see Dangerfield 155–61, 170, 182.

20   Pearse has been variously regarded as a saint and a poseur. For an assessment of his divided nature (and of his concept of blood sacrifice), see Thornley. A slightly different version of this speech is given in Charles Duff 191.

21   In my discussion of this story in the article "Historical Situations in Borges," I construct a whole fictive genealogy for Madden. If I choose not to do so here, it is in order to restore Yu Tsun and Stephen Albert to their rightful place in the discussion. Clearly the story is centrally concerned with genealogy.

22   Madden also considers the relations between literature and society in his prefaces to *The Literary Life and Correspondence of the Countess of Blessington* (1: 1–2) and to *Life and Martyrdom of Savonarola* (1: vi–vii).

23   See Sylvia Molloy on Manzano's autobiography (*At Face Value* 36–54, especially 44–46).

24   See also Madden's own account of his stay in Cuba, in his *Memoirs* (74–85).

25   However, in the preface to *The United Irishmen* Madden writes: "We have outlived the wrongs that made rebels of these men" (1: xii).

26   See, for example, the several essays, including a most interesting one on Father Las Casas, appended to the biography of Manzano (Mullen 168–205).

27   As with the surprisingly accurate detail of the teacher of English at the Hochschule of Tsingtao, so Stephen Albert's description of himself as a "bárbaro inglés" [English barbarian] (477) has been discovered by Mark Millington to be a variant of "the obviously standard phrase 'Western Barbarians'" (180n), used in the first decade of the twentieth century to describe Western residents in Beijing. Millington comments: "This detail seems to suggest the accurate cultural reference of Albert's phrase" (180n).

28   In his *History of Chinese Literature*, a book dear to Borges, Giles adds a further anecdote about the destruction of the Beijing copy of this enormous work: "On the 23rd June 1900, almost while these words were being written, the Han-lin College was burnt to the ground. The writer's youngest son, Mr. Lancelot Giles, who went through the siege of Peking, writes as follows:—'An attempt was made to save the famous *Yung Lo Ta Tien*, but heaps of volumes had been destroyed, so the attempt was given up. I secured vol. 13,345 for myself'" (296n).

29   Again one thinks of Richard Burton, who pursued a career as a spy at the same time that he studied Arabic, Farsi, and a number of the languages of India, and whose study of languages led to a subsequent career as a diplomat and translator. Burton did not ever learn Chinese or go to China, so he is not the only possible model for Stephen Albert. (Another model is the British paleographer Sir Frederic Madden, though he did not venture into the field of espionage as far as I know; see Balderston, "Historical Situations in Borges" 337–38).

30   "Albert" was of course also the name of the prince consort married to Queen Victoria, who was for a time shunned because of his German origin. No doubt the principal association with Stephen Albert's first name is with the Christian martyr Saint Stephen.

31   The book was published under the pseudonym Charles Edmonds.

32   I quote directly from the appendix "Trench Warfare" in Carrington's *Subaltern's War*, as Leed has quoted with considerable inexactitude.

33   Compare Masefield: "Men going into the lines saw little of where they were going" (88).

34   In an essay on *Don Segundo Sombra*, Borges refers to the sense in Europe that the world had entered "en un período de interminable paz. . . . [D]e esa fiesta fueron excluidos los argentinos; *Don Segundo Sombra* quiere compensar esa privación con antiguos rigores. Algo en sus páginas hay del énfasis de *Le Feu*, y la noche que precede al arreo . . . se parece a la noche que precede a una carga de bayoneta" (*Páginas de Jorge Luis Borges* 186) [into a period of endless peace. . . . [T]he Argentines were excluded from that party; *Don Segundo Sombra* tries to compensate for that lack with older travails. Its pages have something of the impact of *Under Fire*, and the night before the roundup . . . resembles the night before a bayonet charge.]

35   Cf. Murillo: "The *Annals*, keeping in mind Borges' purpose in alluding to them, give us an indelible perspective on an epoch of violence and moral degradation, at the disintegrating center of an empire" (149).

36   Valéry would have been heartened by the sight of the young man reading on the train. In "The Outlook for Intelligence" (1935) he writes: "I shall believe in the teaching of ancient languages when, in a railway carriage, I see one passenger out of a thousand take a small Thucydides or a charming Virgil from his pocket and become absorbed in it, trampling under foot the newspapers and the more or less *pulp* stories" (*History* 152).

37   The poems he translates and comments on include one by Johannes Becher on the sinking of the "Lusitania" ("Antología expresionista" 102) and one by Alfred Vagts on a bomb crater (104–6).

38   There is also a reference to trench warfare in "Rusia": "La trinchera avanzada es en la estepa un barco al abordaje / con gallardetes de hurras / mediodías estallan en los ojos" (*Poesía juvenil* 60) [The farthest trench is a ship to be boarded on the steppe with streamers of hurrahs noons exploding in the eyes]. There are also frequent references in the Ultraist poems to bayonets, airplanes, rifles, blood, wounds, morphine, etc.

39   For the opposite view—that war is about the destruction of the material world—see Elaine Scarry's *The Body in Pain,* especially the interesting discussions of Clausewitz and Liddell Hart.

40   Cf. Liddell Hart, in the epilogue to both editions of his history of the Great War: "We are to-day conscious, above all, of the general effects [of the war] on the world and on civilization. In this mood of reflection we are more ready to recognize both the achievements and the point of view of our late enemies, and perhaps all the more because we realize that both the causes and the course of war are determined by the folly and the frailty rather than by the deliberate evil of human nature" (*History* [1934] 501).

4   Prague, March 1939: Recovering the Historicity of "El milagro secreto"

1   A current joke from Eastern Europe is interesting in that it takes the topos of time travel and uses it ironically to talk about history: "An old man was fishing by a river when he caught a golden fish. The golden fish said, 'Throw me back and I'll grant you three wishes.' The old man thought a minute, then asked to be young again and rich and in love with a beautiful woman. He woke up in a bed with silk sheets in a lavishly decorated room, and the young woman lying naked next to him leaned over and said: 'Wake up, Ferdinand, it's time for the parade.'" I heard the joke in August 1990; the *regressus* to the European situation in 1914 is of course chilling.

2   See also the note on Meyrink in *Textos cautivos* 35–36 and the prefaces to *El cardenal Napellus* and *El Golem (Biblioteca personal* 79).

3   Eighteen of his books are listed in Rudolf Havel and Jiří Opelík's dictionary of Czech literature (153).

4   I should clarify that I do not read Czech either, so my knowledge of this literature is limited to what can be gleaned from literary histories, translations, and indexes.

5   A possible additional source for knowledge of Czech culture is revealed in Borges's "Prólogo" to a collection of stories by Meyrink (*El cardenal Napellus*), where he notes that he knew a Czech baroness, Helene von Stummer, in Geneva during World War I (10). It was the baroness who gave Borges a copy of the recent Meyrink novel "que había logrado, increíblemente, distraer la atención de un vasto público, harto de las vicisitudes bélicas" (10) [which had somehow managed to distract the attention of a vast public, sick of the events of the war]. This remark cannot but bring to mind the "secret miracle" of Hladík's dedication to his work in his last moments, or the narrator's devotion to a translation of *Urne Buriall* at the close of "Tlön, Uqbar, Orbis Tertius" (443).

6   Hašek is mentioned by Max Brod in his biography of Kafka (108). For a good discussion of Hašek, see Cecil Parrott's *Jaroslav Hašek*.

7 For a map of Prague with German names for streets, neighborhoods, the river, and so on, see Gruša 126–27.

8 The life of Kafka by Mailloux refers in some detail to the impact of these changes on the Jewish population of Prague (424–25, 449).

9 The language question comes up twice in Karel Čapek's book of conversations with Thomas Masaryk: Masaryk considers linguistic unity as necessary to the functioning of the modern state (169), yet regards a degree of what he calls "cultural syncretism" as inevitable and gives the example of Germanisms used in the Czech language (173). Interestingly, he does not acknowledge here, nor does Čapek point out, that at the time of their conversations Czechoslovakia was a country in which at least three languages were widely spoken: Czech, Slovak, and German. And though we may laugh at Pierre Menard when he collects verses that depend for their effect on their punctuation (446), it is worth remembering that a struggle went on for seventy years over whether the republic in question should be called "Czechoslovakia," "Czecho-slovakia," or the "Czech and Slovak Federative Republic."

10 For a useful introduction to the cultural life of Prague at the time of Kafka, Hašek, and Čapek, see Ivan Klíma's "Čapek's Modern Apocalypse," the introduction to a new translation of *War with the Newts*. For an examination of the ways Jewish, German, and Czech identities overlay one another in the cases of Kafka and some other Prague writers, see Eisner, especially 12–16, 35–51, 69–72, 76–82, 91–100. The same issues are of course also discussed by Brod, Mailloux, and many others.

11 For recent appreciations of Čapek, see Arthur Miller's foreword and Peter Kussi's introduction to *Toward the Radical Center: A Karel Čapek Reader.* Miller writes: "In the old days his tales were possibly more mystifying than frightening; we were more likely to read him as a charming curio. Now his world is far less outrageous or even improbable. We have evolved into his nightmare. In our time his Faustian conviction that nothing is impossible makes him very nearly a realist" (vi).

12 The game of doubles is taken up in "El milagro secreto" when several items of Borges's own work, including his expressionist poems and *Historia de la eternidad,* are attributed to Hladík, the latter under the title *Vindicación de la eternidad* (510). Also, Hladík is accused of being "judaizante"; in reply to a similar charge by Argentine anti-Semites, Borges wrote his remarkable "Yo, judío" in 1934. That text begins: "Como los drusos, como la luna, como la muerte, como la semana que viene, el pasado remoto es de aquellas cosas que pueden enriquecer la ignorancia. Es infinitamente plástico y agradable, mucho más servicial que el porvenir y mucho menos exigente de esfuerzos. Es la estación famosa y predilecta de las mitologías" (*Ficcionario* 87) [Like the Druses, like the moon, like death, like next week, the remote past is one of the things that can be enriched by ignorance. It is infinitely malleable and willing, much more accommodating than the future and much less demanding of effort on our part. It is the famous and favorite season for my-thologies].

13 The English versions of the works mentioned by Borges bear the titles *The Makropoulos Affair, The Absolute at Large, An Atomic Phantasy: Kratatit,* and *The White Plague.* There are two books on Masaryk: *President Masaryk Tells His Story* and *Masaryk on Thought and Life.* The prefatory note by Paul Selver to the English translation of *R. U. R.* makes reference to another work mentioned by Borges, "Criticism of Words," stating that in that work "his capacity for wit, irony, and satire, is exercised to the full" (viii). The same

preface links the fortunes of Czech literature with that of the new Czechoslovak state: "It is significant that at the period when Czechoslovakia is so triumphantly justifying its establishment as an independent State, Čapek is beginning to obtain for Czech literature, of whose vigorous and progressive spirit he is a typical representative, the world-wide attention which it merits, but of which it has hitherto been deprived owing to the adverse circumstances of its development" (viii). For a profound exploration of the relations between culture and nationalism, see Benedict Anderson's *Imagined Communities*.

14   Klíma comments: "In Čapek's works revolutionaries find themselves side by side with dreamers and explorers, demagogues with people's tribunes and redeemers. All these characters, no matter how different or apparently antagonistic their motives, contemplate changing or improving the world by some momentous act" (xi).

15   Klíma comments: "Čapek doubted that anything posed a greater threat to mankind than uncontrolled Faustian desire. A man who feels equal to the creator labors under the delusion that he can and should make the world conform to his own idea. In reality, he simply ceases to perceive its complexity, disturbs one of its subtle, imperceptible structures, and triggers calamity" (xii).

16   Harkins summarizes the plot of the play and says that it depends on a "typically expressionist" device of a return after death of the ghosts of the Mother's husband and sons. He further states: "The point is that the play is in fact a drama within the Mother herself; it is her own feelings that are in conflict, which the author has externalized as the ghosts of her husband and her sons" (*Karel Čapek* 152). The same plot device is used in Hladík's play, which Borges summarizes with the phrase: "El drama no ha ocurrido: es el delirio circular que interminablemente vive y revive Kubin" (510) [The drama has not occurred: it is the circular delirium that Kubin interminably lives and relives].

17   The only one of the early *ficciones* not to appear in *Sur* was "La forma de la espada" [The Shape of the Sword], which appeared in *La Nación* in July 1942.

18   Bradley provides a good short account of the events leading up to the invasion and of the invasion itself. Greater detail is available in Mamatey and Luža's *History of the Czechoslovak Republic* and in Shiela Grant Duff's *A German Protectorate*. These accounts square with the sparse details of the invasion in the Borges story.

19   This is the opera by Dvořák.

20   One example: Hladík's reactions to his imprisonment, first marked by an obsessive imagination of his own death and later by a refuge in his literary creation, are typical of the reactions to extreme situations studied by Bruno Bettelheim in his well-known writings on the death camps (*Informed Heart* 111–15, 187–235). See also his earlier essay, "Individual and Mass Behavior in Extreme Situations."

21   The story was published only a year after the Wannsee Conference, which was held in a Berlin suburb on 20 January 1942. For details of the Wannsee Conference and the formalization of the "Final Solution," see Davidowicz 136–39 and Gilbert 280–93. The mass killings of Jews and others had already begun before the Wannsee Conference (see Gilbert 240–79), but the scale and organization of the killing changed after January 1942. For a brief account of what happened to the Jews of Czechoslovakia, see Davidowicz 375–79.

22   There are many more such remarks that I cite here. See, for instance, the 1940 essays "Algunos pareceres de Nietzsche" [Some of Nietzsche's Opinions] (*Ficcionario* 143–46) and "Definición del germanófilo" [Definition of the Lover of Germany] (*Ficcionario* 166–68).

23   In "Guayaquil," a story to be considered in chapter 8, the following dialogue takes place between the two historians:

—¿Usted es de Praga, doctor?

—Yo era de Praga—contestó.

Para rehuir el tema central observé:

—Debe ser una extraña ciudad. No la conozco, pero el primer libro en alemán que leí fue la novela *El Golem* de Meyrink.

Zimmermann respondió:

—Es el único libro de Gustav Meyrink que merece el recuerdo. Más vale no gustar de los otros, hechos de mala literatura y de peor teosofía. Con todo, algo de la extrañeza de Praga anda por ese libro de sueños que se pierden en otros sueños. Todo es extraño en Praga o, si usted prefiere, nada es extraño. Cualquier cosa puede ocurrir. (1066–67)

"You are from Prague, doctor?"

"I was from Prague," he answered.

To escape from the main topic of conversation, I observed: "It must be a strange city. I am not acquainted with it, but the first book I read in German was Meyrink's novel *The Golem*."

Zimmermann answered: "It is the only one of Gustav Meyrink's books that deserved being remembered. It's better not to like the others, made of bad literature and worse theosophy. For all that, something of the strangeness of Prague is evoked in that book of dreams that are lost in other dreams. Everything is strange in Prague, or, if you prefer, nothing is strange. Anything can happen."

24   Maurice Leblanc (1864–1941) was the author of various detective novels featuring the detective Arsène Lupin, sometimes in nationalistic competition with detectives from other countries (e.g., Sherlock Holmes). Edward Phillips Oppenheim (1866–1946) was another writer of crime fiction, including such titles as *The Adventures of Mr. Joseph P. Cray*. Baldur von Schirach (b. 1907) was a leader of Hitler Youth, author of such works in the 1930s and 1940s as *Die fahne der verfolgten, Revolution der Erziehung, Die Hitler-Jugend: Idee und Gestalt,* and *Zwei Reden zur deutschen Kunst,* as well as of the much later *Ich glaubte an Hitler* (1967).

25   Boileau, *L'Art poétique* 3.48:

Jamais au spectateur n'offrez rien d'incroyable:

Le vrai peut quelquefois n'être pas vraisemblable.

Une merveille absurde est pour moi sans appas:

L'esprit n'est point ému de ce qu'il ne croit pas. (202)

Never offer anything unbelievable to the spectator: what is true is sometimes not verisimilar. An absurd marvel is for me without attraction: the spirit is not moved by what it cannot believe in.

Though the line quoted is a particularly famous line from Boileau's poetic treatise, the whole passage in which it occurs is of interest as it may have informed Borges's thinking about the fantastic and verisimilitude.

26   See King 64–77, 95–101. Beatriz Sarlo offers a somewhat dissenting view (135, 228–30), though her observation that most of the anti-Fascist writings published in *Sur* were translations of European authors does not affect the point made here about the magazine's political orientation.

27   The clearest example is in "La escritura del dios": "Un hombre se confunde, gradual-
      mente, con la forma de su destino; un hombre es, a la larga, sus circunstancias" (598) [A
      human being is confused, little by little, with the form of his or her destiny; a human
      being is, in the long run, his or her circumstances], but the same idea is present in the dis-
      cussions of "rasgos circunstanciales" or "detalles circunstanciales" elsewhere in Borges's
      work (e.g., 217–18, 220, 498, 509, 612). Borges's disdain for Ortega as a philosopher and as
      a writer is well known.

28   I enjoy Bioy's writing, needless to say, but am interested here in the way in which texts
      bounce off one another. Since Bioy and Borges were so closely associated in the crucial
      period of the composition of *Ficciones* and *El Aleph,* many critics have found Bioy's essays
      and reviews of Borges helpful, though fewer have looked to his fiction for clues to the
      elaboration of Borges's own.

29   Pierre Menard, author of another invisible work, also died in 1939. The coincidence does
      not necessarily signify anything, yet noting it already makes it seem to signify something
      (cf. Barthes, "Reality Effect" 142n).

30   See Ricardo Piglia's novel *Respiración artificial* for an ingenious theory of how Kafka's
      writing is prophetic of the rise of fascism (223–72).

31   Compare Borges's meditations on the same subject in "La supersticiosa ética del lector"
      (202–5) [The Superstitious Ethic of the Reader] and "Sobre los clásicos" (772–73) [On
      the Classics].

5   Cryptogram and Scripture: Losing Count in "La escritura del dios"

1   Edmonson and Tedlock gloss this passage as having not to do with the pre-Columbian
     Popol Vuh but with the reader of it. Edmonson translates: "There was once a manuscript
     of it, / And it was written long ago, / Only hiding his face is the reader of it, / The
     mediator of it" (*Book of Counsel* 7), and glosses the passage with a note that reads: "*Eval u
     vach* 'hidden his/its face.' All the translations say that it is the book that is hidden, but
     grammatically *u* refers to *ilol* 'the reader' " (7n). Tedlock's (later) translation reads: "There
     is the original book and ancient writing, but he who reads and ponders it hides his face"
     (71). It would seem from their comments that a special group of initiates would have been
     trained to read and interpret the hermetic writings, and that this group was driven
     underground, imprisoned, or annihilated after the Conquest. It is not unreasonable to
     suppose that Tzinacán, the Jaguar Priest of the Borges story, was a member of this group.

2   For the polemic, see the volumes edited by Leopoldo Zea (*El descubrimiento de América y
     su sentido actual,* tacitly in favor of celebration) and by Heinz Dieterich Steffan (*Nuestra
     América frente al V Centenario,* with texts by Benedetti, Roa Bastos, Chomsky, León-
     Portilla, Fidel Castro, and others against celebration). See also Vargas Llosa, "Questions
     of Conquest."

3   There is an obvious parallel to the Kabbalah in the treatment of the hermetic writing
     here; see Alazraki, Sosnowski, and Aizenberg. But to call the story "a Kabbalistic quest,"
     as Sosnowski does, seems to beg the question of the Maya-Quiché elements in it.
     Unfortunately, those who use the story to argue for Borges as a "Kabbalistic" writer have
     done so by ignoring the specific matter of the story and by ignoring the phrase in the
     story, "El éxtasis no repite sus símbolos" [Ecstasy does not repeat its symbols]. The task

for those who would argue for the "Kabbalistic" nature of the story would be to integrate the explicit Maya-Quiché context with the possible (or implicit) Kabbalistic substrate.

4 One of the only critics to take the highland Guatemalan setting into account is Jaime Giordano (see especially 110, 115). However, though he makes reference to the Maya context of the story and the *Popol Vuh,* he does not bring those references into his argument. Giordano interprets the story in almost existentialist terms.

5 For one example of such a confusion, see Murillo 203–4. In a paper at the Kentucky Foreign Language Conference in April 1991, Joseph Tyler made the same mistake.

6 Long before the Spanish conquest of the Guatemalan highlands, there was strong Mexican influence there, evinced by the use of Nahuatl place names, Mexican influences on architecture and religion, and a mythical history that ties the history of the Quiché and Cakchiquel elites in with the history of Tula and central Mexico. Coe says, for instance: "Utatlán, the Quiché capital which was burned to the ground by the terrible Pedro de Alvarado, or the Cakchiquel centre Iximché . . . are completely Mexican down to the last detail" (135). Thompson says the ruling elites among the Quiché and other groups claimed to be of Toltec descent (*Rise and Fall* 267) and adds that a full conquest of the Maya by the Aztecs would no doubt have occurred had the Spanish conquest not intervened (268). Pérez Brignoli asserts: "The Mexican presence, very strong at the moment of the Spanish conquest (the recent annexation of Soconusco, the commercial enclave on the Gulf of Honduras, merchant-spies in the principal cities of the Guatemalan plateau), was, however, quite old, extending over several centuries" (37–38). In the period immediately prior to the arrival of Alvarado, Moctezuma sent messengers who demanded tribute, first in 1510, then in 1519–20; on the latter visit, the messengers informed the Mayas of the arrival of the Spaniards on the Mexican coast (Bricker 29; cf. Kelly 133). León-Portilla's map of Mesoamerica in 1519 shows the extent of Mexican penetration in the area ("Mesoamerica before 1519" 35); he adds that Nahuatl had become the lingua franca of the whole region (36). Carmack says in his history of Utatlán: "Strong Mexican influence at K'umarcaaj in the years preceding the Conquest had to some extent Nahuatized the town. Before the Spaniards ever saw the place, it was known in Mesoamerican circles as Utatlán" (143).

7 Or should it be "matrimony"? The Maya world was marked by double lines of descent, both patrilineal and matrilineal, and the simultaneous heritage of the Foremothers/Forefathers is one of the problems faced by translators and commentators who write in a Romance or a Germanic language. See this footnote by Recinos, for instance: "*Ri qui chuch oh quiche vinac,* literally 'the mothers of us, the Quiché.' *Chuch,* 'mothers' here has the generic meaning, as the word 'fathers' has in Spanish, and both are understood as the forefathers" (*Popol Vuh* 170n). In the text above, needless to say, he translated "Foremothers" as "Forefathers" (170).

8 This locution is one of the possible translations of the title of the *Popol Vuh* listed by Recinos in his introduction to the Fondo de Cultura Económica edition of the book (15). See also his discussion of the meaning of the title (83n–84n).

9 In his late poetry there are a few references to Uxmal (*Los conjurados* 39, 41, 44). Much earlier, in a 1945 speech accepting the "gran premio de honor" that the Sociedad Argentina de Escritores had granted him for *Ficciones,* Borges said: "Sueños y símbolos e imágenes atraviesan el día; un desorden de mundos imaginarios confluye sin cesar en el mundo; nuestra propia niñez es indescifrable como Persépolis o Uxmal" (*Páginas de Jorge*

Luis Borges 172) [Dreams and symbols and images traverse the day; a disorder of imaginary worlds comes together endlessly in the world; our own childhood is as undecipherable as Persepolis or Uxmal]. Note the adjective "indescifrable" attached implicitly to the Maya civilization, surely as a result of the difficulty in cracking the glyph system.

10 Though Borges often lauds Reyes for the clarity of his prose, this is certainly not a good example thereof!

11 It is now generally conceded that the Quichés and other late cultures from the period of warring principalities just prior to the Conquest had probably lost some of the knowledge of astronomy and mathematics possessed by the Classic period Maya cultures. In any case, Henríquez Ureña's reference to "Mayas and Quichés" is odd, because the Quichés were one of a number of Maya groups that consolidated their position in the Guatemalan highlands after the breakup of the Classic Maya civilization.

12 Borges's own relation with the Fondo de Cultura became closer later when he and Bioy Casares edited a two-volume edition of *Poesía gauchesca,* numbers 29 and 30 of the "Biblioteca Americana" series directed by Henríquez Ureña (1955).

13 Of course Borges could have been acquainted with any number of earlier translations of the *Popol Vuh,* including the French translation by Georges Raynaud (1925), which was rendered into Spanish in 1927 by Miguel Angel Asturias and J. Manuel González de Mendoza. I choose to emphasize the Recinos translation because it circulated more widely, because Reyes and Henríquez Ureña were involved in bringing it out, and because the material in the footnotes, particularly the name of Tzinacán, seems most pertinent to the story.

14 On the *Popol Vuh,* Vasconcelos writes: "The Popol Vuh is a collection of inept digressions, updated a bit by the Spanish compilers after the conquest who improved on the incoherent verbal tradition, already incomprehensible to the degenerate races that succeeded those other not very capable people who created these monuments" (17). Compare also this later comment in the same work: "Read the *Popol Vuh* with the best possible disposition and you will see that it is nothing more than stuttering about first causes represented by absurd giants, as well as business about the 'discovery of maize' and childish hypotheses about the way the elements function. A magical religion and not the most advanced of its kind" (157).

15 According to Kelly, Ahpozotzil was an honorific title for the Cakchiquel king, not the name of a specific king (132, 134). His book was published in 1932 and could easily be one of the sources for the story. Recinos in his translation of the *Anales de los cakchiqueles* says that an individual named Cahí Ymox was elected Ahpozotzil in 1521 (121) and that this same Cahí Ymox was hanged by Alvarado in 1540 (137). More recent studies differ on whether Ahpozotzil was the name of an individual or an honorific title associated with the Cakchiquel kingship, with Bricker, for instance, sustaining the view that the name is that of an individual (35).

16 The Recinos translation of the *Anales* reads: "Right away a messenger arrived from Tunatiuh [Alvarado] to the Cakchiquel kings asking them to send soldiers: 'May warriors come from Ahpozotzil and Ahpoxahil to kill the Quichés,' the messenger told the kings. Tunatiuh's order was obeyed immediately and two thousand soldiers marched to the killing of the Quichés" (125). The author of the *Anales* adds, though, that some Cakchiquel warriors refused to fight for the Spaniards, and that the only benefit the Cakchiquels derived from the alliance was the privilege to pay tribute to the Spaniards (126).

17 Bricker's source here is Domingo Juarros's *Statistical and Commercial History of the*

Kingdom of Guatemala (434, 441); the English translation dates from 1823. Juarros gives the fullest account of the Cakchiquel revolt that I have found, drawing on a number of colonial sources. It is of interest here that one of Juarros's notes reads: "This cacique [Ahpozotzil] revolted in 1526, and was for a long time detained prisoner in Guatemala; in the books of the Cabildo he is called Sinacam [*sic*]" (452n). Another useful account of the Cakchiquel revolt is included in Recinos's *Pedro de Alvarado* (102–19); this book (published in 1952) was not available to Borges at the time of the writing of the story, but Fernández del Castillo's life of Alvarado (published in 1945) covers much of the same material (64–66, 74–75, 90–91, 118–19).

18 This city, now known as Antigua Guatemala, was of course the town where Bernal Díaz was to write his history of the conquest of Mexico later in the century, as shown in his use of "esta ciudad" [this city] in my earlier quotation from the *Historia verdadera*. For a concise (but old) account of the Cakchiquel rebellion, see Kelly 169–72.

19 On the burning of Utatlán in 1524 by Alvarado, see Las Casas (paraphrased by Bricker 33), López de Gómara (22: 400), and Bernal Díaz (2: 183); for modern discussions, see Carmack 143–47 and Bricker 32. Alvarado himself says in his report to Cortés: "And since I knew that they were so badly disposed toward your majesty, and for the good and peace of this land, I burned them, and I ordered that their city be burnt and destroyed down to its foundations; because it was so dangerous and so strong that it seemed to me more like the home of thieves and not of townspeople" (458). Alvarado's letter, excerpts from Bernal Díaz, and some of the associated Quiché and Cakchiquel material were made available in English (by the Cortes Society!) in 1924, in a volume edited by Sedley J. Mackie.

20 The "balam" here means jaguar, as all of these heroes were members of a jaguar cult. Thus, "Chilam Balam" means "Jaguar Priest." This is made explicit in Maud Worcester Makemson's title for her translation of the Book of Chilam Balam of Tizimín, *The Book of the Jaguar Priest* (1951).

21 The Quiché text goes on to describe the wooden men in terms similar to the description of the "son" in "Las ruinas circulares": "They did not have souls, nor minds, they did not remember their Creator, their Maker. . . . It was merely a trial, an attempt at man" (89).

22 Dreams within dreams are a characteristic plot device in a novel Borges mentions frequently, Meyrink's *Der Golem*. See chapter 4 on "El milagro secreto."

23 The expression here is "mi viejo cuerpo doliente," full of pain not only because of the priest's age but also because of the torture he was subjected to by Alvarado, who wanted information about buried treasure. There is a brief reference to torture of Maya rulers by Alvarado because of stories of buried treasure in the *Anales de los cakchiqueles* (Recinos 128n); however, this account has also been influenced by the story of the torture and death of the Aztec leader Cuauhtémoc. See López de Gómara 413, Bernal Díaz 2: 224, 278, and many other accounts.

24 Tzinacán says: "Urgido por la fatalidad de hacer algo, de poblar de algún modo el tiempo, quise recordar, en mi sombra, todo lo que sabía. Noches enteras malgasté en recordar el orden y el número de unas sierpes de piedra o la forma de un árbol medicinal" (596) [Spurred on by the need to do something, to fill up the time in some manner, I tried to remember everything I knew as I lay there in the darkness. I wasted whole nights remembering the order and number of the stone serpents or the form of a medicinal tree]. The references here are to the great representations of the earth crocodile/snake figure (León-Portilla 57–63) on which rest the cosmic ceibas (León-Portilla 64–65, 74–77) and the human universe.

25 Alazraki has discussed possible Hindu influences on the story (*Borges and the Kabbalah* 46–48), making particular reference to the *Bhagavad Gita*. As with the Buddhist and Kabbalistic readings of this story, I would object that the Hindu material is extraneous to the cultural system of the protagonist, and that the critic's first priority should be to establish the coherence of that cultural system. Parallel mythologies that are not founded on attention to the particulars of a given textual web (in the manner of Frazer, Jung, Campbell, and Cirlot) cannot but fail to aid in understanding the specific details of the text.

26 See my article on Buddhist ideas in *Inquisiciones*, "Octuple Allusion." I make brief reference there to this story (76).

27 In the Rendón introduction to the relevant section of prophetic texts of Barrera Vásquez edition of the Chilam Balam books, there is a general discussion of the "ruedas" [wheels] (91), and the chapter titles used are "First Prophetic Wheel of a Fold of Katuns" (95) and "Second Prophetic Wheel . . ." (124). In the Rivera edition of the *Chilam Balam de Chumayel*, the twelfth chapter is called "La rueda de los Katunes" [the Wheel of the Katuns] (127–37). Edmonson is careful to avoid the word "wheel" and prefers "cycle": "The calendrical battle between the Itza and the Xiu is reflected in two cycles of *katun* prophecies (Barrera's first and second wheels) running from 11 to 13 Ahau. The 'first wheel' is Itza and goes from 1539 to 1824. The 'second wheel' is Xiu. It goes from 1539 to 1677" (*Ancient Future* 22n). He also uses the word "cycle" in his discussion of the Mayapan calendar in *The Book of the Year* (70). In *Heaven Born Mérida and Its Destiny: The Book of Chilam Balam of Chumayel*, however, Edmonson uses the word *wheel* without setting it off in quotation marks (112n).

28 Of course, the number fourteen is also used in "La casa de Asterión" [The House of Asterión] to signify infinity (569). Whatever significance the number may have had in ancient Crete, it surely did not refer to the jaguar there; similarly, there is no reason to assume that the Minoan symbolism would function for the Jaguar Priest. "El éxtasis no repite sus símbolos" [Ecstasy does not repeat its symbols].

29 Barrera Vásquez's edition of the Chilam Balam books says of the fourteenth day of the calendar (Ix): "Ix. Brave jaguar. Mouth bloody. Claws bloody. Butcher. Devourer of meat. Killer" (193), and the introduction to the same book contains an extended discussion of the relationships in the various Maya languages between *ix* or *its* and *balam* (54–55). In turn, Recinos includes a note on the sacred days in the Quiché calendar in his edition of the *Popol Vuh*: "14. *Balam*, tiger" (113n). As Edmonson shows in his comparative study of Mesoamerican calendars, the sacred names of the units of time vary from language to language and culture to culture, but there is a high degree of conceptual consistency.

In a personal communication, Professor Edmonson explained: "In a sense the most interesting element is the numeral 14, because the Maya only counted to 13 in their most fundamental cycle. XIV therefore might represent the end of one cycle and the beginning of another. A Maya would never have said it that way, but then Borges was not a Maya. When you get to the end of the Long Count, do you write 13.0.0.0.0? Or simply 0.0.0.0.0? For most purposes, 14.0.0.0.0 is unthinkable in Maya. In other words, 13 = 0 = 1 = God. I believe that even within the Maya system this always remained the ultimate (and world-destroying or world-creating) mystery" (letter to author, 24 January 1992). Apropos of the other number in the story, he writes: "The fleeting reference to 40 may be because if you are counting 20 day months by 13's, the coefficient for any particular day follows the sequence 1, 8, 2, 9, 3, 10, 4, 11, 5, 12, 6, 13, 7. In other words, the coefficient increases by 1 every 40 days. In a sense, this too is a matter of 14: you gain 7 of every 20, or 14 every 40 days, but since you're only counting up to 13, the 14 becomes 1."

30 In the story, Tzinacán twice makes mention of human sacrifice performed by cutting out the heart of the sacrificial victim (596, 599). This is a custom strongly associated in the popular mind with central Mexico, and some Mayanists have asserted that it was not as common in the Maya area, or that it was a cultural import from central Mexico. Thompson, however, asserts that "sacrifice by removal of the heart was the usual method" (*Rise and Fall* 246; see also *Maya History* 176).

31 The date for this destruction is only a *katun* away as I write this. Michael Coe declares: "Thus, following the Thompson correlation, our present universe would have been created in 3113 BC, to be annihilated on December 24, AD 2011, when the Great Cycle of the Long Count reaches completion" (149).

32 Much has been published in recent years on the development of the European/bourgeois notion of individuality; I have particular admiration for Francis Barker's *The Tremulous Private Body*.

33 Compare also Mercedes de la Garza's discussion of "prophecy" (embracing past, present, and future) in the Chilam Balam books (xxxiv–xxxvi).

34 I am grateful to Munro Edmonson and Rolena Adorno for their careful readings of this chapter.

6 Going Native: Beyond Civilization and Savagery in "Historia del guerrero y de la cautiva"

1 Gossman writes that this episode, called "the memorable fable of the SEVEN SLEEPERS" by Gibbon, underscores the "fundamental connection between irony and history writing" (*Empire Unpossess'd* 74), being marked with "an affectation of surprise at the absurdities of human belief" (75).

2 "In qua Droctulft dux a Langobardis confugerat, seque partibus imperatoris tradens, sociatus militibus, Langobardorum exercitui fortiter resistebat" (Paulus Diaconus 101). Foulke's translation: "Thither [to Brexillus] duke Droctulft had fled from the Langobards and surrendering to the emperor's party, and being joined by his soldiers, resisted bravely the army of the Langobards" (118). Paul goes on to explain that Droctulft, though Swabian, had been taken prisoner and raised among the Lombards, who eventually honored him with the title of duke. He only goes to Ravenna when his band of soldiers was forced out of Brexillus by the Lombard army (118); thus, his "conversion" to "civilization" cannot reasonably be ascribed to his encounter with Ravenna.

3 Foulke's translation of the epitaph reads:
> Drocton [*sic*] lies buried within this tomb, but only in body,
> For in his merits he lives, over the orb of the world.
> First with the Langobards he dwelt, for by race and by nature
> Sprung from Suavian stock, suave to all people was he.
> Terrible to be seen was his face, though in heart he was kindly,
> Long was the beard that grew down on his vigorous breast.
> Loving the standards of Rome and the emblems of the republic,
> Aid unto them he brought, crushing the power of his race.
> Love unto us he bore, despising the claims of his kindred,
> Deeming Ravenna his own fatherland, dear to his heart.

First of all his valiant deeds was the glory of captured Brexillus.
There for a time he remains, dreadful to all his foes.
Later when here his power brought aid to the Roman standards
First within his hands rested the banner of Christ.
Afterwards when Faroald withheld by treachery Classis,
'Fleet-town' in hope to avenge, arms for the fleet he prepares,
Struggles in tiny ships on the flowing stream of Badrinus.
Conquers and overcomes numberless Langobard bands,
Vanquishes also in lands of the East the impetuous Avar,
Seeking to win for his lords victory's sovereign palm.
Often to them as a conq'ror, sustained by the aid of Vitalis,
Martyr and holy saint, honored with triumphs he came.
And in the fane of Vitalis he sought the repose of his body,
Pleased that this place should hold, after his death, his remains
When he died, he implored these things of the priest Joannes,
By whose pious love he had returned to these lands. (119–20)

For the Latin original, see Bethmann and Waitz's edition of Paulus Diaconus, "Historia langobardorum."

4   Some examples of Borges's use of material from Gibbon's tenth chapter: (1) "A través de una oscura geografía de selvas y de ciénagas, las guerras lo trajeron a Italia, desde las márgenes del Danubio y del Elba" (557) [Through a dark geography of forests and swamps, the wars took him from the banks of the Danube and the Elbe to Italy] derives from Gibbon's description of the oozing morass (1: 218), the northern forests and sacred woods (1: 200), and the crossing of the Danube by the Goths (1: 208). (2) "Más congruente es imaginarlo devoto de la Tierra, de Hertha, cuyo ídolo tapado iba de cabaña en cabaña en un carro tirado por vacas" (557) [It is more plausible to imagine him a worshiper of the Earth (Hertha), the veiled idol of which was carried from cabin to cabin in a cart drawn by cows] comes from Gibbon's summary of information from Tacitus: "The unknown symbol of the *Earth,* covered with a thick veil, was placed on a carriage drawn by cows" (1: 200). (Cf. Tacitus 40: 728.) (3) ". . . o de los dioses de la guerra y del trueno, que eran torpes figuras de madera" (557) [or of the gods of war and of thunder, which were clumsy figures made of wood] derives from Gibbon's reference to the "uncouth representations of the three principal deities, the god of war, the goddess of generation, and the god of thunder" (1: 210), though Borges omits the reference here to the fertility goddess and adds information about the material from which the images were made. (4) "Era blanco, animoso, inocente, cruel, leal a su capitán y a su tribu, no al universo" (557) [He was white, energetic, innocent, cruel, loyal to his captain and to his tribe, not to the universe], a statement that errs in giving Droctulft's status in the Lombard army, derives its central ideas from Gibbon's discussion of the difference between stable modern nations and the German tribes, characterized as "voluntary and fluctuating associations of soldiers, almost of savages" (1: 206), whose "love of liberty" (1: 223) leads them to a wild sort of democracy, and from Gibbon's discussion of the personalist leadership exerted by the German generals (1: 196). (See also the more specific information on the Lombard mode of electing a sovereign, 2: 405.) (5) "Quizá le basta ver un solo arco, con una incomprensible inscripción en eternas letras romanas" (558) [Perhaps it was enough for him to see a single arch, with an incomprehensible inscription in eternal Roman letters] derives its force from Gibbon's discussion of the lack of literate

culture among the Germans (1: 190). Similarly, the discussion of Droctulft's possible religious beliefs (557) derives from Gibbon's account of the variety of religious practices among the Lombards (2: 389).

5   See Sylvia Molloy for an admirable discussion of blurring in Borges's portrayal of character (*Letras* 17–48).

6   This racist observation, that such a great writer as Dante could not be a mere Italian, was obviously prompted by the pan-German feelings shared by many Anglo-Saxons before World War I (and by some after it).

7   Gossman's admirable third chapter is entitled "The Vacant Space of the Eternal City" (*Empire Unpossess'd* 49–71). His analysis of the late Roman reverence for the abandoned space of the capital, and of the concomitant crisis of authority and representation, though without reference to the passage I just quoted, has obvious bearing on the question of the definition and claims of "civilization."

8   Though other accounts would have Fanny Haslam born two or three years later, the collection of family photographs organized by Miguel de Torre Borges gives 1842 as her birthdate (5).

9   For an account of Colonel Borges's activities as a frontier commander (less favorable to the colonel than biographies by Gutiérrez, Suárez, and his grandson), see Hux 135–74.

10   In a telephone conversation on 6 August 1991, Borges's sister Norah Borges was unable to confirm the grandmother's story; she claimed not to remember any stories that the grandmother had told them about her married life with Colonel Borges.

11   Before riding to his death, Francisco Borges left the following letter to his friend Juan José Lanusse: "My friend: Tell General Mitre that I die respecting him as I always have; that though I leave a young woman a widow and two tender creatures as orphans, it is a very great comfort for me that I die believing that I have fulfilled my duty and acted in accord with my convictions and with the same principles for which I have fought all my life" (Suárez 13). The same source quotes from Borges's last letter to his wife, in which he asked her "to teach English well to her two little sons" (Suárez 13). Suárez's article was first presented as a speech when Colonel Borges's body was moved to the Recoleta Cemetery in Buenos Aires in 1927, then published in the *Revista Crítica, Histórica, Política y Literaria* (Biblioteca Nacional, Buenos Aires, item 126300). Suárez notes that Colonel Borges's widow, sons, daughter-in-law, and grandsons were present for the ceremony, as well as Mitre's daughter.

12   The story does not make clear the tortuous political dilemma in which Francisco Borges found himself. For this, see Eduardo Gutiérrez's portrait of Colonel Borges in *Croquis y siluetas militares* (37, 45), and even better, the Suárez account, which says that Colonel Borges was troubled by the "doubt of this truly Shakespearean problem" (11) because of his divided loyalties to Sarmiento and to Mitre. There is also a reference to Colonel Borges in Newton's study of Mitre (246); in Urién's study of Mitre there is a reference to Lieutenant Colonel "Francisco Bosch" (93), which must be a misprint for Borges.

13   Compare the last words of the maternal grandmother: "Carajo, basta de sufrir" [Shit, enough suffering] (*Ficcionario* 474).

14   In the article by Suárez, Fanny Haslam de Borges thanks the historian for rescuing the memory of her husband from oblivion after so many years:
Distinguished friend:
I have no words sufficient to express my gratitude and affection for your eloquent speech.

I have followed step by step the life of my husband as you have sketched it so fondly. I have been through very bitter times, but now I owe you such lovely memories that the bad times have been erased.

Thanking you with all my heart, I remain, your friend.

Fanny Haslan [*sic*] de Borges

Buenos Aires, 28 November 1927. (14)

15   Had he lived even a bit longer the family would have been eligible for the ten leagues of land granted to the veterans of the Paraguayan war of 1864–70 (Mafud 200). Borges fought in that war, as is recorded in Gutiérrez; the land grant, however, was not approved until March 1874 and presumably took a while to implement.

16   Estela Canto's version of these events is less favorable to Borges's mother: "Doña Leonor exercised her anti-Peronism among her friends, the ladies with whom she chatted and had tea. A typical woman of her generation, she lacked political consciousness: she hated Perón and Evita because she considered them vulgar intruders who were trying to undermine an order that should have been immutable. She never gave speeches in women's clubs against Perón. Her activity had a domestic character" (92). She goes on to tell of the demonstration on Florida Street; in her account, the event appears to have been spontaneous. When I visited Mariana and Adela Grondona on 12 July 1991, however, the two sisters got into a lively discussion of whether it was in fact so spontaneous. Adela Grondona explained that on the day of the demonstration she had just returned from Stockholm and her sister suggested that they go to Florida Street. Once there, they met up with Norah and Leonor Borges and the others, but according to Adela Grondona everyone else knew what was planned except for her. Her sister, she said, had been plotting with various politicians from the Radical party, as had several of the others. Mariana Grondona did not deny this, and seemed to take satisfaction in having tricked Adela into participating.

17   Besides Grondona's diary or novel *El grito sagrado,* written about this event (and discussed briefly below), in her work *La mujer de la independencia y la independencia de la mujer* [Women during Independence and Independence in Women], Grondona writes:

During a certain evil period in our country's history many women citizens suffered unspeakable highhandedness, persecution and imprisonment, losing their teaching positions, having to go into exile.

After long years of suffering the fatherland asked women once more to be heroic and found them ready: ready to carry documents and messages, to conceal arms, to go out to the streets and the squares. Ready to be imprisoned, absolved, exiled. They were brave when they celebrated the liberation of Paris and the fall of Berlin, chased by the mounted police and by tear gas. The women were brave in 1948 when they sang the national anthem on Florida Street in defense of the 1853 Constitution that Perón was going to reform, among whom I have the honor to appear, spending thirty days in the San Miguel Prison Asylum, condemned by the court of the misdemeanor of "making noise in the street and obstructing traffic." (59–60)

In a footnote, Grondona lists her companions in this adventure: Leonor Acevedo de Borges, Norah Borges de [de] Torre, Raquel Pueyrredón de Lastra, Mariana Grondona de Legarreta, María Elina G. A. de Tomkinson, and two Uruguayans, Amanda and Alsacia Moneta. According to Rodríguez Monegal, the two Uruguayans had come to Buenos Aires to buy shoes (*Jorge Luis Borges* 401).

18   This incident is not discussed in Marifran Carlson's *¡Feminismo! The Woman's Movement*

in Argentina from Its Beginnings to Eva Perón, but Carlson does discuss in general terms the troubled relations between the traditional elite feminist intellectuals (e.g., Alicia Moreau de Justo and Victoria Ocampo) and the new Peronist feminist organizations during the period in question (183–97). It should be noted that the new Peronist constitution that the Borges and Grondona "anti-Peronist ladies" were protesting gave women a number of legal rights (in matters of family and property) that they had not previously possessed (190–91). After a half-century of struggle for women's suffrage, the Perón government had given women the right to vote in 1947 (188–89).

19 In a not very well-argued article, "1872: un año clave en la gestación de la Campaña al Desierto" [1872: A Key Year in the Planning of the Campaign to the Desert], Stella Maris Molina Carlotti de Muñoz Moraleda asserts that 1872 was also crucial in Roca's realization that the only way to deal with the so-called Indian problem was by taking the offensive. She calls it "the year of mental elaboration of the campaign, the year of intellectual planning, the year of becoming conscious of the reality of the Indian and the desert" (108). Interestingly, Roca was the "jefe de fronteras" [frontier commander] in 1872 in Río Cuarto, the same post that Francisco Borges occupied farther to the east in Junín.

20 The Tandil incident served to confirm the opinion of the British consul-general, Mr. Macdonell, who had recommended against British immigration in an 1871 report. This report was published in the *Parliamentary Papers* of 1872 (Ferns 368). For a full consideration of the gaps between the theory and practice of European immigration to Argentina in the nineteenth century, see Fishburn's *Portrayal of Immigration.* For some of the documents from the debates on immigration during the period, see Halperín Donghi's *Proyecto y construcción de una nación* (46–47, 89–103, 295–300, 405–7, 461–63).

21 On this story, see Davi Arrigucci's remarkable essay, "Da fama e da infâmia: Borges no contexto literário latino-americano" [Of Fame and Infamy: Borges in the Latin American Literary Context], which has undoubtedly influenced my project here.

22 The striking description in the second part of "La cautiva," "El festín," to which Iglesia refers, is as follows:

> En torno al fuego sentados
> unos lo atizan y ceban;
> otros la jugosa carne
> al rescoldo o llama tuestan;
> aquél come, éste destriza.
> Más allá alguno degüella
> con afilado cuchillo,
> la yegua al lazo sujeta;
> y a la boca de la herida,
> por donde ronca y resuella
> y a borbollones arroja
> la caliente sangre fuera,
> en pie, trémula y convulsa,
> dos o tres indios se pegan;
> como sedientos vampiros
> sorben, chupan, saborean
> la sangre haciendo murmullo
> y de sangre se rellenan. (15)

Sitting around the fire, some of them stir and feed it, while others toast the juicy meat on the embers or the flames; some eat, others tear the meat in strips. Farther off someone cuts the throat of a roped mare with a sharp knife, and at the mouth of the wound, where the mare wheezes and pants, still standing, trembling and confused, and its hot blood flows bubbling out, two or three Indians, like thirsty vampires, sip, suck, and savor the blood, murmuring, filling themselves with blood.

23   The details of the grandmother's account of the life of the Indians on the pampas are close to those in Mansilla's book. Mansilla gives descriptions of the *toldos* (194), the bonfires (203), the banquets (89, 190), the marches at dawn (236), the raids (305, 370), polygamy (200), filth (273, 359), and magic (224–25).

24   This book is unfairly characterized by Rodolfo Borello as a mere chronicle and work of propaganda (*Peronismo* 178n); in fact it merits critical attention for its fascinating rendering of class conflict among the female prisoners.

25   I have not been able to find this poem in Tomaszewski's published works, and Adela Grondona (in a conversation on 12 July 1991) does not remember where the poem was published, or whether it was published at all; it may never have been published at the time because of the censorship imposed by the regime. It is not included in Tomaszewski's book *Versos de ayer y de hoy*.

26   The conjunction of a story of the Argentine frontier and a story from classical Rome is already suggested by José León Suárez in his tribute to Colonel Borges at the family tomb in the Recoleta:

Happier than almost all of Borges's comrades, his noble consort, who lived for three years in marriage and has lived on for 53 years of widowhood, attends with vigor this act of a noble and spontaneous reparation of justice, after having acted like Cornelia, the wife of Sempronius and the mother of the Gracchi, in preserving the full honor of her husband and in bringing up her sons orphaned so early by the death of their father. And happier, still, than the daughter of Scipio the African, she has prolonged her old age surrounded by the affection and the respect of sons who perpetuate the surname and the virtues of their forebear; and surrounded by the consideration of her contemporaries who, in the midst of the abundant material life of this vertiginous semi-Carthage, have taken an hour of their time to come together before this tomb, to concentrate their spirits on the plane of all that is noble and altruistic and to communicate with the great spirit of Borges, who did not die fighting for paltry interests but struggling for high ideals. (3–4)

Suárez goes on to note, with a trace of xenophobia that is somewhat discordant granted that the noble widow before him is herself a foreigner, that unlike those who came from afar and grew rich in Argentina after the Conquest of the Desert, the old Creole "sons of the soil" are those who profited the least from the nation's progress (4).

27   Andrés Avellaneda has written an eloquent analysis of "La fiesta del monstruo" [The Celebration of the Monster] in his *El habla de la ideología* (77–89) [The Discourse of Ideology]. A less compelling reading is that of Rodolfo Borello (*Peronismo* 148–49).

28   This is what Borges argues in "Déle, Déle." When he tells the story of the interview with the police officer that leads to his resignation from the Miguel Cané Library, he says: "'Tendré que renunciar,' repetí, al bajar las escaleras de la Intendencia, pero mi destino personal me importaba menos que ese cartel simbólico" (*Ficcionario* 224) ["I will have to resign," I repeated, while going down the stairs of City Hall, but my personal fate mattered less to me than that symbolic poster]. He goes on to assert that the writer's

mission includes standing for clarity of thought, against the obfuscations and confusions imposed by society (in this case, by dictatorship), and calls individualism "una vieja virtud argentina" (224) [an old Argentine virtue].

29   Cf. Zea on the encounter between Prospero and Caliban in *The Tempest:* "It is a dialectical encounter in which Prospero has only looked in the mirror, projecting onto the other side of the mirror the expressions of what he, Prospero, is in reality. On the other side is not the monster Caliban, but Prospero himself in his monstrosity" (*Discurso desde la marginación* 254).

30   Monegal's wording is interesting here: "Like so many of her compatriots, [Fanny Haslam] carried the *imperial language* with her. She taught English not only to her son but to her grandson as well. Even her daughter-in-law would eventually be *colonized*" (*Jorge Luis Borges* 16, emphasis added).

31   Fanny Haslam's literary tastes in later life ran to such contemporary writers as Arnold Bennett, Galsworthy, and Wells ("Autobiographical Essay" 206).

32   Elsewhere I have explored Borges's faithful devotion to the genre of the adventure novel (*El precursor velado* 13–41), a taste formed early in life and never renounced, despite the fact that literary fashions had changed. What is intriguing in this regard is the extent to which Fanny Haslam's own (if only briefly) adventurous past would influence her grandson's taste for the adventure novels of Stevenson, Wells, Twain, Conrad, Gutiérrez, and so on. Though I earlier remarked on the linking of references to Stevenson with references to Gutiérrez, it should be noted that the one Hispanic author in the above list was brought in partly because of his sketch of Francisco Borges in *Croquis y siluetas militares,* or so at least says Alicia Jurado, though her reference to Gutiérrez is muddled (28).

7   On the Threshold of Otherness: British India in "El hombre en el umbral"

1   Cf. Bertrand Russell in 1916: "We in England boast of the *Pax Britannica* which we have imposed, in this way, upon the warring races and religions in India. If we are right in boasting of this, if we have in fact conferred a benefit upon India by enforced peace, the Germans would be right in boasting if they could impose a *Pax Germannica* upon Europe. Before the war, men might have said that India and Europe are not analogous, because India is less civilized than Europe; but now, I hope, no one would have the effrontery to maintain anything so preposterous" (*Why Men Fight* 104).

2   I cannot find a published source for this famous quip. Even if it may be apocryphal, Gandhi's attitude toward Western civilization was indeed that it would be a good idea; see Chatterjee's analysis of Gandhi's *Hind Swaraj* (1909), in which Gandhi says that modern civilization is "a civilization only in name" (85ff.). Similarly, in 1920 Gandhi wrote: "By Western civilization I mean the ideals which people in the West have embraced in modern times and the pursuits based on these ideals. The supremacy of brute force, worshipping money as God, spending most of one's time in seeking worldly happiness, breath-taking risks in pursuit of worldly enjoyments of all kinds, the expenditure of limitless mental energy on efforts to multiply the power of machinery, the expenditure of crores on the invention of means of destruction, the moral righteousness which looks down upon people outside Europe,—this civilization, in my view, deserves to be altogether rejected" (Martin Green 5), and in 1924 he wrote: "There is no such thing

as Western or European civilization, but there is a modern civilization, which is purely material" (Iyer 293).

3   The eleventh edition of the *Encyclopaedia Britannica,* the one that Borges knew so well, opens with the following dedication: "Dedicated by Permission to His Majesty George the Fifth King of Great Britain and Ireland and of the British Dominions beyond the Seas Emperor of India and to William Howard Taft President of the United States of America" (1: v). The possession of India is here one of the principal attributes of the British king, indeed it is because of India that "king" becomes "emperor," that "king-dom" becomes "empire."

4   Of the many works I consulted on British India, the best account of the British attempts to shape the colonized people is Francis Hutchins's *Illusion of Permanence.*

5   There are many studies of Kipling's representation of India; I have found particularly helpful those by Rao, Moore-Gilbert, and Paffard.

6   Berveiller has already suggested some sort of relation between Kipling's struggle for an English identity and Borges's own situation when, after commenting on Conrad's internationalism, he says that Borges associates his own case with that of "the Eurasian Rudyard Kipling, for Kipling, having being born an Anglo-Indian in Bombay, therefore wanted to be all the more English [and] was devoted to Englishness. Did not [Borges's] own Argentineness proceed from comparable circumstances?" (271). The problem of Borges's relation to British culture is, however, strangely out of focus in Berveiller's discussion.

7   The narrator is unnamed but seems to be Borges by virtue of his friendship with Bioy and his interest in Kipling and in things British.

8   Another account that makes Nicholson sound almost like a model for Kurtz in *Heart of Darkness* is given by Michael Edwardes in *Red Year.* In addition to further details about the native "worship" of the god "Nikalseyn" (especially 49–50), he gives the text of a song on Nicholson's death (179–80) and a theory on Nicholson's latent homosexuality (see especially 237, note on the "sexuality of imperialism").

9   Collier (246–64) gives quite a full account of Nicholson's last weeks, presenting Nich-olson as a larger-than-life hero. See especially his account of Nicholson's charge on the Lahore Gate of Delhi: "All his life he had subdued both mind and body to his iron will; now it was inconceivable he could not spur other men on the path to glory. His mighty frame fought through the press, until he towered at their head. Eyes blazing, he turned to face them" (261). Hibbert is much more critical of Nicholson's actions at Delhi, which he presents as rash and irresponsible (301–9). A heroic painting of the storming of Delhi by W. S. Morgan shows Nicholson urging his men on with sword upraised (Edwardes 45).

10   For examples of the excruciating tortures that were actually applied, see Majumdar 9: 591–602.

11   Nicholson is shown without the beard in Edwardes, *Red Year* 48. A more heroic image (with beard) is given in Edwardes, *Battles of the Indian Mutiny* 21.

12   The spelling of Nicholson's nickname in the Borges story matches Kipling's (Nikal Seyn) and not the encyclopedia's (Nikalsain), thus suggesting that Kipling is the more impor-tant source here. However, Kipling gives little of Nicholson's story and indeed was reproached by his contemporaries for not writing directly on the Mutiny (Rao 16). His passing reference to Nicholson in *Kim* depends on his readers (including Borges) knowing much more about Nicholson, and about the Mutiny of 1857, than is told.

13   The reference to Oudh in the story is fully as interesting as that to Amritsar, though I

pursue the latter in greater detail here. At the time of the Mutiny, Oudh (or Avadh) was as important a center of unrest as the Punjab, and there were great battles between the insurgent and colonial armies for possession of Lucknow (see Edwardes, *Battles of the Indian Mutiny* 57–149; Hibbert 216–66, 347–66; and Majumdar 9: 536–48, 636–37). During the twentieth-century struggle for independence, Oudh did not take as central a role as it had during the Mutiny, partly due to the cozy relationship between the British and the Nizam of Oudh; see, however, Shahid Amin on Gandhi's activities in the Gorakhpur district of eastern Uttar Pradesh in 1921–22. If Borges's intention, then, is to find a city or region that played an important role in both the Mutiny and the struggle for independence, Amritsar is a much more appropriate choice than Oudh.

14 See Sylvia Molloy's comments on another of these narrative disjunctions, the information in the story that the literature of Uqbar "never referred to reality, but instead to the two imaginary regions of Mlejnas or Tlön" (432): "The story is guided by a description of *one* of the two imaginary regions, brought out of a literature in which they serve, in turn, as referents. Mlejnas is cast aside, already without force in the text" (*Letras* 170). The same technique is used at the opening of "Tema del traidor y del héroe" [Theme of the Traitor and of the Hero]: "La acción transcurre en un país oprimido y tenaz: Polonia, Irlanda, la república de Venecia, algún estado sudamericano o balcánico. . . . Digamos (para comodidad narrativa) Irlanda; digamos 1824" (496) [The action takes place in a stubborn, oppressed country: Poland, Ireland, the republic of Venice, some South American or Balkan state. . . . Let's say (for narrative convenience) Ireland; let's say 1824].

15 Cf. Suleri: "An astonishing development in the narratives of Anglo-India is the rapidity with which the British understanding of the dynamics of Indian civilization atrophied into a static and mistrustful interpretation of India as a locus of all things ancient, a backdrop against which the colonizing presence could not but be startled by its own novelty" (33).

16 On the importance of stereotypes to colonialist discourse, see Bhabha, "The Other Question." Bhabha considers such stereotypes in light of Freudian ideas on fetishism.

17 For further details, see Fischer 179–84 and Dodwell, *Indian Empire* 765–70. One odd note: though Fischer says that the Amritsar massacre was a "turning point" in Gandhi's political development, Gandhi's own writings in 1919 mention it only tangentially, since Gandhi was preoccupied at the time with lapses from the discipline of nonviolence by demonstrators in Ahmedabad. One of Gandhi's few references at the time to the massacre at Amritsar is in a letter to J. L. Massey, dated 14 April 1919: "Though the events at Amritsar are, so far as I can see, unconnected with satyagraha and my arrest, I feel sure that had I been able to proceed to these places [Delhi, Amritsar, and Lahore], the awful occurrences could have been avoided" (219).

18 Amritsar is also mentioned in Kipling's "Miss Youghal's Sais" (in a volume of stories often mentioned by Borges, *Plain Tales from the Hills*) as the site of one of the first adventures of Detective Strickland: "His crowning achievement was spending eleven days as a *faquir* or priest in the gardens of Baba Atal at Amritsar, and there picking up the threads of the great Nasiban Murder Case" (32).

19 This notion of a law distinct from and more powerful than British colonial law seems to derive here, oddly enough, from Kipling, particularly from the *Jungle Books*. See Noel Annan's essay, "Kipling's Place in the History of Ideas," in Rutherford, *Kipling's Mind and Art,* for a discussion of Kipling's concept of law (especially 109).

20 Note that the Punjab was partitioned between India and Pakistan when self-rule came,

and that its place in postcolonial India is still a contested one, as witnessed by the frequent clashes over the issue of Sikh independence or autonomy. The "unity" the story speaks of is purely a matter of historical conjuncture, of opposition to the British Raj when it manifested itself in particularly cruel ways.

21   Cf. Suleri on the lama in *Kim:* "The sale of information and the economy of colonial knowledge . . . is by no means beyond the ken of the 'otherworldly' lama. He not only understands the structure of oppression, but furthermore has an intuitive knowledge of the price that very literally accompanies such a reality" (122).

22   Interestingly enough, Borges's single reference to Gandhi in the *Obras completas* places Gandhi and Chaplin in close proximity: "¿Quién iba a atreverse a ignorar que Charlie Chaplin es uno de los dioses más seguros de la mitología de nuestro tiempo, un colega de las inmóviles pesadillas de Chirico, de las fervientes ametralladoras de Scarface Al, del universo finito aunque ilimitado, de las espaldas cenitales de Greta Garbo, de los tapiados ojos de Gandhi?" (222) [Who dares ignore that Charlie Chaplin is one of the most secure gods in the mythology of our time, a colleague of the motionless nightmares of Chirico, of the fervent machine guns of Scarface Al, of the finite but limitless universe of the zenithal back of Greta Garbo, of Gandhi's covered eyes?]. Louis Fischer's biography includes a photograph of a meeting between Gandhi and Chaplin (276).

23   Nandy studies the same "newly created sense of linear history in Hinduism" (26) in the thought of Swami Dayanand Saraswati and Swami Vivekananda (both active in the late nineteenth century).

24   Chatterjee gives a wonderful account of Nehru's problems in getting used to these mythic formulations (146–57).

25   Besides the review of Chaplin's *City Lights,* there are a few other passing references to Gandhi's life and thought in Borges's works (see Balderston, *Literary Universe* 58), none of them very profound. However, it would have been impossible for Borges and Bioy to be altogether immune to Gandhian influences, because Victoria Ocampo considered herself a Gandhian, published articles in *Sur* and elsewhere on India, and sponsored visits to Buenos Aires by Rabindranath Tagore, Lanza del Vasto, and others associated with the Gandhian movement (see King 34, 60, 103, 138, 179, 197). Borges gives his own impression of Tagore in a funny note in *El Hogar,* which opens: "Hace trece años tuve el honor un poco terrible de conversar con el venerado y melifluo Rabindranath Tagore" (*Textos cautivos* 139–40) [Thirteen years ago I had the rather terrible honor of conversing with the venerated and mellifluous Rabindranath Tagore].

26   In chapter 1 I mentioned that the same phrase is used to describe the old gaucho in "El Sur." Thus, in the broader outlines of Borges's work, the question posed by "El hombre en el umbral" is not only the conflict between East and West but one between traditional (eternal, ageless) cultures and historical ones, and he sees Argentina as also caught up in this conflict. But, as noted before, the same sentence, when inscribed in a different context, can mean quite different things, a lesson we learned from Pierre Menard.

27   Once again, here is Chatterjee: "To Gandhi, then, truth did not lie in history, nor did science have any privileged access to it. Truth was moral: unified, unchanging and transcendental. It was not an object of critical inquiry or philosophical speculation. It could only be found in the experience of one's life, by the unflinching practice of moral living" (97).

28   There is perhaps a hint of envy on the narrator's part for Bioy, who had the means in the 1940s and 1950s to travel, which Borges did not, and perhaps also a note of condescension

for Bioy, who has gone all the way to London to bring back that most *criollo* and most *borgeano* of objects, a dagger! Bioy insisted, by the way, in a conversation in July 1991 that he never bought a dagger in London or anywhere else and says that the whole story, and Christopher Dewey himself, were invented by Borges. I have not been able to confirm Dewey's existence or career by other means; the British Council in London could not grant access to personnel records in April 1991, and later in the same year the British Council in Buenos Aires was still putting its records in order after the renewal of relations between Britain and Argentina.

29 Borges began studying Latin at the Collège Calvin in Geneva ("Autobiographical Essay" 214) and later continued with a priest in Majorca (Jurado 33).

30 For a full discussion of this technique, see Balderston, *El precursor velado* 29–41.

31 Kushigian fails to note the irony of this statement, calling the use of details and local color "two unforgivable offences, personally odious to Borges" (36). Molloy's comments are more to the point: "It should be clarified that the story he reconstructs does not disdain either the brief circumstantial detail or interpolation. The paradoxical invocation names two techniques frequently employed by Borges: perhaps those that provide him—as writer or as reader—the greatest pleasure" (*Letras* 171).

32 There is a large and important body of criticism that explores the subtleties and contradictions of Kipling's attitudes toward the empire, including essays by Edmund Wilson and George Orwell in Rutherford, *Kipling's Mind and Art*, and Rao, *Rudyard Kipling's India*. I do not wish to oversimplify the issues involved in the debates here, but clearly Kipling, even in his more critical moments, was still an apologist for the empire.

33 Note Borges's reservations about Kipling's ethical stance even in this comment on *Kim:* "Kipling inventa un Amiguito del Mundo Entero, el libérrimo Kim: a los pocos capítulos, urgido por no sé qué patriótica perversión, le da el horrible oficio de espía. (En su autobiografía literaria, redactada treinta y cinco años después, Kipling se muestra impenitente y aun inconsciente.)" (733) [Kipling invents a little Friend of All the World, the free spirit Kim; a few chapters later, spurred on by I know not what patriotic perversion, he gives him the horrid profession of spy. (In his literary autobiography, written thirty-five years later, Kipling reveals himself to be unrepentant and even unconscious)]. But compare with this later remark from the *Introducción a la literatura inglesa:* "Cuentista, novelista y poeta, RUDYARD KIPLING (1865–1936) se impuso la tarea de revelar a sus distraídos compatriotas la existencia del dilatado Imperio Británico. Esta misión tiene la culpa de que muchos lo juzgaron, y aún lo juzgan, por sus opiniones políticas, no por su genial labor literaria" (*Obras completas en colaboración* 846) [Short-story writer, novelist, and poet, Rudyard Kipling (1865–1936) set himself the task of revealing to his distracted compatriots the existence of the vast British Empire. This mission has the drawback that many people judged him, and judge him even today, for his political opinions, not for his brilliant literary work]. Note that in the earlier comment, Borges does not rigidly separate aesthetic from political judgments. For Kipling's unrepentant backward view, see *Something of Myself* (e.g., 45, 212).

34 Ludmer is perhaps overly optimistic about the possibilities of communication by the oppressed in a colonial society, and it should be remembered that in the last years of her life Sor Juana sold her library and stopped writing. On a similar limit-situation, see Gayatri Chakravorty Spivak, "Can the Subaltern Speak?" (on widow-sacrifice). Another useful reflection on these issues is R. Radhakrishnan's "Negotiating Subject Positions in an Uneven World." My debt to Radhakrishnan is considerable, since the argument of this

chapter came to me during the presentation of his 1989 Modern Language Association paper on Gandhi and Nehru (now published as "Nationalism, Gender, and the Narrative of Identity").

35   Cf. Nehru: "I used to be troubled sometimes at the growth of this religious element in our politics. . . . I did not like it at all" (qtd. in Chatterjee 151).

36   Sandra Kemp says of Wali Dad that he "speaks and writes in the English tradition but cannot 'live' in it" (22). The phrase that Wali Dad is marking as a quotation from an English author, "Demnition Product," is not actually an exact quotation but a new phrase invented on the abundant models provided by Dickens in *Nicholas Nickleby* for use of the American slang term "demnition" for "damned," "damn," and "damnation." In the Dickens novel, the character Mr. Mantalini, who had changed his surname from the original Muntle in an attempt to make a successful name for himself as a London dressmaker (106–7), uses the words "demd" and "demnition" at least once in almost every sentence he speaks. See, for instance, his use of "demnition miserable" (176), "demnition discount" (365), "the demnition gold and silver" (365), "the same little engrossing demnition captivater" (368), and "demnition sweetness!" (494). In his final appearance in the novel, having "gone to the dogs," he says of himself: "It is all up with its handsome friend! He has gone to the demnition bow-wows" (703). What is interesting in Wali Dad's use of the term is his creative application of Mantalini's word to himself as the Product of a colonial establishment, thus emphasizing the links between a dependent economy and a psychocultural condition.

37   Borges's own contribution to the notion of "postcolonial discourse" is most notable in his 1950 speech "El escritor argentino y la tradición" [The Argentine Writer and Tradition], included in later editions of *Discusión*. For a discussion of the uncanny parallels between this Borges essay and an essay from the 1870s by Machado de Assis, "Instinto de nacionalidade" [The Instinct of Nationality], see Davi Arrigucci. At a conference on Borges at Pennsylvania State University in April 1991, Edna Aizenberg gave a fascinating paper on the appropriation of certain ideas and techniques from Borges in various African and Middle Eastern postcolonial writers; her study of this topic is forthcoming.

38   Another sense of this phrase is given by Kipling's sister, in her memoir of being left with her brother as boarders in England: they felt, she says, "almost as much as on a doorstep" (qtd. in Nandy 66). This phrase reminds us of another context in which people find themselves on thresholds: as foundlings. Note the various displacements suffered in the notion of being "on a threshold" or "in a doorstep." Freud significantly called this sense of estrangement a "liminal state"; see Homi Bhabha, "DissemiNation," for a discussion of how "discursive liminality" is characteristic of modern notions of "writing the nation" (295–97).

39   Compare Borges to Irby (and many other similar declarations in other interviews): "Todo lo que yo he hecho está en Poe, Stevenson, Wells, Chesterton y algún otros" (*Encuentro con Borges* 37–38) [Everything I have done is already in Poe, Stevenson, Wells, Chesterton, and some others]. Chatterjee notes the same concern with imitation in the early Bengali nationalist Bankimchandra Chattopadhyay, who wrote: "One cannot learn except by imitation. Just as children learn to speak by imitating the speech of adults, to act by imitating the actions of adults, so do uncivilised and uneducated people learn by imitating the ways of the civilised and the educated. Thus it is reasonable and rational that Bengalis should imitate the English" (qtd. in Chatterjee 65). Gandhi also acknowledges

the impact of the West, but his analysis does not stop where Chattopadhyay's does: "Everyone of the Indians who has achieved anything worth mentioning in any direction is the fruit, directly or indirectly, of western education. At the same time, whatever reaction for the better he may have had upon the people at large was due to the extent of his eastern culture" (qtd. in Nandy 75).

8   Behind Closed Doors: The Guayaquil Meeting and the Silences of History

1   I am of course aware that Vicente Lecuna calls this the "legend of silence" and asserts that Bolívar in three letters written two days after the meeting said everything there was to say about it (*Catálogo* 2: 249). Lecuna's many writings against this "legend of silence" corroborate my point: that silence is intolerable at the center of a major historical event.

2   The texts of the speeches of both Peróns are printed at the beginning of the first volume of the *Actas del Congreso*. Both are fascinating documents. Eva Perón says: "In all of our acts of homage to San Martín we feel only one sorrow: not to have been there, in 1824, for instance, to force him to stay among us . . . when he decided to leave for exile. We are sorry because had we—the poor shirtless people—been there, we would have done with San Martín what we have done with Perón: saved him from the oligarchy and converted him into the Leader and Director of the newborn fatherland" (1: xlviii). Perón says: "A general becomes; a director is born. A general is a technician; a director is an artist" (1: liii). Later, paraphrasing a famous sentence from "El milagro secreto" discussed in chapter 4, Perón adds: "El arte militar, como los demás, presupone creación, que es la suprema condición del arte" (1: liv) [Military art, like the other arts, presupposes creation, which is the supreme condition of art]. The contrast with the original Borges sentence is instructive: "Hladík preconizaba el verso, porque impide que los espectadores olviden la irrealidad, que es condición del arte" (510) [Hladík preferred verse, because it prevents the spectators from forgetting unreality, which is the condition of art]. Perón cannot resist the emphatic adjective "suprema." Instead of "irrealidad," he writes "creación," instead of "verso," "arte militar." So much for the "arms and letters" debate!

3   Vicente Lecuna, in his *Catálogo de errores y calumnias en la historia de Bolívar,* says much the same thing: "We know of no civilized or barbarous country intent on denigrating the personality of the hero of another nation in order to elevate its own hero, without any solid basis" (2: 309). He refers to what he judges the denigration of Bolívar by Argentine historians and writers but then proceeds to denigrate the character of San Martín (see, for instance, his discussion of San Martín's "taciturn or aloof character, inclined to inaction and misanthropy" [2: 275]), all the while protesting that he—like the Argentine historians he is attacking—is aware of "the great positive virtues of the Argentine hero, denied by no one and admired by all" (2: 283).

4   The one historian of note who writes about the entire controversy with equal praise for the two heroes of the independence wars is the Paraguayan historian Julio César Chaves. He writes, for instance: "We are not partisans or adversaries of either Bolívar or San Martín; we are historians, we are Americans, conscious and proud of the greatness and glory of the two liberators" (9).

5   In the Afterword to the English translation of *El informe de Brodie,* Borges suggests what would be a rather unfortunate fantastic reading of the story: "'Guayaquil' can be read in

two different ways—as a symbol of the meeting of the two famous generals, or, if the reader is in a magical mood, as the transformation of the two historians into the two dead generals" (151).

6   T. McAlindon has perceptively commented: "*Nostromo,* of course, is a novel obsessed with history. . . . Continually, the reader is forced to question his [*sic*] authorities, sift the evidence, and draw his own conclusions—of which the most important is that the past goes on repeating itself" (59). Thus, Conrad requires his reader to treat the material in the novel as unauthenticated documents, to read critically as a historian.

7   Cf. Borges, in his essay on Quevedo in *Otras inquisiciones:* "Como la otra, la historia de la literatura abunda en enigmas" (*Obras completas* 660) [Like the other history, the history of literature is full of enigmas].

8   Halperín Donghi says of the narrator of the story that he "is once again the slightly comic character (due to his hesitant shyness) chosen by Borges to represent himself in his stories" ("La imagen argentina" 138).

9   See the eloquent reference to Colonel Suárez's actions in the battle in "Nueva refutación del tiempo" (762) [New Refutation of Time] and in various poems (including "Página para recordar al coronel Suárez, vencedor en Junín" [Page to Remember Colonel Suárez, Victor in Junín]). In Borges's full name, Jorge *Francisco Isidoro* Luis Borges *Acevedo,* the suppressed names refer to military ancestors: Colonel Francisco Borges (discussed in chapter 6 with reference to "Historia del guerrero y de la cautiva"), Colonel Isidoro Suárez, "el héroe de Junín," and Isidoro Acevedo, whose participation in the battles of Cepeda, Pavón, and Puente Alsina is recalled in a wonderful poem in *Cuaderno San Martín.* For Borges's full name, see Miguel de Torre Borges, *Borges: fotografías y manuscritos* (17). Rodríguez Monegal describes the house of Leonor Acevedo and Jorge Guillermo Borges as a "family museum" dedicated to Borges's maternal ancestors, including a case of their swords and uniforms and daguerreotypes of "a parade of dark, sad gentlemen or reserved ladies, many of them prematurely widowed" (*Jorge Luis Borges* 6). Estela Canto has wonderfully evoked the family museum (102–3), particularly the vainglorious pleasure Borges's mother took in mementos of what Canto calls "some frays between local gangs" (103).

10   The most eminent writer and scholar to have taught at the Universidad del Sur was Borges's friend Ezequiel Martínez Estrada, author of important studies of Hudson, Martí, Horacio Quiroga, and José Hernández.

11   The most violent is still General Ramón Camps's reply to Timerman's *Preso sin nombre, celda sin número,* entitled *Caso Timerman: punto final* (1982), a document remarkable even at the time of its publication for Camps's free use of the transcripts from Timerman's interrogation under torture.

12   To accentuate the similarity to Jacobo Timerman's surname, in what follows I will use the spelling of the historian's name found in *El informe de Brodie* instead of the more usual *Obras completas* version.

13   Halperín Donghi restates the conflict in the story as one in which the Argentine protagonist, notable for his "attractive and hesitant shyness," recoils before "the repulsive spectacle offered by that rival possessed of an immoderate hunger for glory who, by persuading him of the essential vanity of that glory, dissuades him from continuing the contest for it" ("La imagen argentina" 138). He notes that the picture of the rival is colored by the hostile views of Bolívar offered in the works of a whole parade of Argentine historians and comments on the Borges story: " 'Guayaquil' offers a testimony

of the extent to which this stubborn inventor of labyrinths—who was at the same time the quintessential Buenos Aires gentleman—persisted in his simple faith in the image of Bolívar invented in the remote and totally forgotten moment when the republic believed itself to be in danger from the paladin of a revolution that was not its own" (138).

14 In this letter Bolívar does not tell Santander about the Guayaquil meeting with San Martín, since he had already written to Santander about that meeting on 29 July and 3 August (see Lecuna, *Cartas* 3: 58–60, 63–68). In the 13 August letter he does, however, say something of interest on the arms and letters question: "I have never been, nor am I at present, nor will I ever be an administrator. . . . I have no talent for diplomacy; less still for economics; less still for letters. I have been, am now and will always be a military man" (3: 70).

15 He writes: "Releo el párrafo anterior para redactar el siguiente y me sorprende su manera que a un tiempo es melancólica y pomposa. Acaso no se puede hablar de aquella república del Caribe sin reflejar, siquiera de lejos, el estilo monumental de su historiador más famoso, el capitán José Korzeniovski, pero en mi caso hay otra razón. El íntimo propósito de infundir un tono patético a un episodio un tanto penoso y más bien baladí me dictó el párrafo inicial" (1062) [I reread the previous paragraph in order to write the next one and am surprised by its manner, at once melancholy and pompous. Perhaps it is impossible to speak of that Caribbean republic without reflecting, even if from afar, the monumental style of its most famous historian, Captain Joseph Korzeniovski, but in my case there is another reason. The secret purpose of infusing a somewhat painful and rather trifling episode with a note of pathos dictated my initial paragraph]. I will have more to say shortly about the reference to Korzeniovski.

16 Sarmiento writes: "The manner in which European and American writers have treated the history of Bolívar is more appropriate to San Martín and others of his kind. San Martín was not a popular *caudillo;* he was truly a general. He had been educated in Europe and came to America when the government was a revolutionary government, and was able to form a European army freely, to train it and plan regular battles for it according to the scientific laws. . . . But if San Martín had had to lead *montoneras* [guerrilla raids], to be beaten here and then raise another army from plainsmen over there, he would have been hanged on his second try" (*Facundo* 18). Sarmiento adds that historians have not yet found the language that would do justice to the career of Bolívar: "Bolívar is still a story shaped from true facts [un cuento forjado sobre datos ciertos]; Bolívar, the real Bolívar, is still not known to the world, and it is very probable that, when he is translated into his native idiom, he will appear even more surprising and greater than ever" (18). Sarmiento's phrase, "un cuento forjado sobre datos ciertos," might seem an apt description of Borges's "Guayaquil," but for the uncertainties on which Borges founds his story.

17 "Goths" is the Spanish American nickname for the Spaniards at the time of the independence wars.

18 " 'My siege is done': the reply given by René Aubert (1655–1735), abbé of Vertot, when he rejected fresh documentation on the siege of Rhodes brought to him after he completed his account of the event (d'Alembert, *Reflexions sur l'Histoire*)" (Fishburn and Hughes 163).

19 On this topos in Borges's stories, especially in "La forma de la espada," see Balderston, "The Mark of the Knife: Scars as Signs in Borges."

20 There were of course numerous other exponents of each position. I have mentioned only

some of the most famous and most prolific authors who have written on the question. The Masonic lodge in question is the "Logia Lautaro," dedicated to the freedom of Spanish America, to which many of the leaders of the struggle for independence belonged. Apart from the discussion of the lodge in Pérez Amuchástegui, there is a brief discussion of the Masonic angle in Sarmiento (for example, *El general San Martín* 17–19; see also Chaves 92). The title of Rojas's book is *El santo de la espada,* and his account of the Guayaquil meeting puts heavy stress on San Martín's "saintly" renunciation of worldly power after the meeting with Bolívar; San Martín is "a self-sacrificing missionary, without precursors in history, who creates the mould of a new kind of heroism" (240). Lecuna frequently refers to San Martín's physical exhaustion and impatience with Peruvian politics (one such reference to San Martín's "cansancio" is in *Catálogo* 2: 201). In addition to the reference to San Martín in *Facundo,* Sarmiento gives a personal reminiscence of the Liberator in his *Viajes* (239–40).

21   For Sarmiento's speech, see Antonio P. Castro, *Sarmiento en el Instituto Histórico de Francia,* especially 21–25.

22   Horacio Juan Cuccorese, in the proceedings of the conference on the centenary of San Martín's death, refers to "the Venezuelan historian Vicente Lecuna—who is willing to go to any lengths [se desvive] to prove the falsity of the letter of the 29th" (283).

23   Chaves, however, concludes that the Lafond letter is probably authentic (100).

24   A very odd species of forgery, to be sure: a letter by San Martín, dated 1822, forged (Lecuna and Irarrázaval Larraín suggest) by San Martín himself some two decades after the event. A Borges story about a rather similar attempt to correct the past—set not during the wars of independence but during the Uruguayan revolution of 1904—is "La otra muerte" (571–75) [The Other Death].

25   In the story, the former ambassador Colombres *Mármol* becomes the ambassador Dr. *Melaza:* "El doctor Ricardo Avellanos, tenaz opositor del oficialismo, se negó a entregar el epistolario a la Academia de la Historia y lo ofreció a diversas repúblicas latinoamericanas. Gracias al encomiable celo de nuestro embajador, el doctor Melaza, el gobierno argentino fue el primero en aceptar la desinteresada oferta" (1062) [Dr. Ricardo Avellanos, the stubborn antagonist of officialism, refused to release the letters to the Academy of History and offered it to various Latin American republics. Thanks to the praiseworthy zeal of our ambassador, Dr. Melaza, the Argentine government was the first to accept the disinterested offer]. Perhaps marble turned to molasses in the hot tropical sun of Sulaco; more likely, the ambassador's marmoreal appearance was cracked and then melted by the rapid fire of the Venezuelan defender of Bolívar's memory, Dr. Vicente Lecuna. (A portrait of Dr. Lecuna—himself rather marmoreal—appears as frontispiece to the first volume of his *Catálogo de errores y calumnias en la historia de Bolívar.*) In the English translation of the story by Borges and di Giovanni, Dr. Melaza inexplicably becomes Dr. Melaza-Mouton (*Doctor Brodie's Report* 119).

26   The last forty pages of the second volume of Lecuna's *Catálogo* consist of a transcription of the chapter on the Guayaquil meeting in José Miguel Irarrázaval Larraín's *San Martín y sus enigmas,* a work by a Chilean historian who goes even farther than Lecuna himself in impugning the character of San Martín.

27   Compare Irarrázaval Larraín: "And just as blood attracts blood, according to the opinion of tragedians, so an initial fiction generates an endless chain of new artifices" (qtd. in Lecuna, *Catálogo* 2: 355).

28 Waldo Frank, whose 1951 study of Bolívar is heavily indebted to Lecuna, comments on the success of Lecuna's first demolition (by "historical, graphological, orthographical, linguistic, and chemical" tests) of the Colombres Mármol papers, *La Entrevista de Guayaquil: Restablecimiento de la verdad histórica* (1948), and adds: "The book had great success, particularly in Argentina. As I write this footnote, I learn from Dr. Vicente Lecuna in Caracas that the building in Buenos Aires, occupied by the publisher of his book exposing the forgeries, has been attacked and burned by a nationalist mob!" (263n).

29 The verb "entrevistarse" is used to describe Zimerman's meeting with the minister; the noun traditionally used to describe the historical meeting between Bolívar and San Martín is "entrevista," as we have seen.

30 In an interview with Richard Burgin in 1967–68, Borges commented on the Argentine side of the dispute: "You know that we have a national hero called José de San Martín, you may have heard of him, no? The Argentine Academy of History decided that no ill could be spoken of him. I mean he was entitled to a reverence denied to the Buddha or to Dante or to Shakespeare or to Plato or to Spinoza and that was done quite seriously by grownup men, not by children. And then I remember a Venezuelan writer wrote that San Martín, *'Tenía un aire avieso.'* And then Capdevila, a good Argentine writer, refuted him in two or three pages, saying that those two words, *avieso*—sly, cunning, no?—and San Martín, were impossible, because you may as well speak of a square triangle" (30). This interview was published in 1970, the same year that "Guayaquil" was published.

31 In the story, Ricardo Avellanos, "tenaz opositor del oficialismo," refuses to give the letter to the Estado Occidental's own Academia de la Historia, hence Dr. Melaza's initiative to acquire copies of the letter for the Argentine government and the Academia Nacional de la Historia to which the narrator belongs—that of Buenos Aires. Note that the titles of the two academies—"Academia Nacional de la Historia" for the Argentine association, "Academia de la Historia" for the corresponding body in Venezuela or the Estado Occidental—perfectly match in Lecuna's account and the Borges story.

32 Halperín Donghi comments on the war between the academies of history: "The contrast between the two heroes . . . provides the need for choice between them in the mock-heroic epic in which those Argentine institutions and their Venezuelan counterparts exchange ever more strident arguments across the distances of a continent that pays them rather bemused attention" ("La imagen argentina" 136).

33 He says: "Confesar un hecho es dejar de ser el actor para ser el testigo, para ser alguien que lo mira y lo narra y que ya no lo ejecutó" (1062) [To confess a fact is to stop being an actor and to be a witness, to be someone who looks at it and tells it and is no longer the one who carried it out], which implies that his account of the meeting with Zimerman is a private exercise, a purgation, a distancing of the events. But he also says at the end of the story, "Releo estas desordenadas páginas, que no tardaré en entregar al fuego" (1067) [I reread these disordered pages, which I will not delay in casting into the fire], words that are difficult to reconcile with the survival of his manuscript.

34 See, for instance, Juliet McLauchlan's comments on the novel: "Decidedly, then, *Nostromo* does not lack 'actuality,' as has been claimed. . . . [T]he greatness of *Nostromo* is that it quite transcends the limitations of even so fine a political novel as Conrad's own *Under Western Eyes*. . . . By a wonderful fusion of the private and public, the internal and external, by superb embodiment of idea in image, *Nostromo* attains timelessness and universality" (15).

35   Conrad's main sources of information on Latin America were his friends W. H. Hudson
and R. Cunninghame Graham, but in what follows it appears that at the very least he read
Mary Mann's translation of *Facundo* and Carlyle's essay on Dr. Francia.

36   Conrad writes: "It was the same Guzman Bento who, becoming later Perpetual President, famed for his ruthless and cruel tyranny, reached his apotheosis in the popular
legend of a sanguinary land-haunting spectre whose body had been carried off by the
devil in person from the brick mausoleum in the nave of the Church of Assumption in
Sta. Marta" (47).

37   On the secession movement in the Occidental Province of Costaguana, see Decoud:
"Therefore the one and indivisible Republic of Costaguana must be made to part with its
western province" (*Nostromo* 215). In addition, the vote taken under duress in Sulaco on
whether to remain part of Costaguana is similar to the vote taken in Guayaquil under
similar circumstances two days after the meeting between Bolívar and San Martín.
Pedrito Montero, the guerrilla leader who takes Sulaco, tells the town officials: "We shall
organize a popular vote, by yes or no, confiding the destinies of our beloved country to
the wisdom and valiance of my heroic brother, the invincible general. A plebiscite. Do
you understand?" (391). For Bolívar's similar manipulation of the Guayaquil plebiscite,
see his letter to Santander in which he says: "I hope that the Electoral Junta which is
going to meet on the 28th of this month will release us from the ambiguous situation in
which we find ourselves. The decision of the junta will no doubt be in our favor, and if it
isn't, I don't yet know what I will do but my mind is made up. . . . In any case, you know
that there is always some way to do things" (qtd. in Madariaga, *Bolívar* 2: 192). In a later
letter to Santander, dated 3 August 1822, Bolívar writes of his success with his "plebiscite":
"The business of Guayaquil has been decided by acclamation and in the best possible
order. The partisans of independence and of Peru have fled to the Peruvian squadron.
Olmedo was the last to leave me a letter in writing" (Lecuna, *Cartas* 3: 64). Olmedo, the
leader of the Guayaquil "letrados," is best known today as a poet, author of an ode on the
victory of the independence forces at Junín. In 1822 he sided with San Martín but later
chose to celebrate the merits of Bolívar, the only one of the two still on the field at the
time of the penultimate battle against Spain in 1824. For Olmedo's public career, see
Aurelio Espinosa Pólit's introduction to his collected poems (x–xxx). The victory at
Junín is, of course, mentioned in the story, in the description of the "family museum"
with its picture of the cavalry charge led by Colonel Isidoro Suárez (1064).

38   For Conrad's description of the Guajira peninsula, see 4. For the Sierra Nevada de Santa
Marta, see 5–6. The description of the immediate surroundings of Sulaco fits Santa Marta
much better than Guayaquil, though the description of the topography between Sulaco
and the inland capital and the unequivocal references to the Pacific Ocean and the west
coast of the continent (hence the name "Occidental Province") suggest Guayaquil more
than Santa Marta. Borges, by the way, seems to have opted for Santa Marta as the model
for Sulaco, since there are references in the story to "cierta república del Caribe" (1062,
1065) [a certain Caribbean republic].

39   This is the direct reference to Bolívar: "As the great Liberator Bolívar had said in the
bitterness of his spirit, 'America is ungovernable. Those who worked for her independence have ploughed the sea'" (186). See Madariaga's biography of Bolívar for the
Liberator's deathbed speech (2: 527).

40   Madariaga is admittedly not the most sympathetic of Bolívar's biographers, but the event
is reported in other accounts as well. The silver that was taken weighed 27,912 ounces,

according to Madariaga (*Bolívar* 1: 460); see also Madariaga's replies to Lecuna's and Larrazábal's versions of this incident, which Lecuna calls a "ridiculous legend" (*Crónica razonada* 1: 460–65).

41 McAlindon suggests that Conrad's main source for his "philosophy of history" is Carlyle (58, 68), but Schopenhauer's skepticism about history would seem equally germane.

42 Alvin Sherman in his article "Confrontation and the Force of Will in Borges's 'Guaya-quil'" considers the influence of Schopenhauer on this story in general terms with reference to Schopenhauer's treatise *On the Freedom of the Will*. He does not, however, consider the section on history in *The World as Will and Representation* (or *Parerga and Paralipomena*) or the historical background of the story.

43 In *Parerga*, however, he says: "Clio, the muse of history, is as thoroughly infected with lies and falsehood as is a common prostitute with syphilis. It is true that the modern critical investigation of history endeavours to cure this, but with its local means it overcomes only isolated symptoms that break out here and there; moreover, much quackery often creeps in which aggravates the evil" (2: 447). The translator explains that "quackery" (*Quacksalberei*) here puns on "mercury" (*Quecksilber*), completing the metaphor (2: 447n).

44 This is the sentence that Borges recalls in "El tiempo y J. W. Dunne": "Ya Schopenhauer escribió que la vida y los sueños eran hojas de un mismo libro, y que leerlas en orden as vivir; hojearlas, soñar" (649) [Schopenhauer already wrote that life and dreams are pages of the same book, and that living is reading them in order, dreaming, flipping through them]. Compare with Decoud in *Nostromo*: "The house, the dark night, the silent children in this dim room, my very presence here—all this is life, must be life, since it is so much like a dream" (249).

45 In a note on "Isidoro Acevedo," one of the many poems about a military ancestor, Borges writes: "No la puntual veracidad de los hechos, sino su valor representativo, es lo problemático." (*Cuaderno San Martín* 56). The choice of "valor representativo" over "puntual veracidad" is pure Schopenhauer.

46 Sarmiento, in his discourse before the French historians, had already referred to Bolívar's "force of will and obstinacy" (Castro 26).

9 Conclusions

1 For an excellent overview of the entire period in which Laprida was involved in public life, see Halperín Donghi's *Argentina de la revolución de la independencia a la confederación rosista*.

2 Sarmiento writes: "Laprida, the illustrious Laprida, president of the Congress of Tucu-mán, came to me right away and warned me in the friendliest of terms of the danger that was growing from moment to moment. Poor man! I was the last one of those who were capable of esteeming and respecting his merits, to hear that voice which was about to be extinguished forever! Had I followed him, it would not be necessary to lament now for the loss of the man who most honored his land, San Juan, and before whom the most eminent personages of the Republic bowed down, as if to one of the fathers of the country, as if to the personification of that Congress of Tucumán which declared the Independence of the United Provinces. A few steps away they murdered him; rumor has it that the murderers were from San Juan, and for many years the tragic end that befell him that day was not known" (*Recuerdos* 137). See Carilla ("San Martín" 147) on the

parallels between this passage and the opening of the poem; of particular interest is Carilla's footnote (147n) on Borges's rereading of *Recuerdos de provincia* in 1943. See also Mary Mann's account of this episode in the life of Sarmiento she appended to her translation of *Facundo* (322).

3   Of particular interest in the *Vida de Aldao* is Sarmiento's narrative of Fray Félix Aldao's decision—as he is performing the last rites for a dying soldier on a battlefield during the wars of independence—to throw down his cassock and take up the sword (*Life in the Argentine Republic* 238).

4   For Sarmiento's humorous self-portrait during the 1852 campaign against Rosas, see his *Campaña en el Ejército Grande,* particularly the wonderful account of the encounters between the dandified narrator and the stern leader of the army, Justo José de Urquiza (141–42), his frolicking the first time he sees the pampas (139), and his self-aggrandizing act of sitting down and writing at Rosas's desk after the defeat of the tyrant (208–9). Sarmiento is eloquent in his discussion of the relation between "arms" and "letters": "A soldier, with pen or with sword, I fight to be able to write, because writing is thinking; I write as a mode and weapon of combat, because combat is the realization of thought" (61).

5   See Molloy for a discussion of the controversy around Sarmiento's erroneous attribution of this epigraph (*At Face Value* 30–32).

6   For a full discussion of this process, see Stallybrass and White's *Politics and Poetics of Transgression.*

7   One of Borges's most persistent fantasies ("Hombre de la esquina rosada," "El Sur," "El tango") is of dying in a knife fight. See Balderston, "Mark of the Knife" and "Dichos y hechos," for discussions of how this fantasy is rooted in a shared mythology in the River Plate region.

8   See for instance Alazraki's comments at the beginning and end of *Borges and the Kabbalah* (xv, 177).

9   For a curious discussion by Borges of the distance between reality and fiction, see his note on violence in *La Prensa* in 1978, "Los hombres no se miden con mapas" [Men Are Not Measured with Maps]:

> En cuanto al copioso arsenal que ha coleccionado a lo largo de una obra de medio siglo el autor del artículo [Manfred Schönfeld], básteme aclarar que no me identifico con esos armamentos. No he exaltado el "sórdido cuchillo" (el adjetivo es mío) de Juan Muraña; mis milongas de orilleros no son didácticos. No soy ninguno de los dos hermanos Nielsen [*sic*] de *La intrusa.* Acusarme de ello sería como acusar de piratería en alta mar a Robert Louis Stevenson, cuyas hermosas páginas abundan en bucaneros. (9)

> As for the well-stocked arsenal that the author of the article [Manfred Schönfeld] has collected from a body of work written over more than half a century, let me clarify that I do not identify with those arms. I have not exalted the "sordid knife" (the adjective is mine) of Juan Muraña; my songs about thugs from the outskirts are not didactic. I am neither one of the two Nielsen [*sic*] brothers in "The Intruder." To accuse me of that would be like accusing Robert Louis Stevenson of being a pirate on the high seas simply because his beautiful pages abound in pirates.

10   As even Elena Poniatowska observes in a recent interview: "I think that all fiction is based on reality, even that of Borges and Marcel Schwob" (Gazarian Gautier 205).

11   Astonishingly, Lionel Gossman attributes these lines to a modern German poet (*Between History and Literature* 15), giving as his source an article by Hans Blumenberg in the 1968 *Actes du Ve Colloque International d'Esthétique* (330).

12   I simplify of course, but White has not modified his stance much from *Metahistory* and *Tropics of Discourse* to *The Content of the Form*.

13   See *Political Unconscious* 35, 82. I doubt, however, that the sort of reading I have done is quite what Jameson had in mind when he exhorts the critic: "Always historicize!" (9). His only reference to Borges in this work is a note that reads: "The motif of treason, in particular, often expresses the classical anxiety of intellectuals at their 'free-floating' status and their lack of organic links with one or the other of the fundamental social classes: this reflexive meaning is explicit in Sartre, but implicit only in writers like Conrad or Borges" (258n). There is of course an explicit link in Borges between the motif of treason and the position of the intellectual in society: the reference to Benda's *La Trahison des clercs* (an anticipation of the Sartrean position) in "Pierre Menard, autor del Quijote."

14   As Žižek puts it, the "Lacanian real" is "a point that never took place 'in (symbolic) reality,' that has never been inscribed in the symbolic texture, but that must nonetheless be presupposed as a kind of 'missing link' guaranteeing the consistency of our symbolic reality" (*Looking Awry* 120).

Works Cited

Actas del Congreso Nacional de Historia del Libertador General San Martín, 1950. 3 vols. Mendoza: Universidad Nacional de Cuyo, 1953.

Adorno, Theodor. *Aesthetic Theory.* 1970. Trans. C. Lenhardt. London: Routledge and Kegan Paul, 1984.

Agheana, Ion T. *Reasoned Thematic Dictionary of the Prose of Jorge Luis Borges.* Hanover, N.H.: Ediciones del Norte, 1990.

Aizenberg, Edna. *The Aleph Weaver: Biblical, Kabbalistic, and Judaic Elements in Borges.* Potomac, Md.: Scripta Humanistica, 1984.

———, ed. *Borges and His Successors: The Borgesian Impact on Literature and the Arts.* Columbia: University of Missouri Press, 1990.

Alazraki, Jaime. *Borges and the Kabbalah and Other Essays on His Fiction and Poetry.* Cambridge: Cambridge University Press, 1988.

———. *La prosa narrativa de Jorge Luis Borges. Temas. Estilo.* Madrid: Gredos, 1968.

Alonso, Carlos J. *The Spanish American Regional Novel: Modernity and Autochthony.* Cambridge: Cambridge University Press, 1990.

Altamirano, Carlos, and Beatriz Sarlo, eds. *Literatura/ Sociedad.* Buenos Aires: Hachette, 1983.

Alvarado, Pedro de. "Relación hecha por Pedro de Albarado a Hernando Cortés, en que se refieren las guerras y batallas para pacificar las provincias de Chapotulan, Checialtenengo y Utlatan, la quema de su cacique, y nombramiento de sus hijos para sucederle, y de tres sierras de acije, azufre y alumbre." *Historiadores primitivos de Indias. Biblioteca de Autores Españoles,* vol. 22. Ed. Enrique de Vedia. Madrid: M. Rivadeneyra, 1858. 457–63.

Amin, Shahid. "Gandhi as Mahatma: Gorakhpur District, Eastern UP, 1921–2." *Selected Subaltern Studies.* Ed. Ranajit Guha and Gayatri Chakravorty Spivak. New York: Oxford University Press, 1988. 288–346.

Anderson, Benedict. *Imagined Communities: Reflections on the Origin and Spread of Nationalism.* London: Verso, 1983.

Anderson, Mark, ed. *Reading Kafka: Prague, Politics, and the Fin de Siècle*. New York: Schocken Books, 1989.

Arrigucci, Davi, Jr. "Da fama e da infâmia (Borges no contexto literário latino-americano)." *Enigma e comentário: ensaios sobre literature e experiência*. São Paulo: Companhia das Letras, 1987. 193–226.

Attridge, Derek, Geoff Bennington, and Robert Young, eds. *Post-Structuralism and the Question of History*. Cambridge: Cambridge University Press, 1987.

Avellaneda, Andrés. *El habla de la ideología: Modos de réplica literaria en la Argentina contemporánea*. Buenos Aires: Editorial Sudamericana, 1983.

Aznar Soler, Manuel, and Luis Mario Schneider, eds. *II Congreso Internacional de Escritores Antifascistas (1937). Ponencias, documentos y testimonios*, vol. 3. Barcelona: Laia, 1979.

Balderston, Daniel. "Dichos y hechos: Borges, Gutiérrez y la nostalgia de la aventura." *La Torre* (new series) 2.8 (1989): 595–615.

———. "Historical Situations in Borges." *Modern Language Notes* 105.2 (1990): 331–50.

———. " 'El jardín de senderos que se bifurcan': un cuento de la guerra." *Perspectives on Contemporary Literature* 14 (1988): 90–96.

———. *The Literary Universe of Jorge Luis Borges*. Westport: Greenwood Press, 1986.

———. "The Making of a Precursor: Carlyle in *Yo el Supremo*." *Symposium* 44.3 (1990): 155–64.

———. "The Mark of the Knife: Scars as Signs in Borges." *Modern Language Review* 83.1 (1988): 67–75.

———. "Octuple Allusion in Borges's *Inquisiciones*." *Transformations of Literary Language in Latin American Literature*. Ed. K. David Jackson. Austin: Abaporu Press/Department of Spanish and Portuguese, University of Texas, 1987. 75–78.

———. *El precursor velado: R. L. Stevenson en la obra de Borges*. Trans. Eduardo Paz Leston. Buenos Aires: Editorial Sudamericana, 1985.

———, ed. *The Historical Novel in Latin America: A Symposium*. Gaithersburg, Md.: Ediciones Hispamérica, 1986.

Barbusse, Henri. *Le Feu (Journal d'une escouade)*. Paris: Ernest Flammarion, 1916.

———. *Under Fire: The Story of a Squad*. Trans. Fitzwater Wray. New York: E. P. Dutton, 1917.

Barker, Francis. *The Tremulous Private Body*. London: Methuen, 1984.

Barrenechea, Ana María. *La expresión de la irrealidad en la obra de Jorge Luis Borges*. 1957. 2nd ed. Buenos Aires: Editorial Paidós, 1967.

———. "On the Diverse (South American) Intonation of Some (Universal) Metaphors." *Borges and His Successors: The Borgesian Impact on Literature and the Arts*. Ed. Edna Aizenberg. Columbia: University of Missouri Press, 1990. 17–25.

Barrera Vásquez, Alfredo, and Silvia Rendón, eds., intro., and trans. *El Libro de los Libros de Chilam Balam*. Mexico City: Fondo de Cultura Económica, 1948.

Barrès, Maurice. *Du sang, de la volupté, et de la mort*. Paris: Librairie Plon-Nourrit, 1921.

———. *Greco ou le secret de Tolède*. Paris: Emile-Paul Editeurs, 1912.

Barthes, Roland. "The Discourse of History." 1967. *The Rustle of Language*. Trans. Richard Howard. Berkeley: University of California Press, 1989. 127–40.

———. "The Reality Effect." *The Rustle of Language*. Trans. Richard Howard. Berkeley: University of California Press, 1989. 141–48.

Benda, Julien. *The Betrayal of the Intellectuals (La Trahison des clercs)*. French ed., 1927. Trans. Richard Aldington. Boston: Beacon Press, 1955.

———. *Les Cahiers d'un clerc (1936–1949)*. Paris: Editions Emile-Paul Frères, 1949.

————. *La Jeunesse d'un clerc, suivi de Un Régulier dans le siècle et de Exercice d'un enterré vif.* Paris: Gallimard, 1968.

————. *Précisions (1930–1937).* Paris: Gallimard, 1937.

————. *La Trahison des clercs.* Paris: Editions Bernard Grasset, 1927.

Berveiller, Michel. *Le Cosmopolitisme de Jorge Luis Borges.* Paris: Didier/Publications de la Sorbonne, 1973.

Bettelheim, Bruno. "Individual and Mass Behavior in Extreme Situations." *Surviving, and Other Essays.* New York: Knopf, 1979. 48–83.

————. *The Informed Heart: Autonomy in a Mass Age.* Glencoe: Free Press, 1960.

Betts, R. R. "Masaryk's Philosophy of History." *Essays in Czech History.* London: Athlone Press, University of London, 1969. 285–303.

Bhabha, Homi K. "DissemiNation: Time, Narrative, and the Margins of the Modern Nation." *Nation and Narration.* Ed. Homi K. Bhabha. London: Routledge, 1990. 291–322.

————. "The Other Question: Difference, Discrimination, and the Discourse of Colonialism." *Literature, Politics, and Theory: Papers from the Essex Conference, 1976–84.* Ed. Francis Barker, Peter Hulme, Margaret Iversen, and Diana Loxley. London: Methuen, 1986. 148–72.

Billington, Ray Allen. *The Far Western Frontier, 1830–1860.* New York: Harper Torchbook, 1962.

Bioy Casares, Adolfo. "El otro laberinto." *La trama celeste.* 1948. Buenos Aires: Sur, 1970. 101–42.

Blackburn, Richard James. *The Vampire of Reason: An Essay in the Philosophy of History.* London: Verso, 1990.

Bloom, Harold, ed. *Joseph Conrad's Nostromo.* Modern Critical Interpretations. New York: Chelsea House, 1987.

————, ed. *Paul Valéry.* Modern Critical Views. New York: Chelsea House, 1989.

Boileau. "L'Art poétique." *Oeuvres de Boileau avec un choix de notes des meilleurs commentateurs.* Ed. M. Amar. Paris: Librairie de Paris, n.d. 189–220.

Borello, Rodolfo. "Modernismo y narrativa. Enrique Larreta." *Historia de la literatura argentina,* vol. 3. Ed. Susana Zanetti. Buenos Aires: Centro Editor de América Latina, 1981. 49–72.

————. *El peronismo (1943–1955) en la narrativa argentina.* Ottawa Hispanic Studies 8. Ottawa: Dovehouse Editions, 1991.

Borges, Jorge Luis. *The Aleph and Other Stories (1933–1969).* Trans. Norman Thomas di Giovanni with the author. New York: Dutton, 1970.

————. "Antología expresionista." *Cervantes* (1920): 110–12.

————. "Autobiographical Essay." *The Aleph and Other Stories, 1933–1969.* New York: Dutton, 1970. 203–60.

————. *Biblioteca personal (prólogos).* Madrid: Alianza Editorial, 1988.

————. *Los conjurados.* Madrid: Alianza Editorial, 1985.

————. *Cuaderno San Martín.* Buenos Aires: Cuadernos del Plata, 1929.

————. *Doctor Brodie's Report.* Trans. Norman Thomas di Giovanni with the author. New York: Bantam, 1973.

————. "Ensayo de imparcialidad." *Sur* 61 (1939): 27–29.

————. *Fervor de Buenos Aires.* Buenos Aires: n.p., 1923.

————. *Ficcionario: Una antología de sus textos.* Ed. Emir Rodríguez Monegal. Mexico City: Fondo de Cultura Económica, 1981.

————. "Los hombres no se miden con mapas." *La Prensa* 6 September 1978: 9.

————. *El idioma de los argentinos*. Buenos Aires: M. Gleizer Editor, 1928.

————. *El informe de Brodie*. Buenos Aires: Emecé, 1970.

————. *Inquisiciones*. Buenos Aires: Editorial Proa, 1925.

————. *El jardín de senderos que se bifurcan*. Buenos Aires: Ediciones Sur, 1942.

————. *Labyrinths: Selected Stories and Other Writings*. Ed. Donald A. Yates and James E. Irby. New York: New Directions, 1964.

————. *Luna de enfrente*. Buenos Aires: Editorial Proa, 1925.

————. "1941." *Sur* 87 (1941): 21–22.

————. *Nueve ensayos dantescos*. Intro. Marcos Ricardo Barnatán and Joaquín Arce. Madrid: Espasa-Calpe, 1982.

————. *Obras completas*. Buenos Aires: Emecé, 1974.

————. *Obras completas en colaboración*. Buenos Aires: Emecé, 1979.

————. *Páginas de Jorge Luis Borges, seleccionadas por el autor*. Intro. Alicia Jurado. Buenos Aires: Editorial Celtia, 1982.

————. "Pierre Menard, autor del Quijote." *Sur* 56 (1939): 7–16.

————. *Poesía juvenil de Jorge Luis Borges*. Ed. Carlos Meneses. Pequeña Biblioteca Calamus Scriptorius 18. Barcelona: José J. de Olañeta Editor, 1978.

————. "Prólogo." *El cardenal Napellus*. By Gustav Meyrink. Ed. Jorge Luis Borges. Madrid: Ediciones Siruela, 1984. 9–13.

————. *El tamaño de mi esperanza*. Buenos Aires: Editorial Proa, 1926.

————. *Textos cautivos: Ensayos y reseñas en El Hogar (1936–1939)*. Ed. Enrique Sacerio-Garí and Emir Rodríguez Monegal. Barcelona: Tusquets, 1986.

Borges, Jorge Luis, and Adolfo Bioy Casares, eds. and intro. *Poesía gauchesca*. 2 vols. Mexico City: Fondo de Cultura Económica, 1955.

Boswell, James. *Boswell's Life of Johnson*. Ed. Chauncey Brewster Tinker. 2 vols. New York: Oxford University Press, 1933.

Bradley, J. F. N. *Czechoslovakia*. Edinburgh: Edinburgh University Press, 1971.

Bricker, Victoria Reifler. *The Indian Christ, the Indian King: The Historical Substrate of Maya Myth and Ritual*. Austin: University of Texas Press, 1981.

Britton, R. K. "History, Myth, and Archetype in Borges's View of Argentina." *Modern Language Review* 74.3 (1979): 607–16.

Brod, Max. *Franz Kafka: Eine Biographie (Erinnerungen und Dokumente)*. 1937. New York: Schocken Books, 1946.

Brombert, Victor. *The Intellectual Hero: Studies in the French Novel, 1880–1955*. Philadelphia: J. B. Lippincott, 1961.

Burgin, Richard. *Conversations with Jorge Luis Borges*. New York: Avon Books, 1970.

Butler, Arthur John. "Dante." *Encyclopaedia Britannica*, vol. 7. New York: Encyclopaedia Britannica Company, 1910. 810–17.

Camps, Ramón J. A. *Caso Timerman: punto final*. Buenos Aires: Tribuna Abierta, 1982.

Canto, Estela. *Borges a contraluz*. Madrid: Espasa Calpe, 1989.

Čapek, Karel. *Intimate Things*. Trans. Dora Round. London: George Allen and Unwin, 1935.

————. *Masaryk on Thought and Life: Conversations with Karel Čapek*. Trans. M. and R. Weatherall. New York: Macmillan, 1938.

————. *The Mother: A Play in Three Acts*. Trans. Paul Selver. London: George Allen and Unwin, 1939.

————. *R. U. R. (Rossum's Universal Robots): A Fantastic Melodrama*. Trans. and intro. Paul Selver. Garden City, N.Y.: Doubleday, Page, 1923.

———. *Toward the Radical Center: A Karel Čapek Reader.* Ed. and intro. Peter Kussi. Foreword by Arthur Miller. Highland Park, N.J.: Catbird Press, 1990.

———. *War with the Newts.* Intro. Ivan Klíma. Trans. M. and R. Weatherall. Evanston, Ill.: Northwestern University Press, 1985.

Carilla, Emilio. *Jorge Luis Borges, autor de "Pierre Ménard" (y otros estudios borgesianos).* Publicaciones del Instituto Caro y Cuervo 85. Bogotá: Instituto Caro y Cuervo, 1989.

———. "San Martín: Sus mensajes de historia. La personalidad moral." *Actas del Congreso Nacional de Historia del Libertador General San Martín, 1950.* Mendoza: Universidad Nacional de Cuyo, 1953. 463–502.

Carlson, Marifran. *¡Feminismo! The Woman's Movement in Argentina from Its Beginnings to Eva Perón.* Chicago: Academy Chicago Publishers, 1988.

Carmack, Robert M. *The Quiché Mayas of Utatlán: The Evolution of a Highland Guatemala Kingdom.* Norman: University of Oklahoma Press, 1981.

Carrington, Charles [pseud. Charles Edmonds]. *A Subaltern's War, Being a Memoir of the Great War from the Point of View of a Romantic Young Man, with Candid Accounts of Two Particular Battles, Written Shortly after They Occurred, and an Essay on Militarism.* London: Peter Davies, 1929.

Castro, Antonio P., ed. and intro. *Sarmiento en el Instituto Histórico de Francia. Discurso sobre San Martín y Bolívar: Reproducción facsimilar.* Facsimile of *Discurso presentado para su recepción en el Instituto Istórico de Francia por D. F. Sarmiento.* 1848. Buenos Aires: Museo Histórico Sarmiento, 1951.

Cédola, Estela. *Borges o la coincidencia de los opuestos.* Buenos Aires: Editorial Universitaria de Buenos Aires, 1987.

Certeau, Michel de. *The Writing of History.* Trans. Tom Conley. New York: Columbia University Press, 1990.

Cervantes Saavedra, Miguel de. *Don Quijote de la Mancha.* Ed. Martín de Riquer. 2 vols. Barcelona: Editorial Juventud, 1968.

Chadwick, C. "Paul Valéry." *The Twentieth Century. French Literature and Its Background,* vol. 6. Ed. John Cruickshank. London: Oxford University Press, 1970. 41–54.

Charvet, P. E. *The Nineteenth and Twentieth Centuries, 1870–1940. A Literary History of France,* vol. 5. Ed. P. E. Charvet. London: Ernest Benn, 1967.

Chatterjee, Partha. *Nationalist Thought and the Colonial World: A Derivative Discourse?* London: Zed Press, 1986.

Chaves, Julio César. *La Entrevista de Guayaquil.* Buenos Aires: Editorial Universitaria de Buenos Aires, 1965.

Chávez, Fermín. *Civilización y barbarie en la cultura argentina.* 1956. 2nd ed. Buenos Aires: Ediciones Theoría, 1965.

Chirol, Valentine. "China: History from 1875 to 1902." *Encyclopaedia Britannica,* vol. 6. New York: Encyclopaedia Britannica Company, 1910. 200–207.

Christ, Ronald. *The Narrow Act: Borges' Act of Allusion.* New York: New York University Press, 1969.

Clemens, Samuel Langhorne [pseud. Mark Twain]. *Adventures of Huckleberry Finn.* Norton Critical Edition. Ed. Sculley Bradley, Richmond Croom Beatty, and E. Hudson Long. New York: W. W. Norton, 1962.

Coe, Michael D. *The Maya.* Ancient Peoples and Places 52. New York: Frederick A. Praeger, 1966.

Cohen, Sande. *Historical Culture: On the Recoding of an Academic Discipline*. Berkeley: University of California Press, 1986.

Colbrook, E. W., ed. *Odhams' A.B.C. of the Great War*. London: Odhams Limited, 1919.

Collier, Richard. *The Great Indian Mutiny: A Dramatic Account of the Sepoy Rebellion*. New York: E. P. Dutton, 1964.

Collingwood, R. G. *The Idea of History*. Oxford: Clarendon Press, 1946.

Colombres Mármol, Eduardo L., ed. *San Martín y Bolívar en la Entrevista de Guayaquil a la luz de documentos definitivos*. Intro. Rómulo D. Carbia. Buenos Aires: Plus Ultra, 1979.

Conrad, Joseph. *Nostromo: A Tale of the Seaboard*. 1904. Garden City, N.Y.: Doubleday, Page and Company, 1926.

Cook, Albert. *History/Writing*. Cambridge: Cambridge University Press, 1988.

Cordua, Carla. "Borges y la metafísica." *La Torre* (new series) 2.8 (1988): 629–38.

Croce, Benedetto. *La poesia: Introduzione alla critica e storia della poesia e della letteratura. Opere di Benedetto Croce*, vol. 6. Bari: Editori Laterza, 1966.

Cruickshank, John, ed. *The Twentieth Century. French Literature and its Background*, vol. 6. London: Oxford University Press, 1970.

Cuccorese, Horacio Juan. "Historia de San Martín en el Perú." *Actas del Congreso Nacional de Historia del Libertador General San Martín, 1950*, vol. 2. Mendoza: Universidad Nacional de Cuyo, 1953. 267–303.

D'Amico, Robert. *Historicism and Knowledge*. London: Routledge, 1989.

Dangerfield, George. *The Damnable Question: A Study in Anglo-Irish Relations*. Boston: Little, Brown and Company, 1976.

Davidowicz, Lucy S. *The War against the Jews, 1933–1945*. New York: Holt, Rinehart and Winston, 1975.

Debray, Régis. *Teachers, Writers, Celebrities: The Intellectuals of Modern France*. Intro. Francis Mulhern. Trans. David Macey. London: New Left Books, 1981.

Derrida, Jacques. "Freud and the Scene of Writing." Trans. Jeffrey Mehlman. *Yale French Studies* 48 (1972): 74–117.

Desan, Philippe, Priscilla Parkhurst Ferguson, and Wendy Griswold, eds. *Literature and Social Practice*. Chicago: Chicago University Press, 1989.

Descartes, René. *Selected Philosophical Writings*. Ed. and trans. John Cottingham, Robert Stoothoff, and Dugald Murdoch. Cambridge: Cambridge University Press, 1988.

Descombes, Vincent. "The Quandaries of the Referent." *The Limits of Theory*. Ed. Thomas M. Kavanagh. Stanford: Stanford University Press, 1989. 51–75.

Díaz del Castillo, Bernal. *Historia verdadera de la conquista de la Nueva España*. 2 vols. Crónicas de América 2b. Madrid: Historia 16, 1985.

Dickens, Charles. *Nicholas Nickleby*. New York: Dodd, Mead and Co., 1947.

Dodwell, H. H., ed. *British India, 1497–1858. The Cambridge History of India*, vol. 5. Delhi: S. Chand, 1968.

———, ed. *The Indian Empire, 1858–1918, with Additional Chapters, 1919–1969. The Cambridge History of India*, vol. 6. Delhi: S. Chand, 1969.

Duff, Charles. *Six Days to Shake an Empire*. South Brunswick, N.J.: A. S. Barnes, 1966.

Duff, Shiela Grant. *A German Protectorate: The Czechs under Nazi Rule*. London: Macmillan, 1942.

Echeverría, Esteban. *La cautiva. El matadero. Ojeada retrospectiva*. Ed. Carlos Dámaso Martínez. Buenos Aires: Centro Editor de América Latina, 1979.

Edmonson, Munro S., ed. and trans. *The Ancient Future of the Itza: The Book of Chilam Balam of Tizimin*. Austin: University of Texas Press, 1982.

——, ed., intro., and trans. *The Book of Counsel: The Popol Vuh of the Quiche Maya of Guatemala*. New Orleans: Middle American Research Institute, Tulane University, 1971.

——. *The Book of the Year: Middle American Calendrical Systems*. Salt Lake City: University of Utah Press, 1988.

——, ed. and trans. *Heaven Born Mérida and Its Destiny: The Book of Chilam Balam of Chumayel*. Austin: University of Texas Press, 1986.

Edwardes, Michael. *Battles of the Indian Mutiny*. New York: Macmillan, 1963.

——. *Red Year: The Indian Rebellion of 1857*. London: Hamish Hamilton, 1973.

Eisner, Pavel. *Franz Kafka and Prague*. New York: Golden Griffin Books, 1950.

Encyclopaedia Britannica. 11th ed. 29 vols. New York: Encyclopaedia Britannica Company, 1910–11.

Espinosa Pólit, Aurelio. "Prólogo." *Poesías completas*. By José Joaquín de Olmedo. Mexico City: Fondo de Cultura Económica, 1947. vii–lxviii.

Fernández del Castillo, Francisco. *Don Pedro de Alvarado*. Mexico City: Ediciones de la Sociedad Mexicana de Geografía y Estadística, 1945.

Ferns, H. S. *Britain and Argentina in the Nineteenth Century*. Oxford: Clarendon Press, 1960.

Ferrer, Manuel. *Borges y la nada*. London: Támesis, 1971.

Fischer, Louis. *The Life of Mahatma Gandhi*. New York: Harper and Brothers, 1950.

Fishburn, Evelyn. *The Portrayal of Immigration in Nineteenth Century Argentine Fiction (1845–1902)*. Berlin: Colloquium Verlag, 1981.

Fishburn, Evelyn, and Psiche Hughes. *A Dictionary of Borges*. London: Duckworth, 1990.

Fló, Juan, ed. *Contra Borges*. Buenos Aires: Galerna, 1978.

Franco, Jean. " 'The Utopia of a Tired Man': Jorge Luis Borges." *Social Text* 2.1 (1981): 52–78.

Frank, Roslyn M., and Nancy Vosburg. "Textos y contra-textos en 'El jardín de senderos que se bifurcan.' " *Revista Iberoamericana* 100–101 (1977): 517–34.

Frank, Waldo. *Birth of a World: Bolívar in Terms of His Peoples*. Boston: Houghton Mifflin Company, 1951.

Franzius, Georg. *Kiautschou: Deutschlands Erwerbung in Ostasien*. Berlin: Alfred Schall and Grund, [1901].

Frow, John. *Marxism and Literary History*. Cambridge: Harvard University Press, 1986.

Fussell, Paul. *The Great War and Modern Memory*. New York: Oxford University Press, 1975.

Gandhi, Mohandas Karamchand. *August 1918–July 1919. The Collected Works of Mahatma Gandhi*, vol. 15. Ahmedabad: Navajivan Press/Publications Division, Ministry of Information and Broadcasting, Government of India, 1965.

Gane, Mike, ed. *Ideological Representation and Power in Soical Relations*. London: Routledge, 1989.

Garza, Mercedes de la, ed. *Literatura maya*. Caracas: Biblioteca Ayacucho, 1980.

Gazarian Gautier, Marie-Lise. *Interviews with Latin American Writers*. Elmwood Park, Ill.: Dalkey Archive Press, 1989.

Gearhart, Suzanne. *The Open Boundary of History and Fiction: A Critical Approach to the French Enlightenment*. Princeton: Princeton University Press, 1984.

Genette, Gérard. *Palimpsestes: La littérature au second degré*. Paris: Seuil, 1982.

Gianello, Leoncio. *Historia del Congreso de Tucumán*. Biblioteca de Historia Argentina y Americana 14. Buenos Aires: Academia Nacional de la Historia, 1966.

Gibbon, Edward. *The Decline and Fall of the Roman Empire*. 2 vols. New York: Modern Library, n.d.

Gibson, R. "The First World War and the Literary Consciousness." *The Twentieth Century. French Literature and Its Background*, vol. 6. Ed. John Cruickshank. London: Oxford University Press, 1970. 55–72.

Gilbert, Martin. *The Holocaust: A History of the Jews during the Second World War*. New York: Holt, Rinehart and Winston, 1986.

Giles, Herbert Allen. "China: Literature." *Encyclopaedia Britannica*, vol. 6. New York: Encyclopaedia Britannica Company, 1910. 222–30.

———. *History of Chinese Literature*. With supplement on twentieth-century literature by Liu Wu-chi. New York: Frederick Ungar, 1967.

Giordano, Jaime. "Forma y sentido de 'La escritura del dios' de Jorge Luis Borges." *Revista Iberoamericana* 78 (1972): 105–15.

González, Eduardo. *The Monstered Self: Narratives of Death and Performance in Latin American Fiction*. Durham, N.C.: Duke University Press, 1992.

González Echevarría, Roberto. *Myth and Archive: A Theory of Latin American Narrative*. Cambridge: Cambridge University Press, 1990.

———, ed. *Historia y ficción en la narrativa latinoamericana: Coloquio de Yale*. Caracas: Monte Avila, 1984.

Gossman, Lionel. *Between History and Literature*. Cambridge: Harvard University Press, 1990.

———. *The Empire Unpossess'd: An Essay on Gibbon's Decline and Fall*. Cambridge: Cambridge University Press, 1981.

Grafton, Anthony. *Forgers and Critics: Creativity and Duplicity in Western Scholarship*. Princeton: Princeton University Press, 1990.

Green, Howard. "The Battle of the Somme." *The Old Front Line*. Ed. John Masefield. Bourne End, Eng.: Spurbooks, 1917. 11–74.

Green, Martin, ed. *Gandhi in India in His Own Words*. Hanover, N.H.: University Press of New England, 1987.

Griffith, Samuel B. Introduction. *The Art of War*. By Sun Tzu. London: Oxford University Press, 1963. 1–62.

Griffiths, Percival. *Modern India*. 4th ed. New York: F. A. Praeger, 1965.

Grondona, Adela. *El grito sagrado (30 días en la cárcel)*. Buenos Aires: Francisco A. Colombo, 1957.

———. *La mujer de la independencia y la independencia de la mujer*. Buenos Aires: Editoria Theoría, 1982.

Gruša, Jiří. *Franz Kafka of Prague*. Trans. Eric Mosbacher. New York: Schocken Books, 1983.

Gutiérrez, Eduardo. "El coronel Borges." *Croquis y siluetas militares: seleccióne*. Buenos Aires: Editorial Universitaria de Buenos Aires, 1960. 37–45.

Halperín Donghi, Tulio. *Argentina de la revolución de la independencia a la confederación rosista*. Buenos Aires: Editorial Paidós, 1972.

———. "La imagen argentina de Bolívar, de Funes a Mitre." *El espejo de la historia: Problemas argentinos y perspectivas hispanoamericanas*. Buenos Aires: Editorial Sudamericana, 1987. 111–39.

———, ed. and intro. *Proyecto y construcción de una nación (Argentina 1846–1880)*. Caracas: Biblioteca Ayacucho, 1980.

Harkins, William E., ed. *Anthology of Czech Literature*. New York: King's Crown Press, Columbia University, 1953.

————. *Karel Čapek*. New York: Columbia University Press, 1962.

Hašek, Jaroslav. *The Good Soldier Švejk and His Fortunes in the World War*. Trans. Cecil Parrott. New York: Thomas Y. Crowell, 1974.

Havel, Rudolf, and Jiří Opelík, eds. *Slovník českých spisovatelů: Zpracoval ústav pro českou literaturu ČSAV*. Prague: Československý Spisovatel, 1964.

Haverkamp, Anselm. "Poetic Construction and Hermeneutic Tradition in 'Le Cimetière marin.'" *Paul Valéry*. Ed. Harold Bloom. Modern Critical Views. New York: Chelsea House Publishers, 1989. 161–80.

Henríquez Ureña, Pedro. *Historia de la cultura en la América hispánica*. 1947. Mexico City: Fondo de Cultura Económica, 1966.

Hernández, José. *Martín Fierro*. 1872–79. *Poesía gauchesca*, vol. 2. Ed. Jorge Luis Borges and Adolfo Bioy Casares. Mexico City: Fondo de Cultura Económica, 1955. 571–751.

Hibbert, Christopher. *The Great Mutiny: India 1857*. New York: Viking Press, 1978.

Hollier, Denis, ed. *A New History of French Literature*. Cambridge: Harvard University Press, 1989.

Horowitz, Irving Louis. *Radicalism and the Revolt against Reason: The Social Theories of Georges Sorel with a Translation of His Essay on the Decomposition of Marxism*. 2nd ed. Carbondale: Southern Illinois University Press, 1968.

Hunt, Lynn. "History as Gesture; or, The Scandal of History." *Consequences of Theory*. Ed. Jonathan Arac and Barbara Johnson. Baltimore: Johns Hopkins University Press, 1991. 91–107.

————, ed. *The New Cultural History*. Berkeley: University of California Press, 1989.

Hutcheon, Linda. "Metafictional Implications for Novelistic Reference." *On Referring in Literature*. Ed. Anna Whiteside and Michael Issacharoff. Bloomington: Indiana University Press, 1987. 1–13.

Hutchins, Francis G. *The Illusion of Permanence: British Imperialism in India*. Princeton: Princeton University Press, 1967.

Hux, Meinrado. *Coliqueo, el amigo indio de Los Toldos*. 1966. 3rd ed. Buenos Aires: Editorial Universitaria de Buenos Aires, 1980.

Iglesia, Cristina. "Conquista y mito blanco." *Cautivos y misioneros: Mitos blancos de la Conquista*. By Cristina Iglesia and Julio Schvartzman. Buenos Aires: Catálogos, 1987. 13–88.

Irby, James. "Borges and the Idea of Utopia." *The Cardinal Points of Borges*. Ed. Lowell Dunham and Ivar Ivask. Norman: University of Oklahoma Press, 1971. 35–45.

Irby, James, Napoleón Murat, and Carlos Peralta. *Encuentro con Borges*. Buenos Aires: Galerna, 1968.

Isbister, Rob, and Peter Standish. *A Concordance to the Works of Jorge Luis Borges (1899–1986), Argentine Author*. Vol. 3: E-H. Lewiston, N.Y.: Edwin Mellen Press, 1991.

Iser, Wolfgang. *The Act of Reading: A Theory of Aesthetic Response*. Baltimore: Johns Hopkins University Press, 1978.

————. *The Implied Reader: Patterns of Communication in Prose Fiction from Bunyan to Beckett*. Baltimore: Johns Hopkins University Press, 1974.

Iyer, Raghavan, ed. *The Moral and Political Writings of Mahatma Gandhi*. Oxford: Clarendon Press, 1986.

James, William. *Essays in Pragmatism*. Ed. Alburey Castell. New York: Hafner Publishing Company, 1969.

————. "The Moral Equivalent of War." 1910. *The Writings of William James: A Comprehensive Edition*. Ed. John J. McDermott. New York: Modern Library, 1968. 661–71.

Jameson, Fredric. *Fables of Aggression: Wyndham Lewis, the Modernist as Fascist.* Berkeley: University of California Press, 1979.

——. *The Ideologies of Theory: Essays, 1971–1986.* Intro. Neil Larsen. 2 vols. Minneapolis: University of Minnesota Press, 1988.

——. *The Political Unconscious: Narrative as a Socially Symbolic Act.* Ithaca: Cornell University Press, 1981.

Jennings, J. R. *Georges Sorel: The Character and Development of His Thought.* New York: St. Martin's Press, 1985.

Jitrik, Noé. "Bipolaridad en la historia de la literatura argentina." *Ensayos y estudios de literatura argentina.* Buenos Aires: Editorial Galerna, 1970. 222–49.

——. "Sentimientos complejos sobre Borges." *La vibración del presente: Trabajos críticos y ensayos sobre textos y escritores latinoamericanos.* Mexico City: Fondo de Cultura Económica, 1987. 13–37.

Jones, Julie. "Borges and Browning: A Dramatic Dialogue." *Borges the Poet.* Ed. Carlos Cortínez. Fayetteville: University of Arkansas Press, 1986. 207–18.

Juarros, Domingo. *A Statistical and Commercial History of the Kingdom of Guatemala in Spanish America: containing important particulars relative to its productions, manufactures, customs, &c. &c. &c. with an Account of its Conquest by the Spaniards and a Narrative of the Principal Events Down to the Present Time: From Original Records in the Archives, Actual Observation; and other Authentic Sources.* Trans. J. Baily. London: John Hearne, 1823.

Jurado, Alicia. *Genio y figura de Jorge Luis Borges.* Buenos Aires: Editorial Universitaria de Buenos Aires, 1964.

Juvenal. *Thirteen Satires with a Commentary.* Ed. John E. B. Mayor. 2 vols. London: Macmillan, 1888.

Kaplan, Marina. " 'Tlön, Uqbar, Orbis Tertius' y 'Urn Burial.' " *Comparative Literature* 36.4 (1984): 328–42.

Katra, William H. *Contorno: Literary Engagement in Post-Peronist Argentina.* Rutherford, N.J.: Fairleigh Dickinson University Press, 1988.

Kelly, John Eoghan. *Pedro de Alvarado, Conquistador.* Princeton: Princeton University Press, 1932.

Kemp, Sandra. *Kipling's Hidden Narratives.* Oxford: Basil Blackwell, 1988.

Kennan, George F. *From Prague after Munich: Diplomatic Papers, 1938–1940.* Princeton: Princeton University Press, 1968.

King, John. *Sur: A Study of the Argentine Literary Journal and Its Role in the Development of a Culture, 1931–1970.* Cambridge: Cambridge University Press, 1986.

Kipling, Rudyard. *Kim. The Writings in Prose and Verse of Rudyard Kipling,* vol. 19. New York: Charles Scribner's Sons, 1920.

——. "On the City Wall." *In Black and White. The Writings in Prose and Verse of Rudyard Kipling,* vol. 4. New York: Charles Scribner's Sons, 1920. 302–39.

——. *Plain Tales from the Hills. The Writings in Prose and Verse of Rudyard Kipling,* vol. 1. New York: Charles Scribner's Sons, 1916.

——. *Something of Myself for My Friends Known and Unknown. The Writings in Prose and Verse of Rudyard Kipling,* vol. 36. New York: Charles Scribner's Sons, 1937.

Klíma, Ivan, intro. "Čapek's Modern Apocalypse." Trans. Robert Streit. *War with the Newts.* By Karel Čapek. Evanston, Ill.: Northwestern University Press, 1985. v–xxi.

Koch, Dolores M. "El texto en la encrucijada de los senderos." *Texto/Contexto en la literatura iberoamericana*. Ed. Keith McDuffie and Alfredo Roggiano. Pittsburgh: Instituto Internacional de Literatura Iberoamericana, 1980. 181–88.

Kruger, Barbara, and Phil Mariani, eds. *Remaking History*. Dia Art Foundation Discussions in Contemporary Culture 4. Seattle: Bay Press, 1989.

Kundera, Milan. *The Art of the Novel*. Trans. Linda Asher. New York: Harper and Row, 1988.

Kushigian, Julia. *Orientalism in the Hispanic Literary Tradition: In Dialogue with Borges, Paz, and Sarduy*. Albuquerque: University of New Mexico Press, 1991.

LaCapra, Dominick. *History and Criticism*. Ithaca: Cornell University Press, 1985.

———. *History, Politics, and the Novel*. Ithaca: Cornell University Press, 1987.

———. *Rethinking Intellectual History: Texts, Contexts, Language*. Ithaca: Cornell University Press, 1983.

———. *Soundings in Critical Theory*. Ithaca: Cornell University Press, 1989.

Lacouture, Jean. *Léon Blum*. Trans. George Holoch. New York: Holmes and Meier, 1982.

Lafon, Michel. *Borges ou la réécriture*. Paris: Seuil, 1990.

Lanzmann, Claude. *Shoah: An Oral History of the Holocaust, the Complete Text of the Film*. New York: Pantheon, 1985.

Larreta, Enrique. *La gloria de don Ramiro (Una vida en tiempos de Felipe II)*. 1908. 2nd ed. Buenos Aires: Espasa-Calpe Argentina, 1941.

———. *La Lampe d'argile*. Buenos Aires: Editions Coni, 1918.

Lecuna, Vicente, ed. *Cartas del Libertador*. 12 vols. Caracas: Litografía y Tipografía del Comercio, 1929–59.

———. *Catálogo de errores y calumnias en la historia de Bolívar*. 3 vols. New York: Colonial Press, 1956.

———. *Crónica razonada de las guerras de Bolívar*. 3 vols. New York: Colonial Press, 1950.

———. *La Entrevista de Guayaquil: restablecimiento de la verdad histórica*. Caracas: Ediciones del Ministerio de Educación Nacional, Dirección de Cultura, 1952.

Leed, Eric J. *No Man's Land: Combat and Identity in World War I*. Cambridge: Cambridge University Press, 1979.

Leenhardt, Jacques. *Lecture politique du roman: La Jalousie d'Alain Robbe-Grillet*. Paris: Minuit, 1973.

León-Portilla, Miguel. "Mesoamerica before 1519." *Cambridge History of Latin America*, vol. 1. Ed. Leslie Bethell. Cambridge: Cambridge University Press, 1984. 3–36.

———. *Time and Reality in the Thought of the Maya*. Spanish ed., 1968. Trans. Charles L. Boilès and Fernando Horcasitas. Boston: Beacon Press, 1973.

Liang, Hsi-Huey. *The Sino-German Connection: Alexander von Falkenhausen between China and Germany, 1900–1941*. Van Gorcum's Historical Library 94. Amsterdam: Van Gorcum, Assen, 1978.

Liddell Hart, Basil Henry. Foreword. *The Art of War*. By Sun Tzu. London: Oxford University Press, 1963. v–vii.

———. *A History of the World War, 1914–1918*. London: Faber and Faber, 1934.

———. *A History of the World War, 1914–1918*. Boston: Little, Brown and Company, 1935.

———. *The Real War, 1914–1918*. London: Faber and Faber, 1930.

———. *The Real War, 1914–1918*. Boston: Little, Brown and Company, 1931.

Littman, Enno, ed. and trans. *Die Erzählungen aus den Tausend und Ein Nächten*, vol. 4. Leipzig: Insel-Verlag, 1923.

López de Gómara, Francisco. "Conquista de Méjico: Segunda parte de la Crónica General de

Indias." *Historiadores primitivos de Indias*. Biblioteca de Autores Españoles 22. Ed. Enrique de Vedia. Madrid: M. Rivadeneyra, 1858. 295–455.

Lowenthal, David. *The Past Is a Foreign Country*. Cambridge: Cambridge University Press, 1985.

Lowes, John Livingston. *The Road to Xanadu*. Boston: Houghton Mifflin, 1927.

Ludmer, Josefina. *El género gauchesco: Un tratado sobre la patria*. Buenos Aires: Editorial Sudamericana, 1988.

———. "Las tretas del débil." *La sartén por el mango*. Ed. Patricia González and Eliana Ortega. Río Piedras, Puerto Rico: Ediciones Huracán, 1984. 47–54.

Lukács, Georg. *The Historical Novel*. Trans. Hannah and Stanley Mitchell. Lincoln: University of Nebraska Press, 1983.

Lützow, Count. "Bohemia." *Encyclopaedia Britannica*, vol. 4. New York: Encyclopaedia Britannica Company, 1910. 121–35.

———. "Prague." *Encyclopaedia Britannica*, vol. 22. New York: Encyclopaedia Britannica Company, 1911. 248–50.

Mackie, Sedley J., ed. *An Account of the Conquest of Guatemala in 1524 by Pedro de Alvarado*. New York: Cortes Society, 1924.

Madariaga, Salvador de. *Bolívar*. 2 vols. Buenos Aires: Editorial Sudamericana, 1951.

———. Introduction. *History and Politics. The Collected Works of Paul Valéry*, vol. 10. Ed. Jackson Mathews. New York: Pantheon Books, 1962. xxi–xxxvi.

Madden, Richard Robert. *The History of Irish Periodical Literature*. 1867. 2 vols. New York: Johnson Reprint Corporation, 1968.

———. *The Life and Martyrdom of Savonarola, Illustrative of the History of Church and State Connexion*. 2 vols. London: Thomas Cautley Newby, 1853.

———. *The Literary Life and Correspondence of the Countess of Blessington*. 2 vols. New York: Harper and Brothers, 1855.

———. *Memoirs of Dr. R. R. Madden*. Ed. T. More Madden. London: Ward and Downey, 1891.

———. *The United Irishmen, Their Life and Times*. 2 vols. London: J. Madden and Co., 1842.

Mafud, Julio. *Psicología de la viveza criolla: contribuciones para una interpretación de la realidad social argentina y americana*. Buenos Aires: Distal Librería-Editorial, 1984.

Mailloux, Peter. *A Hesitation before Birth: The Life of Franz Kafka*. Newark: University of Delaware Press, 1989.

Majumdar, R. C., ed. *British Paramountcy and Indian Renaissance. The History and Culture of the Indian People*, vols. 9–10. Bombay: Bharatiya Vidhya Bhavan, 1963–65.

Makemson, Maud Worcester, ed. and trans. *The Book of the Jaguar Priest: A Translation of the Book of Chilam Balam of Tizimin, with Commentary*. New York: Henry Schuman, 1951.

Mamatey, Victor, and Radomír Luža, eds. *A History of the Czechoslovak Republic, 1918–1948*. Princeton: Princeton University Press, 1973.

Man, Henry de. *The Remaking of a Mind: A Soldier's Thoughts on War and Reconstruction*. New York: Charles Scribner's Sons, 1919.

Mann, Mrs. Horace [Mary Peabody Mann]. "Biographical Sketch of the Author." *Life in the Argentine Republic in the Days of the Tyrants*. By Domingo Faustino Sarmiento. 1868. New York: Hafner Press, 1974. 276–396.

Mansilla, Lucio V. *Una excursión a los indios ranqueles*. 1870. Ed. Saúl Sosnowski. Caracas: Biblioteca Ayacucho, 1984.

Martín, Marina. "Visión escéptica en 'Tlön, Uqbar, Orbis Tertius.'" *Revista de Estudios Hispánicos* 24.1 (1990): 47–58.

Masefield, John. *The Old Front Line*. Bourne End, Eng.: Spurbooks, 1917.

Masiello, Francine. *Between Civilization and Barbarism: Women, Nation, and Literary Culture in Modern Argentina*. Lincoln: University of Nebraska Press, 1992.

Mason, Philip. *The Men Who Ruled India*. New York: W. W. Norton, 1985.

Masur, Gerhard. *Simón Bolívar*. Rev. ed. Albuquerque: University of New Mexico Press, 1969.

Matamoro, Blas. "Historia de Borges." *Cuadernos Hispanoamericanos* 424 (1985): 129–48.

———. *Jorge Luis Borges o el juego trascendente*. Buenos Aires: A. Peña Lillo, 1971.

Mattalía Alonso, Sonia, and Juan Miguel Company Román. "Lo real como imposible en Borges." *Cuadernos Hispanoamericanos* 431 (1986): 133–42.

McAlindon, T. "*Nostromo*: Conrad's Organicist Philosophy of History." *Joseph Conrad's Nostromo*. Ed. and intro. Harold Bloom. New York: Chelsea House Publishers, 1987. 57–68.

McGann, Jerome J., ed. and intro. *Historical Studies and Literary Criticism*. Madison: University of Wisconsin Press, 1985.

McLauchlan, Juliet. *Conrad: Nostromo*. London: Edward Arnold, 1969.

Mehlman, Jeffrey. "1898: The Dreyfus Affair." *A New History of French Literature*. Ed. Denis Hollier. Cambridge: Harvard University Press, 1989. 824–30.

Menard, Pierre. *L'Ecriture et le subconscient: Psychanalyse et graphologie*. Paris: Librairie Félix Alcan, 1931.

Merrell, Floyd. *Unthinking Thinking: Jorge Luis Borges, Mathematics, and the New Physics*. West Lafayette, Ind.: Purdue University Press, 1991.

Měštan, Antonín. *Česká literatura, 1785–1985*. Toronto: Sixty-Eight Publishers, 1986.

Meyrink, Gustav. *The Golem*. German ed., 1915. Trans. M. Pemberton. Intro. Robert Irwin. London: Dedalus, 1985.

Miller, Christopher L. "1847, 23 December: Orientalism, Colonialism." *A New History of French Literature*. Ed. Denis Hollier. Cambridge: Harvard University Press, 1989. 698–705.

Millington, Mark. "The Importance of Being Albert or the Borgesian Alternative to History." *Ibero-Amerikanisches Archiv* 14.2 (1988): 173–86.

Mitre, Bartolomé. *Historia de San Martín y de la emancipación sudamericana. Obras completas de Bartolomé Mitre*, vol. 4. Buenos Aires: Congreso de la Nación Argentina, 1939.

Molina Carlotti de Muñoz Moraleda, Stella Maris. "1872: Un año clave en la gestación de la Campaña al Desierto (1879)." *Congreso Nacional de Historia sobre la Conquista del Desierto: Celebrado en la ciudad de General Roca del 6 al 10 de noviembre de 1979*. Buenos Aires: Academia Nacional de Historia, 1980. 107–18.

Molloy, Sylvia. *At Face Value: Autobiographical Writing in Spanish America*. Cambridge: Cambridge University Press, 1991.

———. *La Diffusion de la littérature hispano-américaine en France au XXe siècle*. Paris: Presses Universitaires de France, 1972.

———. *Las letras de Borges*. Buenos Aires: Editorial Sudamericana, 1979.

Moore-Gilbert, B. J. *Kipling and "Orientalism"*. New York: St. Martin's Press, 1986.

Mukařovský, Jan, ed. *Déjiny Česke Literatury*. 3 vols. Prague: Nakladaťelství Československé Akademie Věd, 1959–61.

Mullen, Edward J., ed. *The Life and Poems of a Cuban Slave: Juan Francisco Manzano, 1797–1854*. Hamden, Conn.: Archon Books, 1981.

Murillo, L. A. *The Cyclical Night: Irony in James Joyce and Jorge Luis Borges.* Cambridge: Harvard University Press, 1968.

Nandy, Ashis. *The Intimate Enemy: Loss and Recovery of Self under Colonialism.* Delhi: Oxford University Press, 1983.

Newton, Jorge. *Mitre: Una vida al servicio de la libertad.* Buenos Aires: Editorial Claridad, 1965.

New York Times. September–October 1934.

Nicholson, Irene. *The Liberators: A Study of Independence Movements in Spanish America.* New York: Frederick A. Praeger, 1968.

"Nicholson, John." *Encyclopaedia Britannica,* vol. 19. New York: Encyclopaedia Britannica Company, 1911. 657–58.

Novalis [Freiherr Friedrich von Hardenberg]. *Fragmente.* Ed. Ernst Kamnitzer. Dresden: Wolfgang Jess Verlag, 1929.

Ó Buachalla, Séamus, ed. *The Letters of P. H. Pearse.* Gerrards Cross: Colin Smythe, 1980.

O'Leary, Daniel Florencio. *Bolívar and the War of Independence: Memorias del General Daniel Florencio O'Leary.* Ed. and trans. Robert F. McNerney, Jr. Austin: University of Texas Press, 1970.

Orgambide, Pedro. *Borges y su pensamiento político.* Mexico City: Comité de Solidaridad con el Pueblo Argentino, 1978.

Ortega y Gasset, José. *Meditaciones del Quijote.* 1914. In *Obras completas,* vol. 1. Madrid: Revista de Occidente, 1953. 308–400.

Orwell, George. "Reflections on Gandhi." *In Front of Your Nose, 1945–1950. The Collected Essays, Journalism, and Letters of George Orwell,* vol. 4. Ed. Sonia Orwell and Ian Angus. New York: Harcourt, Brace and World, 1968. 463–70.

Paffard, Mark. *Kipling's Indian Fiction.* New York: St. Martin's Press, 1989.

Parrott, Cecil. *Jaroslav Hašek: A Study of "Švejk" and the Short Stories.* Cambridge: Cambridge University Press, 1982.

Paulus Diaconus [Paul the Deacon]. "Historia langobardorum." *Scriptores rerum langobardicarum et italicarum saec. VI–IX.* Monumenta Germaniae historica. Ed. L. Bethmann and G. Waitz. Hannover: Societas aperiendis fontibus rerum germanicarum medii aevi, 1878. 12–192.

———. *History of the Lombards.* Ed. Edward Peters. Trans. William Dudley Foulke. Philadelphia: University of Pennsylvania Press, 1974.

Pérez Amuchástegui, A. J. *La "Carta de Lafond" y la preceptiva historiográfica.* Buenos Aires: Editorial Siglo Veinte, 1962.

Pérez Brignoli, Héctor. *Breve historia de Centroamérica.* Madrid: Alianza Editorial, 1985.

Perón, Eva. "Discurso de la señora Eva Perón." *Actas del Congreso Nacional de Historia del Libertador General San Martín, 1950.* Mendoza: Universidad Nacional de Cuyo, 1953. xlv–xlix.

Perón, Juan Domingo. "Discurso del Excelentísimo Señor Presidente de la Nación General Juan Perón." *Actas del Congreso Nacional de Historia del Libertador General San Martín, 1950.* Mendoza: Universidad Nacional de Cuyo, 1953. li–lvi.

Piglia, Ricardo. *Respiración artificial.* Buenos Aires: Editorial Pomaire, 1980.

Pohorský, Miloš, ed. *Literatura druhé poloviny devatenáctého století. Dějiny České Literatury,* vol. 3. General editor, Jan Mukařovský. Prague: Nakladařelství Ceskoslovenské Akademie Ved, 1961.

Poster, Mark. *Critical Theory and Poststructuralism: In Search of a Context.* Ithaca: Cornell University Press, 1989.

Prieto, Adolfo. *Borges y la nueva generación*. Buenos Aires: Letras Universitarias, 1954.

Quevedo, Francisco de. "La hora de todos y la fortuna con seso." *Los sueños,* vol. 2. Ed. Julio Cejador y Frauca. Clásicos Castellanos 34. Madrid: Espasa-Calpe, 1960. 65–283.

Radhakrishnan, R. "Nationalism, Gender, and the Narrative of Identity." *Nationalisms and Sexualities*. Ed. Andrew Parker, Mary Russo, Doris Sommer, and Patricia Yaeger. New York: Routledge, 1992. 77–95.

———. "Negotiating Subject Positions in an Uneven World." *Feminism and Institutions: Dialogues on Feminist Theory*. Ed. Linda Kauffman. Cambridge: Basil Blackwell, 1989. 276–90.

Rao, K. Bhaskara. *Rudyard Kipling's India*. Norman: University of Oklahoma Press, 1967.

Recinos, Adrián, ed. and intro. *Memorial de Sololá, Anales de los Cakchiqueles, Título de los Señores de Totonicapán*. Biblioteca Americana. Mexico City: Fondo de Cultura Económica, 1950.

———. *Pedro de Alvarado: Conquistador de México y Guatemala*. Mexico City: Fondo de Cultura Económica, 1952.

———, ed., intro., and trans. *Popol Vuh: las antiguas historias del Quiché*. Mexico City: Fondo de Cultura Económica, 1947.

Recinos, Adrián, Delia Goetz, and Sylvanus L. Morley, eds. and trans. *Popol Vuh: The Sacred Book of the Ancient Quiché Maya*. Norman: University of Oklahoma Press, 1950.

Remarque, Erich Maria. *All Quiet on the Western Front*. Trans. A. W. Wheen. New York: Fawcett Crest, 1982.

Rest, Jaime. *El laberinto del universo: Borges y el pensamiento nominalista*. Buenos Aires: Ediciones Librerías Fausto, 1976.

Reyes, Alfonso. *Letras de la Nueva España*. 1948. *Obras completas de Alfonso Reyes,* vol. 12. Mexico City: Fondo de Cultura Económica, 1955. 280–395.

Ricoeur, Paul. "Narrated Time." *A Ricoeur Reader: Reflection and Imagination*. Ed. Mario J. Valdés. Toronto: University of Toronto Press, 1991. 338–54.

———. *Time and Narrative*. Trans. Kathleen McLaughlin and David Pellauer. 3 vols. Chicago: University of Chicago Press, 1985.

Riffaterre, Michael. *Fictional Truth*. Baltimore: Johns Hopkins University Press, 1990.

Rivera, Miguel, ed. *Chilam Balam de Chumayel*. Crónicas de América 20. Madrid: Historia 16, 1986.

Rodríguez Monegal, Emir. *Jorge Luis Borges: A Literary Biography*. New York: E. P. Dutton, 1978.

———. *El juicio de los parricidas: la nueva generación argentina y sus maestros*. Buenos Aires: Editorial Deucalión, 1956.

Rojas, Ricardo. *Los gauchescos. Historia de la literatura argentina: Ensayo filosófico sobre la evolución de la cultura en el Plata,* vol. 2. 1924–25. Buenos Aires: Editorial Guillermo Kraft, 1960.

———. *El santo de la espada: Vida de San Martín*. Buenos Aires: Editorial Losada, 1950.

Rolland, Romain. *Above the Battle*. Trans. C. K. Ogden. Chicago: Open Court Publishing Company, 1916.

———. *The Forerunners*. Trans. Eden Paul and Cedar Paul. New York: Brace and Howe, 1920.

Roth, Jack J. *The Cult of Violence: Sorel and the Sorelians*. Berkeley: University of California Press, 1980.

Ruffinelli, Jorge. "Borges y el ultraísmo: un caso de estética y política." *Cuadernos Americanos* (new series) 2.3 (1988): 155–74.

Rumazo González, Alfonso. *El general San Martín: Su vida y su acción continental en relación con la historia de Bolívar*. Caracas: Ministerio de Educación, Dirección de Información y Relaciones, División de Publicaciones, 1982.

Russell, Bertrand. *The Basic Writings of Bertrand Russell, 1903–1959*. Ed. Robert E. Egner and Lester E. Denonn. New York: Simon and Schuster, 1967.

———. *A History of Western Philosophy*. New York: Simon and Schuster, 1972.

———. *Why Men Fight: A Method of Abolishing the International Duel*. New York: Century Company, 1917.

Rutherford, Andrew, ed. *Kipling's Mind and Art: Selected Critical Essays*. Stanford: Stanford University Press, 1964.

Said, Edward. *Orientalism*. New York: Oxford University Press, 1978.

Sarlo, Beatriz. *Una modernidad periférica: Buenos Aires, 1920 y 1930*. Buenos Aires: Ediciones Nueva Visión, 1988.

Sarmiento, Domingo Faustino. *Campaña en el Ejército Grande Aliado de Sud América*. 1852. Ed. and intro. Tulio Halperín Donghi. Mexico City: Fondo de Cultura Económica, 1958.

———. *Facundo o Civilización y barbarie*. 1845. Ed. Noé Jitrik. Caracas: Biblioteca Ayacucho, 1977.

———. *El general San Martín*. Ed. Fermín Estrella Gutiérrez. Buenos Aires: Editorial Kapelusz, 1950.

———. *Life in the Argentine Republic in the Days of the Tyrants; Or, Civilization and Barbarism*. 1868. Trans. Mrs. Horace Mann. New York: Hafner Press, 1974.

———. *Recuerdos de provincia*. 1850. Buenos Aires: Editorial Sopena Argentina, 1966.

———. *Viajes I.—De Valparaíso a París*. 1849. Ed. Alberto Palcos. Buenos Aires: Librería Hachette, 1958.

Scarry, Elaine. *The Body in Pain: The Making and Unmaking of the World*. New York: Oxford University Press, 1985.

Schalk, David L. *The Spectrum of Political Engagement: Mounier, Benda, Nizan, Brasillach, Sartre*. Princeton: Princeton University Press, 1979.

Schopenhauer, Arthur. *Parerga and Paralipomena: Short Philosophical Essays*. Trans. E. F. J. Payne. 2 vols. Oxford: Clarendon Press, 1974.

———. *The World as Will and Representation*. Trans. E. F. J. Payne. 2 vols. New York: Dover, 1966.

Schrameier, Wilhelm. *Kiautschou: seine Entwicklung und Bedeutung*. Berlin: Verlag von Karl Curtius, 1915.

Schrecker, John E. *Imperialism and Chinese Nationalism: Germany in Shantung*. Harvard East Asian Series 58. Cambridge: Harvard University Press, 1971.

Schwartz, Jorge. "Borges e Joyce (via Salas Subirat, Antonio Houaiss e Haroldo de Campos)." *Boletim Bibliográfico Biblioteca Mário de Andrade* 45.1–4 (1984): 143–55.

Sedgwick, Eve Kosofsky. *Epistemology of the Closet*. Berkeley: University of California Press, 1990.

Seifert, Jaroslav. *Selected Poetry of Jaroslav Seifert*. Trans. Ewald Osers. Ed. George Gibian. New York: Macmillan, 1986.

Selver, Paul. Introduction. *R. U. R.* By Karel Čapek. Garden City, N.Y.: Doubleday, Page and Company, 1923. vii–viii.

Shaw, Donald L. "Jorge Luis Borges: *Ficciones*." *Landmarks in Modern Latin American Fiction*. Ed. Philip Swanson. London: Routledge, 1990. 27–49.

Sherman, Alvin F., Jr. "Confrontation and the Force of Will in Borges's 'Guayaquil.'" *La*

Chispa '89: Selected Proceedings. Ed. Gilbert Paolini. New Orleans: Tenth Louisiana Conference on Hispanic Languages and Literatures, Tulane University, 1989. 297–303.

Slatta, Richard W. *Gauchos and the Vanishing Frontier.* Lincoln: University of Nebraska Press, 1983.

Sorel, Georges. *Reflections on Violence.* 1915. Ed. Edward A. Shils. Trans. T. E. Hulme and J. Roth. New York: Collier Books, 1967.

Sosnowski, Saúl. *Borges y la cábala: la búsqueda del verbo.* Buenos Aires: Ediciones Hispamérica, 1976.

———. "'The God's Script'—A Kabbalistic Quest." *Modern Fiction Studies* 19.3 (1973): 381–94.

Soufas, Christopher. *Conflict of Light and Wind: The Spanish Generation of 1927 and the Ideology of Poetic Form.* Middletown: Wesleyan University Press, 1989.

Spear, Percival. *India: A Modern History.* Ann Arbor: University of Michigan Press, 1972.

Spivak, Gayatri Chakravorty. "Can the Subaltern Speak? Speculations on Widow-Sacrifice." *Wedge* 7–8 (1985): 120–30.

Stallybrass, Peter, and Allon White. *The Politics and Poetics of Transgression.* Ithaca: Cornell University Press, 1986.

Stange, Hans D. H. "Die deutsch-chinesischen Beziehungen in Kultur und Wissenschaft." *Mitteilungen: Akademie zur Wissenschaftlichen Erforschung und zur Pflege des Deutschtums: Deutsche Akademie* 12.1 (1937): 61–70.

Steffan, Heinz Dieterich, ed. and intro. *Nuestra América frente al V Centenario: Emancipación e identidad de América Latina: 1492–1992.* Mexico City: Joaquín Mortiz/Planeta, 1989.

Steiner, Wendy. "Collage or Miracle: Historicism in a Deconstructed World." *Reconstructing American Literary History.* Ed. Sacvan Bercovitch. Cambridge: Harvard University Press, 1986. 323–51.

Stich, Sidra. "Anxious Visions." *Anxious Visions: Surrealist Art.* Ed. Sidra Stich. Berkeley: University Art Museum/Abbeville Press, 1990. 11–175.

Stortini, Carlos R. *El diccionario de Borges.* Buenos Aires: Editorial Sudamericana, 1986.

Strawson, P. F. "On Referring." *Mind* 49 (1950): 1–27.

Sturrock, John. *Paper Tigers: The Ideal Fictions of Jorge Luis Borges.* Oxford: Clarendon Press, 1977.

Suárez, José León. *El coronel Francisco Borges.* Buenos Aires: Talleres Gráficos de G. Pesce, 1928.

Suleri, Sara. *The Rhetoric of English India.* Chicago: University of Chicago Press, 1992.

Sun Tzu. *The Art of War.* Ed., intro., and trans. Samuel B. Griffith. Foreword by Basil Henry Liddell Hart. London: Oxford University Press, 1963.

Tacitus. *The Complete Works of Tacitus.* Ed. Moses Hadas. Trans. Alfred John Church and William Jackson Brodribb. New York: Modern Library, 1942.

Taylor, A. J. P. *The First World War: An Illustrated History.* New York: Capricorn Books, 1972.

Tedlock, Dennis, ed., trans., and intro. *Popol Vuh: The Mayan Book of the Dawn of Life.* New York: Simon and Schuster, 1985.

Theweleit, Klaus. *Male Fantasies.* Trans. Stephen Conway, Erica Carter, and Chris Turner (vol. 1) and Anson Rabinbach and Jessica Benjamin (vol. 2). 2 vols. Minneapolis: University of Minnesota Press, 1987–89.

Thomas, W. Beach. *With the British on the Somme.* London: Methuen, 1917.

Thompson, J. Eric S. *Maya History and Religion.* Norman: University of Oklahoma Press, 1970.

———. *The Rise and Fall of Maya Civilization.* Norman: University of Oklahoma Press, 1954.

Thornley, David. "Patrick Pearse—the Evolution of a Republican." *Leaders and Men of the Easter Rising: Dublin, 1916*. Ed. F. X. Martin. Ithaca: Cornell University Press, 1967. 151–63.

Tilley, Christopher, ed. *Reading Material Culture: Structuralism, Hermeneutics, and Post-Structuralism*. Oxford: Basil Blackwell, 1990.

Todorov, Tzvetan. "Les hommes-récits." *Poétique de la prose*. Paris: Seuil, 1971. 78–91.

Tomaszewski, María Sara. *Versos de ayer y de hoy*. Buenos Aires: Kraft, 1949.

Torre Borges, Miguel de. *Borges: fotografías y manuscritos*. Buenos Aires: Ediciones Renglón, 1987.

Travers, Tim. *The Killing Ground: The British Army, the Western Front, and the Emergence of Modern Warfare, 1900–1918*. London: Allen and Unwin, 1987.

Tsao Hsueh-Chin. *Dream of the Red Chamber*. Trans. Chi-Chen Wang. New York: Twayne, 1958.

Urién, Carlos M. *Mitre: contribución al estudio de la vida pública del Teniente General Bartolomé Mitre*. Buenos Aires: Talleres Tipográficos de A. Molinari, 1919.

Valéry, François. Preface. *History and Politics. The Collected Works of Paul Valéry*, vol. 10. Ed. Jackson Mathews. New York: Pantheon Books, 1962. ix–xx.

Valéry, Paul. *History and Politics. The Collected Works of Paul Valéry*, vol. 10. Ed. Jackson Mathews. Trans. Denise Folliot and Jackson Mathews. New York: Pantheon Books, 1962.

———. *Monsieur Teste. The Collected Works of Paul Valéry*, vol. 6. Ed. and trans. Jackson Mathews. Princeton: Princeton University Press, 1973.

———. *Oeuvres*. Ed. Jean Hytier. 2 vols. Bibliothèque du Pléïade. Paris: Editions Gallimard, 1957.

Vargas Llosa, Mario. "Questions of Conquest: What Columbus Wrought, and What He Did Not." *Harper's* December 1990: 45–53.

Vasconcelos, José. *Breve historia de México*. Mexico City: Editorial Continental, 1956.

Vedia, Enrique de, ed. *Historiadores primitivos de Indias*. Biblioteca de Autores Españoles 22. Madrid: M. Rivadeneyra, 1858.

Veeser, H. Aram, ed. *The New Historicism*. London: Routledge, 1989.

Veyne, Paul. *Writing History: Essay on Epistemology*. Middletown: Wesleyan University Press, 1984.

Viñas, David. *Indios, ejército y fronteras*. Mexico City: Siglo XXI Editores, 1982.

Wells, H. G. *Italy, France, and Britain at War*. New York: Macmillan, 1917.

White, Hayden. *The Content of the Form: Narrative Discourse and Historical Representation*. Baltimore: Johns Hopkins University Press, 1987.

———. *Metahistory: The Historical Imagination in Nineteenth-Century Europe*. Baltimore: Johns Hopkins University Press, 1973.

———. *Tropics of Discourse: Essays in Cultural Criticism*. Baltimore: Johns Hopkins University Press, 1978.

Whiteside, Anna, and Michael Issacharoff, eds. *On Referring in Literature*. Bloomington: Indiana University Press, 1987.

Yates, Timothy. "Jacques Derrida: 'There is nothing outside of the text.'" *Reading Material Culture: Structuralism, Hermeneutics, and Post-Structuralism*. Ed. Christopher Tilley. Oxford: Basil Blackwell, 1990. 206–80.

Yeats, William Butler. *The Poems: A New Edition*. Ed. Richard J. Finneran. New York: Macmillan, 1983.

Zea, Leopoldo, ed. and intro. *El descubrimiento de América y su sentido actual*. Mexico City: Instituto Panamericano de Geografía e Historia/Fondo de Cultura Económica, 1989.

———. *Discurso desde la marginación y la barbarie*. Mexico City: Fondo de Cultura Económica, 1990.

Žižek, Slavoj. *Looking Awry: An Introduction to Jacques Lacan through Popular Culture*. Cambridge: MIT Press, 1991.

———. *The Sublime Object of Ideology*. London: Verso, 1989.

Index

Daniel Balderston is Associate Professor of Spanish and Portuguese and Chair of the Department of Spanish and Portuguese at Tulane University. Recent books include *El precursor velado: R. L. Stevenson en la obra de Borges* (1985), *The Literary Universe of Jorge Luis Borges* (1986), and *The Latin American Short Story: An Annotated Guide to Anthologies and Criticism* (1992). He has edited a volume entitled *The Historical Novel in Latin America: A Symposium* (1986) and has translated books by José Bianco, Silvina Ocampo, Sylvia Molloy, and Juan Carlos Onetti. His translation of Ricardo Piglia's *Artificial Respiration* is forthcoming from Duke University Press.

Library of Congress Cataloging-in-Publication Data
Balderston, Daniel, 1952–
Out of context : historical reference and the representation of reality in Borges / Daniel Balderston.
Includes bibliographical references and index.
ISBN 0-8223-1289-1. — ISBN 0-8223-1316-2 (pbk.)
1. Borges, Jorge Luis, 1899– . 2. Borges, Jorge Luis, 1899– — Criticism and interpretation.   3. Reality in literature.   4. History in literature.   I. Title.
PQ7797.B635Z623   1993
868—dc20   92-23417 CIP